Sportster/Buell Engine Hop-Up Guide

Kip Woodring

Published by:
Wolfgang Publications Inc.
Stillwater, MN 55082
www.wolfpub.com

First published in 2003 by Wolfgang Publications Inc., Stillwater MN 55082

© Timothy Remus, 2003, 2011

All rights reserved. With the exception of quoting brief passages for the purposes of review no part of this publication may be reproduced without prior written permission from the publisher.

The information in this book is true and complete to the best of our knowledge. All recommendations are made without any guarantee on the part of the author or publisher, who also disclaim any liability incurred in connection with the use of this data or specific details.

We recognize that some words, model names and designations, for example, mentioned herein are the property of the trademark holder. We use them for identification purposes only. This is not an official publication.

ISBN 13: 978-1-929133-09-3

Printed and bound in the USA

Sportster/Buell Engine Hop-Up Guide

Chapter One
       History 6

Chapter Two
       Planning 12

Chapter Three
       Exhaust 22

Chapter Four
       Induction 28

Chapter Five
       Ignition 44

Chapter Six
       Charging/Starting .56

Chapter Seven
       Gearing 66

Chapter Eight
       Valvetrain 70

Chapter Nine
       Cam Shafts 74

Chapter Ten
       Cylinder Heads 84

Chapter Eleven
       Pistons & Cylinders 90

Chapter Twelve
       Flywheels 104

Chapter Thirteen
       Oil 116

Chapter Fourteen
       Transmission & Clutch 132

Sources 144

Acknowledgements

Acknowledgements to Custom Chrome, Nallin Racing, Modesto Harley-Davidson/Buell, South Coast H-D, Millennium Technologies, John Massengil, Harley-Davidson Motor Co., Buell Motorcycle Co., Biker's Choice, Santa Cruz Harley-Davidson/Buell, and a host of others who have made the unsung contributions to 'X' engine information, lore and legend over the years. Thanks also to Nallin Racing for the photos of the big bore kits.

I'd like to dedicate this book to Feline Francesca without whom it wouldn't have been possible and with whom all things are probable.

Introduction

This is a book about an engine that needs no introduction - so naturally this is the introduction! Not for the engine, but for the book.

There's an old saying, "catch a man a fish and he eats for a day. Teach a man to fish and he can eat for life!" Teaching, is what I hope this book is about. In this case the lessons are about the enduring and endearing Evolution 'X' engine, in all it's variations. It's not a reference book, yet I hope you'll refer to it over and over. It's not a shop manual, but it might make a good companion for one. It's not a step-by-step guide, though perhaps it will get you a step or two closer to understanding the intricacies, idiosyncrasies, internals, even a bit of the soul of one of the best overall powerplants ever designed.

But regardless of how much or how little you learn, the real purpose is to get you interested in learning more. Because you can never know too much! You may get a great insight from the mechanic at the shop, or the guy down the block, or someone you ride with (or would like to) - wisdom and education can come from anywhere, if you want to look for it.

Maybe in the end, the first place you'll look is in these pages. If so, this book has done it's job.

Chapter One

History

The X Engine Past and Present

The first Superbike is still a super bike, though perhaps not as many folks recognize the fact as should. Since it's birth back in 1957, the Sportster has been everywhere and done everything that a motorcycle possibly can. It has been successful at everything it's ever tried and won every competition in which it could possibly be entered. It has been customized outrageously and hot-rodded mercilessly. It has survived and prospered while virtually all its contemporaries have faded into memory. It is the

Some designs withstand the years better than others. The X engine is one, with roots that go all the way back to 1957 with the introduction of the Sportster. Today the design is still going strong, largely because of Eric Buell's efforts to extract every last horse from the old pushrod V-twin. Kip Woodring collection

first and last of its kind. It is the machine against which all its competitors were, and in many cases are, measured. It has been cloned, imitated, and envied for decades. It is loved for what it is, and liked in spite of what it is. It is unique. Counting its new incarnation as a Buell it has also come full circle. In that iteration it is as it was, America's Sportbike. Yet, it can be nearly all things to nearly all people. Touring bike, muscle bike, cruiser, sport bike, commuter bike, working bike - and more. It will never be perfect. It will always be desirable. It is a machine of fable and foible, yet the most honest and most accurate definition of "Motor" . . . "Cycle." The many legends that exist, and will exist about this bike serve its owners and its maker well. The truth serves better.

When it first appeared it was the fastest motorcycle on the planet, inheriting the mantle from the fabulous Vincent. Journalist-testers of the time were driven to goggle-eyed, raving superlatives in their attempts to describe the feeling. "The Sportster will grow hair on your chest, and if you already have hair on your chest . . . it will part it down the middle." Today, people tend to forget that nearly fifty years ago, with only moderate fiddling and fettling, the Iron Sportster could run 12 second quarter miles.

Following in those fabled footsteps the Evolution 1200 Sportster engine, in the emission-regulated, performance-hampered twenty-first century, will still run low 13's . . . bone stock. In absolute terms that's still plenty fast, with more (often much more) to be had for the asking. In the car world only the most expensive and exotic types can even come close. And, V-Rods not withstanding, the Sportster has always been the Harley with the performance "rep". Evolution 1200's can, and often do, make more power than the traditional air-cooled Big Twin motors. And more torque than anything else it's

size. This fact, coupled with it's relatively light weight, means a sharp big bore 'X' can still run with the big dogs and often lead the pack to boot. The Sportster chassis works well enough to be road raced and dirt tracked virtually un-modified. The Buell chassis just kicks the whole concept of street performance and chassis competence up a notch or two.

Whether in a Sportster or Buell chassis the 'X' engine is the only "quadruple under head cam" engine in production anywhere in the world. This unique feature, more than any other, has allowed tuners to tailor the breathing characteristics of each valve. This spawned the greatest "breather" in dirt track racing history - the XR750. Not to mention the rare street version, the XR1000. An X-engine's unit construction (engine and transmission in the same set of cases) makes for a strong, bullet proof tool that weighs very little for its displacement. It's a dead simple powerplant to work on as well. The fact that it has continued to evolve (sorry, that just slipped out) over all these years means it holds no dark secrets and bears no hidden malice. As engines go, it is a known and workable commodity, much like the equally venerable and amazing small-block Chevy.

From the very beginning, X-engined machines have provided riders with a platform they could massage into any kind of bike imaginable.

The latest improvements, like moving the alternator out from behind the clutch, adding a gear to the tranny, and a derby cover on the primary are just the beginning. Consider also the one-piece no-leak pushrod tubes, hydraulic lifters good to 7000+ rpm, belt drive, and a myriad of details I've probably forgotten to list. Taken together, all these improvements make the newest "X" engines the most desirable ever. In many ways they are vastly preferable to the "F" engines. And, if water jackets and "engine management" aren't your cup of tea, perhaps even a better engine than the VRSC over the long run.

If you doubt it pay close attention to the tricks Eric Buell has conjured up for the venerable 'X' engine - let alone Buell's state of the art chassis. The Firebolt represents a lot more than a trick frame holding a traditional (albeit hot-rodded) Evo XL engine. Look closely and you'll see that almost everything about the Firebolt version of the powerplant is somehow different no matter how much the concept remains the same. From the beginning Buell versions of the Sportster engine were hotter, tricker and really responsible for the resurgence of interest in the performance potential of the 'X' engine.

For the record - 1200cc Buell engines differ from 1200cc Sportster engines in several major ways we'll get into in detail in these pages. For now, the "cliff notes" would read something like this:
• High-flow heads
• Lighter flywheels
• Hotter cams
• High performance exhaust

The 984cc Buell Firebolt engine differentiates even further. In fact, it is unique, with virtually no interchangeability of major components with its older cousins. The notable differences are:
• Short 3.15-inch stroke (in fact the only 'X' engine without a 3.81-inch stroke.)
• Even lighter flywheels
• Shallow chamber heads with unique valve sizes
• Plastic pushrod covers
• Redesigned primary cover and cam cover
• Revised engine oiling system
• Fuel injected with "down draft" intake manifolding
• One-piece pushrod covers
• Special cams set

Put another way – there are very few parts left that any XL or 'big" Buell owner would recognize and the only thing left from the original Sportster is the primary chain. We've come a long, long way.

What I don't understand, is why the 'X' engine stuff doesn't out sell the Big Twins? I mean, Chevy and Ford have just about done away with their "big-block" motors, and when was the last time you saw one of Chrysler's 426 Hemis on the street? These old favorites have faded away for many reasons; some political, some technical, most logical. Big Blocks are inherently less efficient, require more materials to manufacture, use more fuel, and don't necessarily offer any major tangible benefit, let alone power advantage. I mean, the day that GM perfected the 350 small block the need for a big block just went away, at least for street applications. It's much the same with

Like the Sportster, the more advanced Buell can be modified to fit an owner's vision.

Harley. A modern 1200 Sportster motor has better flowing heads, superior valve train geometry, more potential and greater durability. Since it's better to "build" and cheaper to buy it ought to be more popular. The engine/chassis combination is stiffer, stronger, lighter, and better handling, not even counting the Buell. What gives?

Maybe it's because The Motor Company simply hasn't lavished the time, money and marketing on Sportsters that it has on the Big Twins. When you consider the chassis options available for the Big Twin buyer it becomes a little clearer. In spite of the hole in H-D's price range between the point where the 1200 XL leaves off and the Super Glide starts, there are no Softail Sportsters. We don't have any rubber mount Sportsters (not counting the Buell which as good as it is, isn't exactly a mainstream-type "hog"), whereas there are three for Big Twins. Sportsters get no optional "fat" tanks or fenders either, as do the Big Twin models. There is nothing like a Springer XL, or a Wide Glide option. About all Sportster lovers get to pick out from the factory are color and displacement. Other trendy, modern motorcycles as good as Honda's VFR, Kawasaki's Ninja, Suzuki's GSXR, Yamaha's R1, to name but a contemporary few only sell in relatively small numbers most years. Yet, H-D sells tens of thousands of supposedly "low tech" Sportsters year-in year-out. This is crazy. Imagine what the factory could do if they tried?

Well, maybe they are trying. The dedicated Sportster assembly line they created a few years ago in Kansas city can't be a sheer coincidence, can it? Perhaps the prospect of forthcoming counter-balanced or rubber-mounted X-engined models (and who knows what from Eric Buell) isn't far-fetched after all. It sure is tantalizing. Especially considering that they could probably be priced in the $8-11,000 range. I believe there's a lot more to the Sportster/Buell future. Fifty years from now we'll have more legends - and better truths. But that's then, this is here and now.

This book is about what we need to know as the Evolution X engine continues to improve and evolve.

Don't be surprised if this new 1000cc version of the X, as delivered in the Buell Firebolt, winds up in a more "contemporary" Sportster. The revised crankcases are for rubber mounting, which would eliminate the last major "pain in the butt" of Sportsters.

One long-time believer in the worth of X-engined bikes is Steve Storz from Storz Performance Accessories.

Aftermarket Engines

Now that you know a little more about the factory engine, with all it's flaws and virtues, you have to be wondering why, unlike the situation with Big Twin Harley motors, there just aren't a lot of aftermarket alternatives for X engine assemblies. Beats me, too.

Actually, the perception in the aftermarket is that folks who own Sporty's just aren't willing to pony up the dough for enhancements that Big Twin owners will. That includes crate motors. Face it, most scratch built custom bikes are designed and constructed around the 'F' engines. So where's the real market for a big-inch, high dollar, nasty Sporty motor? I submit that it's really hidden in the high-performance minority that owns a 1994-2002 Buell. Hell, Eric Buell himself is largely responsible for the resurgence of X engines as a performance powerplant.

That said, there are aftermarket parts out there that enable one to build some really humongous, nasty motors. S&S Cycles in particular has enough stuff to supply your wildest fantasies. Including "long-block" engines in 91-inch (3-5/8" stroke x 4" bore) and 100-inch (4" x4") displacements.

But be aware... these are not the same as stock only bigger. S&S has decided for a number of reasons to base these crate motors on their "Super Stock" crankcases. A good thing in most ways, but it also means that these engines are "morphs" - using some design elements of the 4-speed X motor and some of the 5-speed. For example, they use replaceable tappet blocks and all its attendant design features on the cam side, but the primary side is all 5-speed in it's execution.

And the S&S isn't a complete engine.

All S&S Sportster-style cases are patterned after the 1991 and up cases with 5 speed transmission. There are differences - the case shown here, Super Stock Sportster Style Crankcase, is designed for engines with a bore of up to 3-5/8 inch.

Aftermarket Engines

Unlike replacement motors from the factory you'll have to budget for things you need to finish the build. Like a transmission, oil pump, clutch and primary drive, and the charging system. Just to name a few of the biggies.

Add the fact that the 100-inch version is too tall to fit in Buell frames, perhaps marginal for some (aftermarket) Sportster frames, and you begin to see this isn't the answer for everyone. The expense, approximately $8000 for the long block, plus another $2000-2500 to "finish" these engines should be enough to make that clear. If not, maybe the fact that they are virtually a "tailor-made" proposition before it's over, will.

In short, these "long block" set-ups are for the hardcore speed freak with enough bankroll to back it up. One other thing is sure, they offer a rush you wouldn't believe when you twist the throttle.

STD Development is the other player in big-bore Sportster cases, but STD goes one step further than S&S. They only offer cases for 4-speed models. The foundation for killer motors is certainly there. But factor in the lack of a fifth gear in the gearbox, (let alone the option to drop an overdrive sixth in these cases) and having the charging system live behind the clutch (never a brilliant idea, even when the factory tried it) and the appeal would almost certainly be for drag racers only.

We'll get into the nuances of dealing with this level of involvement in different areas of the book, but this ought to give you enough of a "cliff notes" overview on the pros and cons of aftermarket engines. At least you can be thinking about the sheer work and expense required to make this kind of "monster motor" dream a reality.

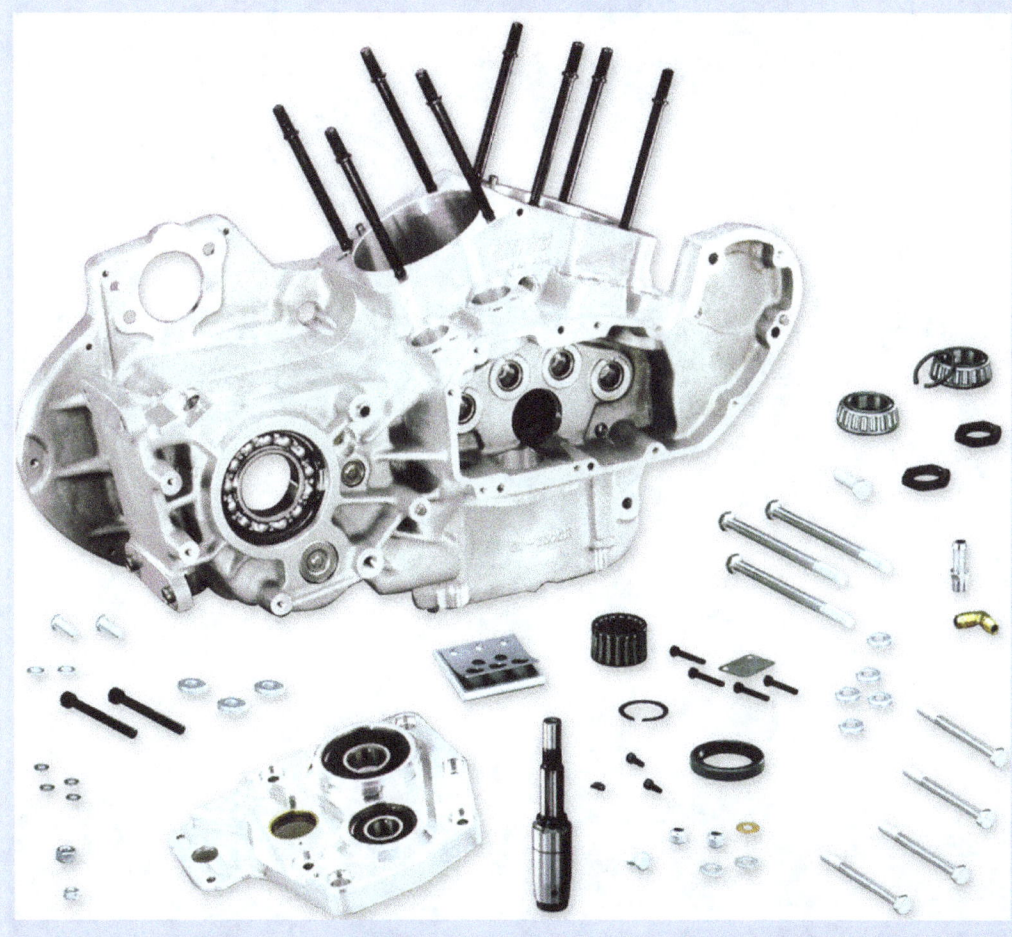

The Special application Sportster style cases shown here will accommodate a bore size up to 4 inches, though you are required to use a +.500 inch pinion shaft.

Chapter Two

Planning

Almost Too Many Options

Before picking up any wrenches you need to plan the actual hop up of that Sportster or Buell. To help you decide which parts are best and why we've set out a planning chapter with three perspectives on the idea of making that hot Sportster even hotter. First we provide a series of combinations that are known to work, from the inexpensive to the, well, the very expensive. Second, we've taken a look at the various components like cams and carbs that are typically replaced or updated as

There are no silver bullets. Good horsepower and torque come from the careful selection and installation of parts chosen to work with each other. And while you're doing all that engine work don't forget the aesthetic considerations.

part of a hop-up project. And finally, because there's no replacement for cubic inches, we've taken a long look at boring and stroking that X engine.

To Begin

You could look at it this way, there are levels of performance that are definitely more suited to a particular riding style or intended use than others. Building an engine for peak power, *lots of it*, at the expense of all else is nearly useless to anyone who isn't drag racing or road racing. And, the key word is expense. The old adage about "speed costs money, how fast do you want to spend" is true. As is the law of diminishing returns. With X engines the first 20% horsepower gain can be had for as little as $300-$400. The last tenth of a horsepower to be had could cost you $10,000. You see where this leads?

It's not tough to get ample power gains from X engines. But your expectations should include the realization that most of it comes from "optimizing" what H-D hath wrought, rather than thinking you can re-engineer it. The simple fact is Sportster engines, even more than Buell engines, and like all Harley engines, are delivered to the owner in a relatively mild state of tune. On top of that, most are hampered by carb jetting or EFI metering that's clearly for clear air, not peak performance. If you also

If you plan to do some hop-up work, it's a good idea to do before and after dyno runs, at the same facility if possible. That way you know how much extra power you actually obtained and where it is in the rpm range.

Don't forget the basics. Like a good air filter capable of moving the additional air your new leaned-on engine is going to require. Filter kits often work with existing factory air cleaner covers. Ness

There are at least 5 carburetors available for your X engined hot rod. None are bad, though one might be better for your application.

come to terms with the reality that a pushrod, air-cooled engine is never going to generate triple digit horsepower without quadruple digit effort and even then not for long, you begin to see what's really probable. Knowing that piston speeds on an engine with a 3.81-inch stroke will exceed the "safe" limit of 4,000 feet per minute, well before you can exceed 8000rpm on the tach, should give you a clue as to *where* to concentrate your power enhancing efforts.

In other words, the first step in planning your engine build is to know your engine. The second is to be realistic in your expectations of the results. The third might be to look for the most bang for the buck once you get past the first two steps. You might also find it cheaper, easier and more rewarding to duplicate combinations of power enhancing parts that are known to work, rather than embark on expensive and not necessarily successful experiments. One important factor in all this that's not talked about much is disabusing yourself of friendly fables about horsepower and torque and how much you can get from an X engine. For example, you'll learn that torque is the big advantage of X engines, even though that's never really talked about in the magazines. You'll learn that a power band is much more useful than peak power. You might even learn that a well tuned, well-ridden 883 can run off and hide from a 1200 Buell because half the success of any "power combination" is the rider's ability to use it.

What I'm saying is that speed comes from tires, suspension, chassis set-up, gearing, riding skill, and a hundred other details. Not just from engine power. That said, and I feel better for saying it, this book is about the

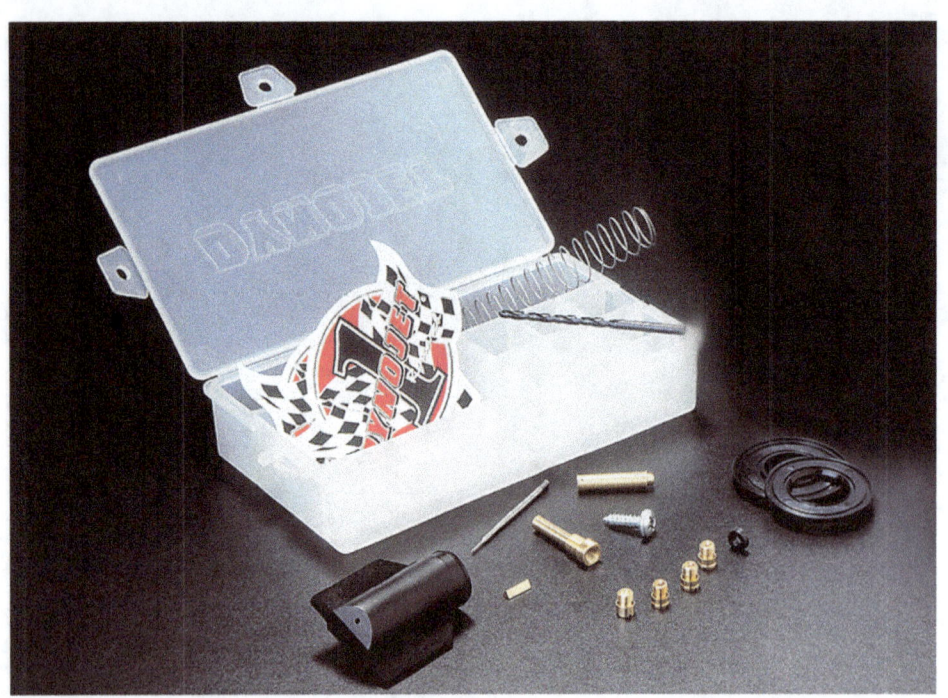

If you change the pipes you're probably going to have to re-jet the carburetor. Kits range from true "jet" kits to more sophisticated kits that include a new slide and spring.

engine. So without further ado - here's a list of some effective power enhancing combinations and what you can expect from them.

COMBINATIONS THAT WORK

Level One
    High flow air cleaner
    Slip-on mufflers
    Jet kit
    High voltage ignition coil
    Upgraded sparkplug wires
    Cost: $300-500 = 10-15% increase in torque and horsepower and improved driveability.

Level Two
    1200cc conversion (883 only)
    Upgraded Ignition module
    Cost: $700-$1000 = 20-40% increase in torque and horsepower (20% over a stock 883, closer to 40% with 1200 heads and/or valves sizes)

Level Three
    Performance 2-1 exhaust
    'Bolt-in' cams
    Cost: $1200-$1500 = 40-60% increase in torque and horsepower. At this point you've most likely reached the "safe" limits of the engine's potential and maximum fun factor.

Level Four
    High performance heads
    Higher compression
    Roller rockers
    Lightened valve train/pushrods
    Upgraded tappets
    Cost: $2000-$3000 or more = 60-70% to perhaps as much as double the power of a stock machine. Reliability is slightly reduced and driveability might be also. Durability is mostly determined by how far you go with the compression and the throttle, but don't expect 100,000 miles.

Level Five
    Increased displacement
    Cams
    Cost: The sky's the limit

as long as you don't blow it, literally. At this point only you can determine if the sheer expense and decreased reliability is worth it for a maximum effort engine build of this sort. Some opt for big-inch motors in mild tune instead. This typically means 95% of the thrills with 50% of the heartache.

Another dose of reality for Sportster lovers. No matter what you do you're not likely to outrun a Buell. There are a number of reasons for this, not least of which is the rubber engine mounts that let a Buell rider run effortlessly at higher engine speeds. But since this is an engine book, let me just put it this way: The best thing to do with any 1200 Sportster engine is build it like a 1200 Buell S1W engine. Same cams, heads, flywheels, ignition module, and so on. The reason, even after all this effort, you won't make as much power as the Lightning—comes down to exhaust systems. You can read more about the details in the exhaust section, but in a nutshell the Buell's have VERY efficient headers, which for "packaging" reasons can't be duplicated on the XL chassis. As always, there are ways around this obstacle. We'll talk about that elsewhere in these pages.

Everybody loves straight pipes (except maybe your neighbors), yet the one design that consistently provides the best power gains, especially in the mid-range, is the two-into one.

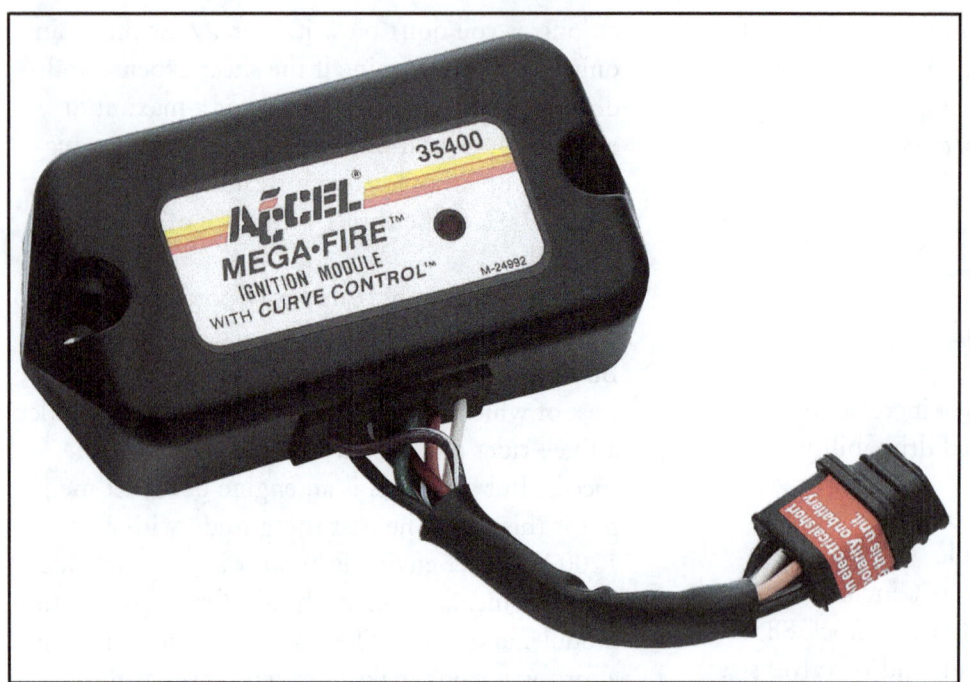

Curve control has nothing to do with your waistline. The better modules provide a number of possible advance curves so you can find one tailored to the exact needs of your particular engine.

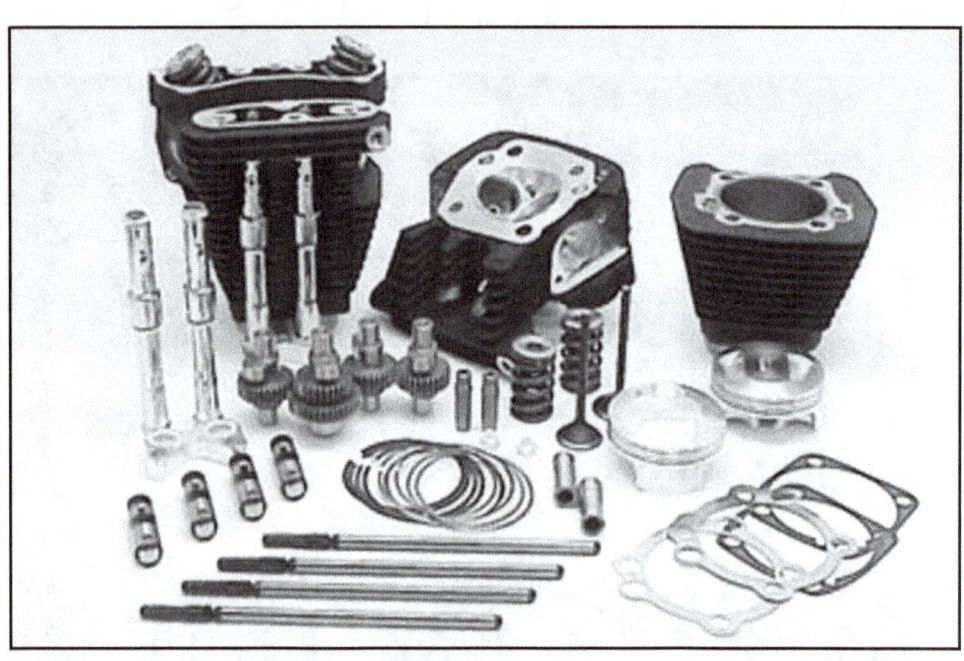

Zipper's 5-speed only, 88 inch big-bore kit, with stock stroke, does a good job of balancing horsepower and torque. This is a square engine, 3-13/16 inch bore and 3-13/16 inch stroke. Comes complete with Aluminum barrels, forged pistons (weight the same as stock) Red Shift cams, heads, pushrods, tubes and gaskets.

MORE PERFORMANCE OPTIONS - BY COMPONENT

I'm not claiming to be THE X-pert, but still, if I were to build a Hyper-Sportster for the street I'd be thinking along these lines, broken down by component.

INTAKE

Choose from Branch Flow-metrics, or Ex-trude-Honed stock manifold, stock CV carb suitably jet-kitted with Yost Master kit, Dynojet, Factory Iron, or possibly a Thunderslide kit and a Screamin' Eagle air cleaner kit. Total expenditure, between $160 and $220. Don't get nuts here. Do the homework. Some of these kits work with minimal changes from stock, some for far more "hotted up" engines. The burden of choice is proper selection. Speaking of which, you can buy a big, nasty Mikuni, Quicksilver, or S&S carb, and who knows? You may even prefer that to a kitted CV. But overall, don't count on it. Save the money for other things.

EXHAUST

You probably don't want to hear this, but if you really want power you're stuck with something like Vance & Hines, Thunderheader, or a SuperTrapp. Regular shorty duals don't cut it. I know you like the looks and the sound of traditional pipes, even (shudder) drag pipes. It won't help. All else being equal, the guy with the V&H (H-D #65269-97) will smoke you, period. And forget the factory "label" about the pipe being for 883s, it works on all Sportys. Most decent exhaust systems cost between $350 and $500.

CAMS

Did you know that all the factory's Screamin' Eagle cam grinds were actually designed for the 1200? Not that it matters much, because they do just fine in 883s as well. But it is curious. The V&H pipes are supposedly for 883s, but work on 1200s and the cams are for 1200s, but work on 883s. Smacks heavily of marketing jargon more than anything else,

An X engine is an X engine, at least at this level of involvement. So which cam goes in that Spam can, ma'am? Well, that would be one cam (#25648-91) for five-speeds, and another (#25628-89) if you have a four speed. (Actually, 2000 and newer models take #25648-01, but don't let it throw you, they are the same.) Either costs about $275. The main reason I seem so certain about the cam choice is the dyno time. It is very difficult to do any better job overall than this grind does. That said, there's not much to choose between the Harley cams, and say, #4 or #8 Andrews, or #230 or #231 Siftons. Most any other grind moves too far away from the notion of broad power bands, let alone the bolt-in concept. This Harley SE bolt-in cam being standard issue in Buells (except the M2), and having seen 85 to 90 horses at the back tire on a dyno more than once, I'd have to say if it's good enough for Erik Buell, it's probably good enough. Buell owners can save their money for other things. Sportster owners, you've been alerted.

HEADS

Thunderstorm cylinder heads are "big valve" versions of the trusty Lightning head, currently available from both Buell and Harley, as Screamin' Eagle. The Thunderstorm heads, as of this writing, are Buell exclusive. All I can say about that is: if you are even remotely considering trick heads for your Sporty, go find a friendly Buell dealer. These things are the performance bargain of the decade, at something like $270 each, assembled. Nail down a set for yourself before they realize how much money they *could* get for these babies. Then send them to Extrude Hone and spend another $350, (if you've got it). You won't regret it. Unless you own an 883, that is.

DISPLACEMENT

883 to 1200 is such a good deal I don't understand why all 883 owners don't go there. As with most things in life, there are options and opinions about the best way to get from 55" to 74". Presuming you're going to buy Screamin' Eagle 1200 or Lightning heads, using factory flat-top pistons is fine and relatively cheap at $140 a pair.

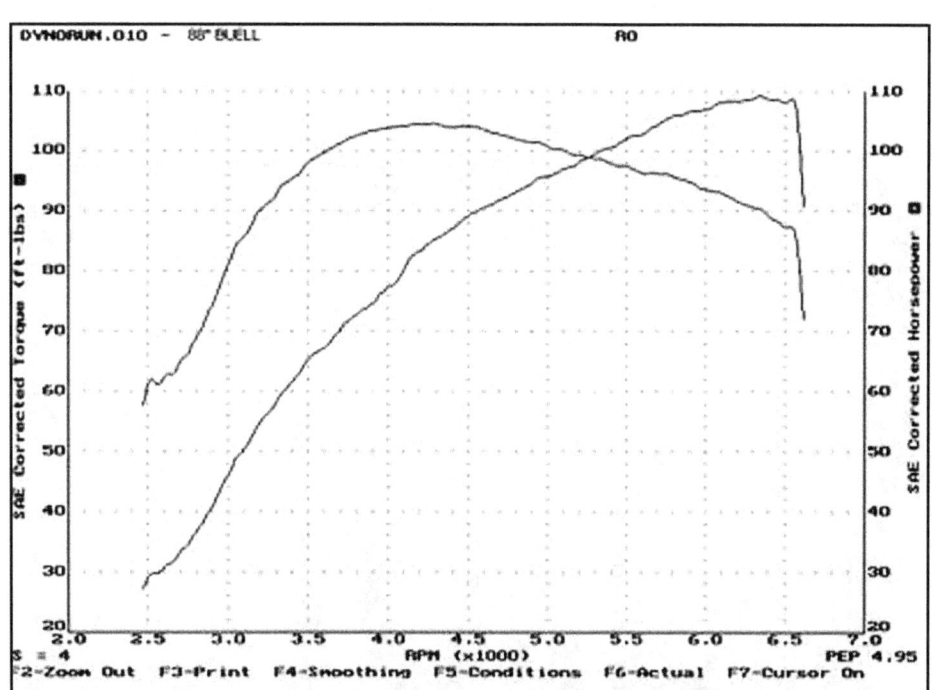

The dyno chart illustrates what Zipper's is talking about when they describe the 88 inch kit seen on the preceding page as having good "middle range power." This engine makes massive torque right where you can use it most often - and makes plenty of top end power to boot.

Using stock 883 heads isn't pointless, but the small valve sizes leave you with not much more than good mid-range and the need to use dished-top pistons. Better to spend the extra for the bigger valves and better ports.

CYLINDERS

Unless you find a deal on the boring, it may actually be cost effective to replace the 883 cylinders with a set of unpainted 1200 conversion barrels (H-D #16554-92A) or black without highlighted fins (#16871-99Y). But, let's do the math to see if we're on the right track. Two flat-top 1200 piston assemblies (H-D #22243-88A), will set you back $140, and the conversion barrels amount to $290, totaling about $430. The alternative would be a pair of regular 1200 cylinder assemblies (H-D #16447-88A), complete with pistons and black wrinkle finish, at—surprise, surprise—$480.

SPORTSTER TO BUELL

Same game, round two. Try adding Buell Thunderstorm parts; like 2 required pistons (H-D #22676-98Y) at the same $140 a pair, and heads (H-D #16797-98Y, front; H-D #16827-98Y, rear) at $550-and change a set. Or, use the twin-plug Screamin' Eagle heads (#16556-96B black, #16457-96B silver) for about the same money. Add a top end gasket kit (H-D #17032-91) at $70-80, and about a day later, you're there. For a total of approximately $700.

ANCILLARIES

Thought you were done, did ya? How about the ignition? The 883 and 1200 ignition advance curves are completely different. Retaining the 883 module after a conversion is a serious handicap to peak performance. Personally, I'd opt for an appropriate "street legal" 1200 S.E. ignition module, (or the Buell Race module if you opt for Thunderstorm heads) then add a hot coil and quality plug wires, and call it good to go. Sure the "racing" modules with their 7500 rpm limits sound neat, but you can't use 'em without blowing things up. (If vibration is an issue, consider Balance Masters on the clutch and compensator before you haul off and buy a single-fire ignition.)

The total dollars involved here, depend more on what you choose than what really does the job, but based on Screamin' Eagle components, looks like this: Plug wires $15, Coil $60, Module $120. Total—a couple hundred bucks.

AN ORDER OF DISPLACEMENT... TO GO.

In the Middle Ages, world maps were less than comprehensive. Back then, mapmakers marked terra incognito with the cryptic and intimidating phrase, "Beyond here, there be dragons." Building big-inch, fire-breathing Harley motors can be a lot like that.

These big-inch *dragon* motors are not for everybody. Certainly not those who prefer to stick to familiar turf and leave the land of fire breathers to the more adventurous ones. You see,

Axtel's 88 inch Mountain motor marches to a different drummer: cylinders are cast from G3000 cast iron. Cast iron is more dimensionally stable when hot, but doesn't shed heat as well as aluminum. Kits include pistons, cylinders, gaskets, wrist pins and teflon buttons.

as simple as the concept is and as good as it looks on paper, it is not easy. It leaves the fiscally challenged gasping in the rarefied atmosphere of big-time expense. So you say to yourself, before we proceed one cubic inch further, if all this is such a pain for the gain, why bother? Because, all else equal, a good Big'un will beat a good Lil'un—every time. So for those who persevere, it's worth it. There really is "no replacement for displacement." The question is, how do you go about creating your own fire breather with maximum terra and minimum incognito?

There are three ways: increase stroke, increase bore, or increase both. Stroke is the distance the piston moves up and down in the cylinder, and bore is the size of the hole in the cylinder. One multiplied by the other equals displacement—simple but deceptive (where Harley V-twins are concerned). Not unlike the ubiquitous small-block Chevy V-8, where every possibility has been tried in GM's 30-year trek from 265 inches to the 350 inches (and more) that are familiar today. And relatively few have been completely successful. In other words, just because any old combination is possible doesn't make it practical.

X engines are no different. Frankly, certain bore/stroke combinations are likely to turn your motor into a hand grenade. Others, even of equal displacement, offer vastly superior reliability, economy, and output. And if you fail to plan, plan to fail. Strokers, in particular, offer no shortcuts; they have to be done right. Doing it right can mean anything and everything, from molehills (like modifying crankcase breather timing), to mountains (like the possible necessity of using aftermarket crankcases).

All stock Harley motors are under-square. Simply, the bore is smaller than the stroke. A 74-inch X-engine, for instance, has a 3.5-inch bore and a 3.81-inch stroke. Generally, any engine laid out like this is meant to operate at lower rpm and generate its maximum torque lower in the powerband than a square or oversquare engine of the same displacement. No surprise, then, that the opposite is true of over-square engines. They like to do their thing at proportionately higher rpm.

Let's suppose you want to increase torque and, therefore, power. The most effective way, as opposed to the most efficient way (more about that later), is to increase stroke. For decades this has been the preferred method. Here's why. Increasing stroke essentially increases leverage at the connecting rod. Moving the big end of the rod farther out toward the edge of the flywheel (which is how you make a stroker) increases the angle the piston has to push on. So in addition to extra displacement, you get a uniform increase in torque clear through the rev range. Sounds great, but as always, there are both mechanical and practical limits to this kind of engineered enhancement.

The angularity (sideways push) of the rod and

Millennium Technologies makes a big-bore kit for the Buell XB9. Cases must be bored to accept the bigger spigots on the bottom of the new Nickle Carbide treated cylinders (no steel liners). Options include various compression rations and re-mapped EFI controls.

the sheer speeds at which the piston must travel create more heat and more wear and tear. If the engine has a stock stroke of 3.81 inches and a 6500-rpm redline, piston speed is 4225 feet per minute (fpm). Now, stroke it half of an inch and piston speed jumps to 5603 fpm at the same rpm. You begin to see the problem?

Sure, modern pistons have improved the ability to withstand this kind of treatment, but until they repeal the laws of physics. You are pushing your luck, not just your piston. Now, try a 5-inch stroke, for example, and you quickly see the law of diminishing returns at work. In fact, durability with strokes this long can usually be measured in hours not years.

Speaking of pushing, high-rev loads on the connecting rods increase at the square of their velocity. The SQUARE of the velocity. Think about that—it's the same as saying a (hypothetical) 50 percent chance of a rod failing at 6,000 rpm goes immediately to the point of near certainty at a mere 1,000 rpm more. It's all you can reasonably expect of a part that accelerates to the top of a nearly 4-inch stroke at a staggering velocity, stops cold with a shock load measured in many tons of force, and then flies back down to repeat the assault. And with every other trip, it has an explosion going on upstairs to boot.

It follows then that one of the most significant (but overlooked) items in a stroker's repertoire are those stiff, strong connecting rods. Just the same, the longer the stroke (especially relative to the bore), the lower the safe engine speed.

If you're not the type to wring out your bike, who cares? There's plenty of reliability in reserve if you prefer bottom end to high revs. In short, the monstrous low-down power this type of engine offers is best suited to riding styles and riders that spend most of their lives at relatively low rpm, but must labor under the burden of their own (not inconsiderable) bulk—plus the weight of a passenger and luggage. Getting away from traffic (and traffic lights) and long, low-velocity pulls up steep grades becomes a snap with enough stroke.

Still, what works great for hauling a load may not be worth a damn for haulin' ass. So let's just increase the bore and forget this stroker stuff for a minute. Big-bores favor horsepower at the expense of low-speed torque, but are able to run at higher rpm. Buells and Sportsters can successfully surrender a little low-end grunt for a bodacious midrange and top-end rush. In fact, we know of at least one individual, a character named Eric Buell, who destrokes his latest version of the X engine to a mere 3.125-inches—the theory being to generate enough horsepower and enough *safe* revs (7,500-plus) to do business with "Rising Sun Rockets" for sustained periods of time. It may not be a bad idea. The

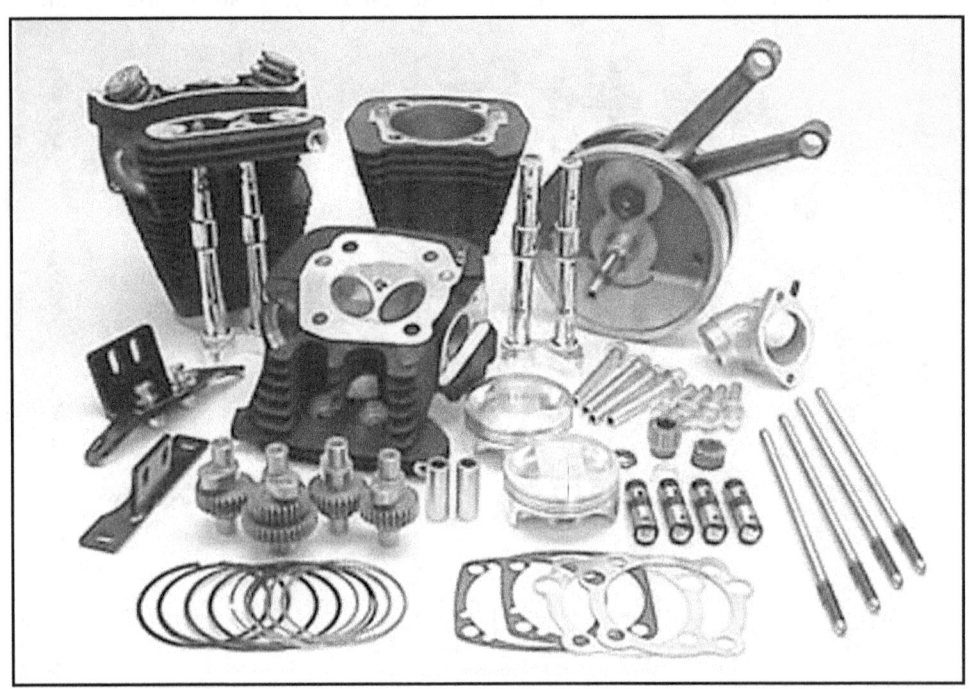

Virtually as big as you can go in a stock case and frame, 99 inches using a 4-5/16 inch stroke crank and special length con rods with aluminum 3-13/16 inch cylinders and pistons. Includes ported Thunderstorm heads, Red Shift cams and special length pushrods. Zipper's

typical big-bore engine will last longer since the piston speeds stay lower and the rod angle is less severe at elevated engine speeds.

The only limits on bore size tend to be sheer reciprocating mass (how heavy is that big slug anyway?) and detonation (spark can only travel so far, so fast) in an extra-wide combustion chamber. And the fact that in a 45 degree V-twin, these two megawide pistons could potentially meet each other, at the same time, in the same place—the bottom of the V.

In short, where bigger is concerned "better" can be pretty subjective. There's a lot to contemplate, mostly little details. And that's just in terms of the motor you want to build. Let's not forget that a really good stroker or big-bore can crowd and/or exceed the limits of other little things like clutches, trannies, and starter motors, too.

So, whether it's for leaping tall buildings in a single bound or going faster than a speeding bullet (or both), it all depends on what you want to do. Whether you build it or buy it, you must ask yourself:
• What is the engine intended to do?
• Were the correct parts used?
• How well has it been put together?
• How well has it been broken in?
• How well has it been maintained?
• Will the rest of the machine hold up?

If you are completely satisfied with the answers, congratulations. The world just got a lot smaller, thanks to a real *fire-breathing dragon*. Your very own.

Displacement conversions

883cc = 53.9ci
900cc = 55ci
1000cc = 61ci
1100cc =67.2ci
1200 =73.3ci (commonly rounded to 74")
1340cc = 81.8ci (commonly rounded to 80")
1450cc = 88.48ci
1550cc = 95ci
1573cc = 96ci
1622cc = 99ci
1638cc =100ci

From here on out – you can figure it out:
Cubic Inches = Cubic Centimeters divided by 16.387
Liters = Cubic Inches multiplied by 0.016387 (or to get cubic centimeters multiply by 16.387)
CC=Cubic Centimeters
CI = Cubic Inches

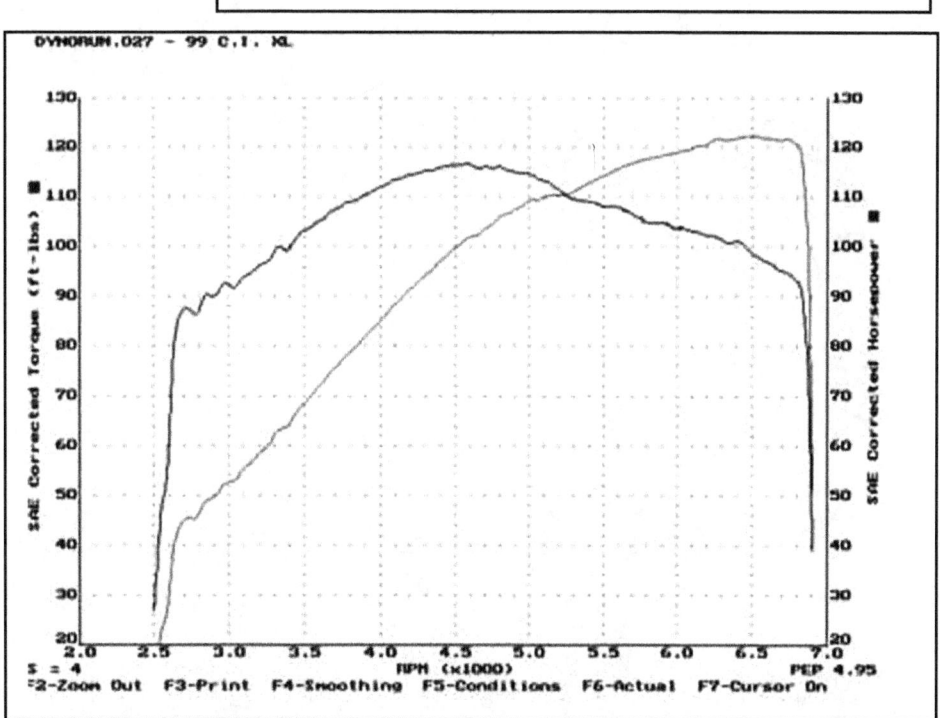

This is what happens when you twist the wrist on a 99 inch Zipper's Sportster! More torque than your tires can likely handle. There is a price to be paid however, in longevity as well as in dollars.

Chapter Three

Exhaust

Getting More Out - To Get More In

It's a fascinating by-product of image that Harleys aren't "fast" and thus don't warrant efficient exhausts. And if that weren't enough, H-D's are so hide-bound with tradition that almost everybody's given up on the idea that exhaust is the key that unlocks the power potential. Yet, strangely, it's also tradition that exhaust is the first thing changed on any Harley… got to be loud and proud to keep up the "other" tradition. Pity about not having the first clue about real performance potential. It was

In various forms, staggered duals have been the exhaust system of choice for most riders for a long, long time. Though there may be more efficient designs, some of these do very well in the power department. Most of these systems run better throughout the RPM band when the baffles are left in place.

absolute fact less than a decade ago for any Harley. Then the Buell Lightning came along and things changed BIG TIME for the Evolution X-motor. Suddenly 100 horsepower was not out of reach, 90 damn near common on a well-tuned 1200 Buell.

Face it, we now know there's a better way to extract power from any H-D engine without having to spend your way into oblivion on hot rod engine parts. And which makes more sense? I'd make a cash money bet right now. There's more power to be had from a proper exhaust and intake than from any number of cam, carb and compression tricks forced to puff through an 89 decibel soda straw. That notion however, leads directly to the third myth… that noise equals horsepower, so louder must be better.

The path to pony power, as distinct from phony power, is clearly along a different line. Buell has shown the way, largely based on accepted tricks the (horrors) Japanese have taught the rest of the motorcycle world. Namely, a properly designed header connected to a large volume muffler, that only cuts noise not power. The trouble with Buell's approach is that "look" only a mother could love. We be talkin' OOGLY . But in this case ugly's only skin deep, while beauty goes clear to the core.

Look for just a moment or two at the differences between exhausts on two X-motored siblings, the Sportster Sport and the Buell

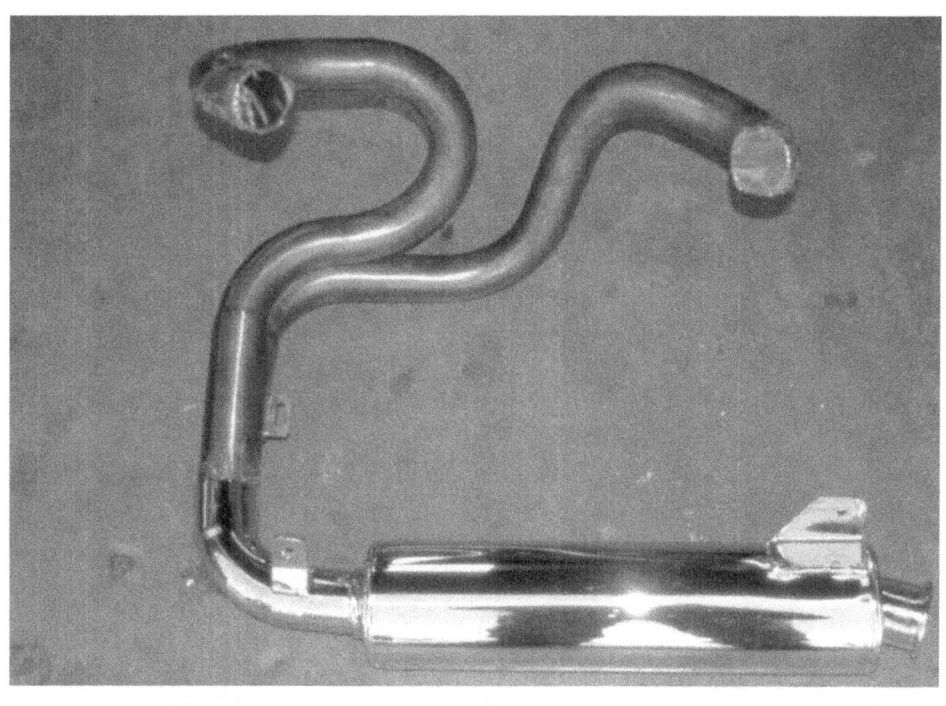
Buell exhaust systems are more efficient and make more power than nearly anything offered for a Sportster.

This OEM Buell two-into-one proves that a modern system designed from scratch to comply with noise regulations can also be plenty efficient.

Thunderbolt. Ponder for that same moment or two that you can build identical engine configurations for the XL and the S3, and the Thunderbolt will quietly thunder off and hide from the noisier and notably slower Sporty. Aside from the Buell's lighter flywheels, or even allowing that you could build those wheels into the XL, the ONLY difference that the Sportster is saddled with is that few feet of 1 3/4 inch tubing stuffed into mufflers no bigger than the average dry Salami. Whereas the Sportster's younger cousin has the benefit of a tuned length header, coming into that ever so important 2 1/2 inch collector. Add a muffler actually big enough to muffle and you've got a very happy thoroughly "exhausted" engine breathing free, running wild. In fact, dyno tests on Buell's confirm that the header/collector is THE thing that makes power. The only task the muffler has is to keep from cutting the "heart" out of all that boost.

So, if header design is so bloody crucial, why-oh-why doesn't The Motor Co. or the aftermarket... anybody (besides Mr. Buell, that is) bother to get it right?

Well, they haven't exactly got it wrong. We do.

Mufflers

The first thing to do is separate the myth from the fact where the relationship of noise to power is concerned. Let's face it, we usually start with a simple muffler change. In fact, it's a fairly safe bet that no Harley makes it past the break-in service without some modification to make the machine "sound like a Harley". A couple of things about that: First, almost anything you do in the way of an exhaust swap will seem to be an improvement. That's because the only way for the factory to comply with Federal noise standards and maintain the "look" of traditional shorty duals is with a baffle design that chokes the power severely .

Next, most of the time if you can't afford replacement mufflers you'll settle for punching holes in the stockers. There's a right way and wrong way, even with something this simple. It can be done with nothing more than a long piece of 1/2-3/4-inch diameter rod and the proverbial BIG hammer. Just pound away. No... on second thought... don't . If you're certain you want to mutilate the OEM muffler, better to buy a 1 1/2-inch holesaw and cut the welds away at the rear of the muff. Bingo. One very throaty and surprisingly potent system.

If your ideas run more towards keeping those pricey stock parts wrapped up on the shelf in the garage "just in case" (you can guess why), then buying new mufflers is on your list. It's dead certain that anything you can look into and see out the other side of will boost noise. That leaves a pretty open field of aftermaket muffs, especially those with removable baffles. Here's the bad news – 1) They won't really make any more power than something a little more "civilized", yet will get you tickets for being uncivilized. 2) You're pretty much wasting your time and your power gains, unless and

The Shark is pretty popular in Europe where they take performance without ... ahem!... "compromise," seriously. This pipe has proven to give a really flat, potent torque curve and a broad healthy powerband.

until, you add a high performance air cleaner.

Think of H-D's old tried and true "off road" mufflers as a baseline. These are known to work well, period. Yet, they are smaller in diameter than the stock stuffed-up units. Doesn't it stand to reason they'd work a damn sight better than they already do, yet not be so loud if they were the same diameter? Maybe even a larger diameter than the stockers? Well, Harley has thought of that. They now sell accessory muffs measuring the same diameter as the stockers. Perhaps not as powerful as the originals, but better than nothing for those performance seekers with a social conscience. I hope it's obvious by now that any amount of muffler swapping is really only making the best out of a bad situation.

HEAD PIPES

Let's talk about how the head pipe plays into the plan, shall we? Whether anyone wants to admit it or not the stock head pipe is pretty decent given its mission parameters. More often than not, the only real objection to the OEM headers is the look. Nobody's a big fan of the crossover pipe. That's too bad, as it does a lot of good in terms of spreading out the powerband. Once again the name of the game is volume, and the crossover "fools" the exhaust pulse into thinking it has got more area than it really has to escape through. Some would even argue there's a scavenging effect. Most folks would surrender a difference you can hardly feel for the cleaner look of either drag pipes or the non-crossover head pipes that Harley (and almost everyone else) will be happy to sell you. Of course the aftermarket seems to specialize in one-piece "systems", wherein the head pipes and mufflers (such as they are) are one. The advantage here is largely that there's no chance the muffs will fall off. The disadvantage? Dent, ding, scratch or scuff any part and you replace the whole (damn) system.

The thing is, we've only dealt with variations on a theme to this point. We already know that peak power, if that's all you care about, can be had with nothing more than a set of straight through, baffleless drag pipes, roughly 38-40 inches long. That bit has been a fact since dirt was mud, in H-D circles. Like most "facts" there's more to it than meets the eye. For instance, if you want to know how long a straight pipe's tuned length should be, for a given engine configuration, you can do all kinds of math, burn up a CPU or two with all sorts of formulas, or use a crayon. Mark a nice thick line the length of the header. Fire the bike up, rev it, and watch closely to see where the crayon mark melts first. It's an old hot-rodder's trick to see where the exhaust wave "reverts". It works, too. Just don't be surprised if the "off the shelf" pipe turns out to be a few inches too short or way too long. Parallel wall tubing tends to behave like that. The better plan is divergent walls,

The SuperTrapp two-into-one combines an efficient design with a tunable muffler. An exhaust that can be setup to be nearly all things to all people. The logic of this tunable system is so inescapable that other aftermarket brands have switched to a similarly flexible arrangement.

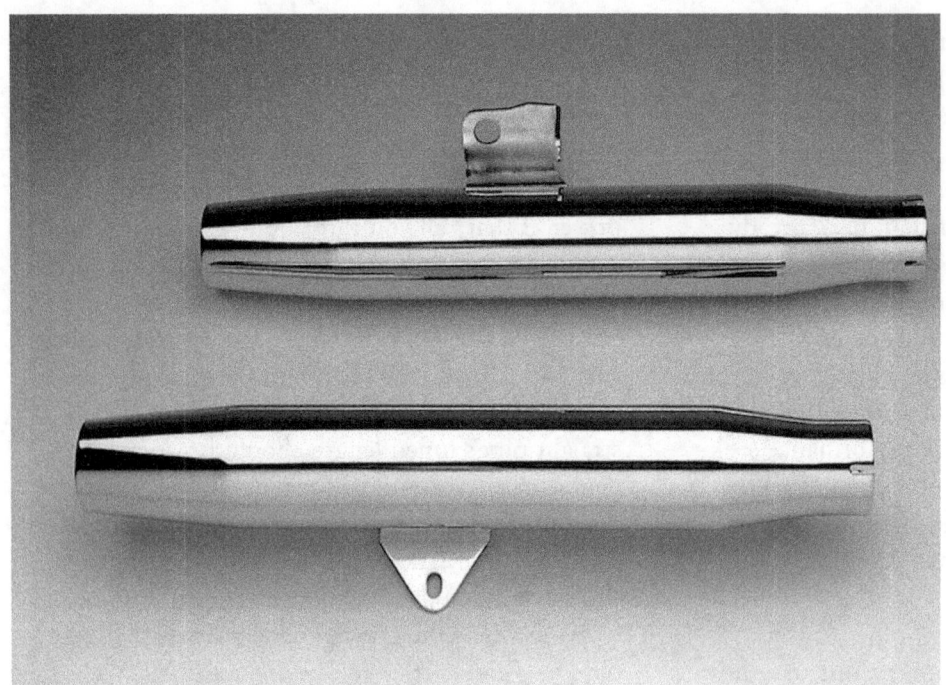

Those who aren't into figuring out baffle adaptation on stock mufflers can swap to any number or aftermarket and factory SE offerings. These are a what you see is what you get sorta thing.

From Hooker Headers comes this two-into-one system. Full length head shields and double-wall mufflers ensure a minimal amount of blueing. Mufflers can be tuned to affect sound and runnability.

aka tapered header pipe design. It is two stroke stuff really, and nobody builds anything like that for Harleys or Buells. Six or seven degrees would probably do, but it is not going to happen. Instead we get step-up diameters. 1 3/4 inches out of the port, jumping to about two inches a-ways down stream. Some H-D performance pipe purveyors are doing this kind of thing, and the scheme has merit.

TWO-INTO-ONE COLLECTORS & SYSTEMS

The most practical way to get a power band and still have nearly as much peak power is to mess around with a system incorporating the aforementioned tubing in a proper tuned length, but add a collector pipe of something at least 2-plus inches in diameter. One of the best examples of this notion in practice is the Pro-Race header from Buell. A carbureted S1 Lightning with the rest of the Pro Race kit (circa 1998) installed, pulled 90 peak horsepower at 6800rpm, and over 85 ft-lbs. max torque at a paltry 3500rpm. This is courtesy of an ignition module with a high rev limit, a free breathing air cleaner, a needle change in the CV carb, and the header alone. The best part is the muffler, once re-installed on the same bike, same dyno, same day, made exactly the same power. Meaning, the muffler was doing it's job keeping power up and noise down. Much more to the point, the spread of power is huge. Consider that the motorcycle in question makes over 70 ft-lbs. of torque, from 3500 rpm to 6500rpm. That's more torque than most motorcycles can make at all… available over two thirds of the rev range. It's also pretty handy to have over 80 horsepower at your command from 4000 rpm on.

Trying not to belabor the point, I still can't emphasize enough that if you want the broadest spread of power, the most useable performance, you cannot beat a well designed collector system with a muffler large enough to be non-restrictive. Well enough for Buell owners, they've got theirs, so to speak. But those systems don't adapt to Sportsters. You have to look around for a system that embodies these crucial elements of design, and can still be wrapped around an XL frame. The good news is that as the renaissance in 'X' engine performance forges ahead, so does less traditional looking, more functionally contemporary exhaust systems. Even conservative H-D has finally decided a clean two-into-one is worth having, not just in the Screamin' Eagle section of the P&A catalog, but on a stock model.

At first it may seem strange that the model of choice for the factory's marketing of this exhaust system is an 883. The XL883R is never going to be a contender for horsepower champion. But, since The Motor Company is pushing image with this little beast they figured it needed all the help it could get to pull it off. Well, it does. That its bigger brothers will benefit from a swap to little brother's "Zorst" is frosting on the performance cake. It's a pity the XL 2-1 systems are still cursed with too small mufflers, regardless of how well the header configuration might work. It means you're still going to have a noisier exhaust to get the max bang for your buck. On top of all that, there are subtle but crucial details to be aware of if you want to run with the Buells. Look, for instance, at H-D's own offerings. Two 2-1 exhausts cohabitate the Screamin' Eagle section of the accessory catalog, the one-piece and the two-piece (or more precisely the slip-on muffler that goes on the stock head pipe collector of the 2002 XL883R.) The head pipe designs are not the same. It would be an interesting exercise to run the one-piece 2-1 and the stock 883R collector with S.E muffler on the same machine in back to back tests. I'm betting the S.E. 883R setup has the beans. So do some of the aftermarket systems that adhere to the same principles. The Vance & Hines SSR 2-1 (formerly a Screamin' Eagle part itself) is one such example. So is the lesser known Shark system from Germany. I think it's safe to predict there will be more.

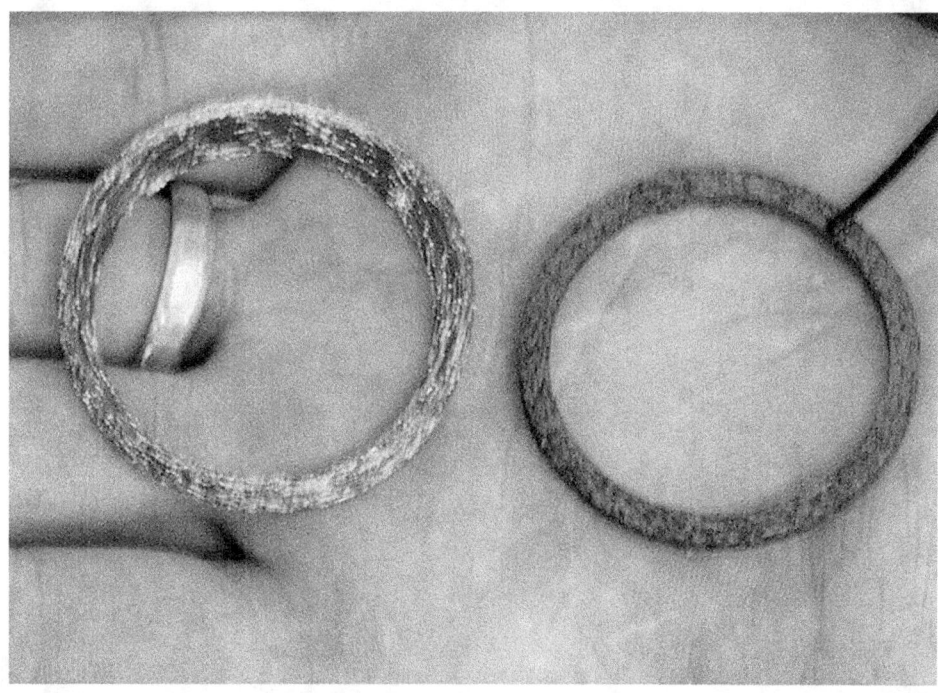

You can have the bumpiest bumpsticks, trickest heads and an exhaust that flows like the Nile flood, yet the factory gasket on the left can virtually negate any power gains from all that good stuff if it's crushed to the point that it protrudes into the port after you cinch the pipe down. The one on the right doesn't have that problem and won't cut airflow. Let that detail Devil you, and you begin to see there's quite a bit of science even in the dark art of exhaust tuning.

Chapter Four

Induction

Plenty of Clean Air & Just Enough Gas

AIR CLEANERS

Any carb needs a good air cleaner to give it's best. Kuryakyn, Screamin' Eagle, even S&S or H-D's own "Teardrop" air cleaners to name but a few, will help a ton. The stock air cleaner, particularly the California bikes with their "trapdoor" are extremely restrictive. But, don't even *think* of running any of these good air cleaners without a *great air filter* like one from K&N. On top of that, dyno testing has shown that X motors respond

Hot rod Sportsters and Buells can, and often do, run the factory Keihin CV carburetor. No matter what you run, just be sure the air cleaner has enough capacity to provide the engine with plenty of clean, unrestricted air.

really well to deep K&Ns (say 2-inches) with lots of surface area. One of the better examples of this is the racing air cleaner for Buells. There are others that work, but *plenty* of others that don't. It would be a lot less confusing if you could get flow numbers (CFM) on the air cleaner you'd like to try. But barring that, just try to keep this tidbit in mind. A carb that flows 250 cfm, can't with an air filter that only flows 150.

Factory Manifolds

The intake on 1986-87 XLs was okay. Well, maybe not quite. If you want to improve the flow of that device there are ways and means. Most of you (and you know who you are) have already swapped for an S&S, or a secondhand CV and manifold, or some such. If not, stick around and we'll get to it.

Up front the stock intake manifold on CV-equipped Sportsters and Buells is a far better piece than the one fitted to Big Twins, or early Sportys. It's shape is conducive to velocity and pretty good mass flow, when you come right down to it. In fact, with the exception of porting (or better yet, Extrude honing… more about that later), there's not all that much you can do to improve on it. Not that it hasn't been tried.

A number of air cleaner kits are designed to work with existing air cleaners, replacing only the backing place and the filter element itself.

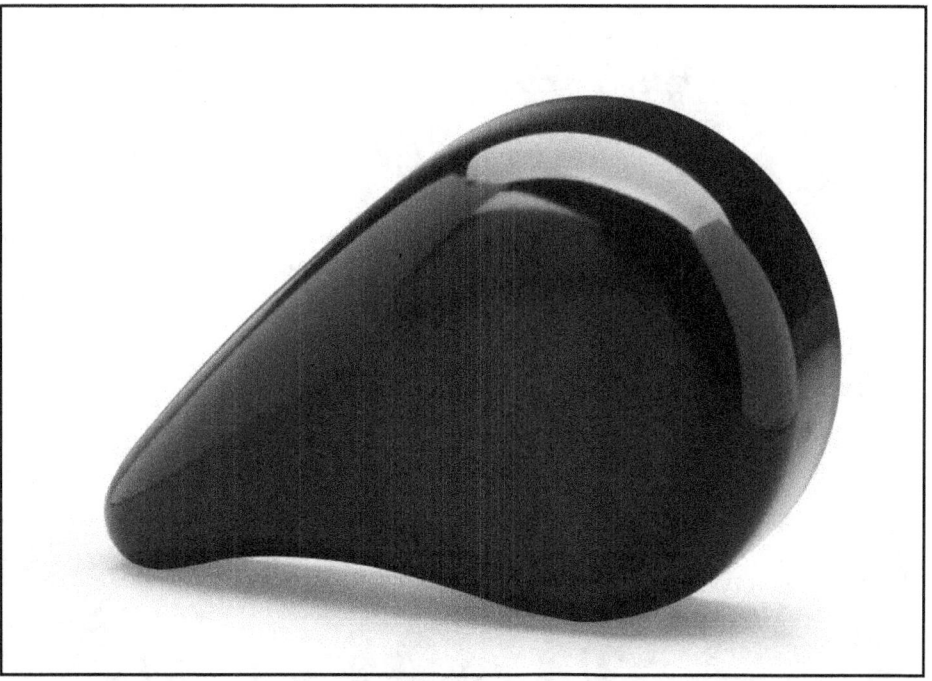

From Dave Perewitz comes this stylish and paintable cover designed to slip over an S&S air cleaner cover for a whole new look.

AFTERMARKET MANIFOLDS

Aftermarket manifolds are surprisingly few and far between for the X engine. Zipper's and S&S offer them, typically for big-inch motors. Bartel's also sells a high performance replacement intake manifold for a maximum effort motor, which makes some sense. As long as you realize that you lose low end tractability to gain top end rush, no free rides here. Therein lies a tale, because frankly one of the most common errors on 883's and even 1200cc engines is over-carburation. This is something of a double-edged sword. If you need more carb you need a high flow manifold to match, or why bother? On the other hand, porting a stock manifold can reveal that the performance restriction wasn't really the carb in the first place. Speaking of which, read on:

FACTORY CARBS

Evolution Sportsters were endowed with a Keihin "butterfly" carburetor when they burst on the scene in 1986. Fortunately the factory realized its mistake by 1988 and the marginal mixer was jettisoned in favor of a much better proposition, the Keihin CV. Frankly, about all you can do with one of the older butterfly Keihins is jet it properly, adjust the accelerator pump and ride. The CV turned out to be much better proposition and the factory has stayed with them ever since.

Not that H-D got the CV totally right from the onset either. California models in particular were afflicted with poor jetting choices and the elimination of the accelerator pump (for a year or so) to meet CARB smog standards. But the fact is dollar for dollar, pound for pound, a properly re-jetted, performance-tuned CV takes some beating for 95% of us street riders. Especially if those

This chrome plated design from Kuryakyn combines a new look with a claimed 35% increase in flow as compared to other high-performance air cleaners. Biker's Choice

streets are much above sea level. We'll talk about that soon.

For now, if you simply must have more carburetor don't overlook the CVs 44mm version (H-D #27934-99). Supposedly intended for use on big-inch Twin Cam motors, I'll tell you right now it fits on Sportys and Buells with the stock (ported?) intake manifold just fine. The option of course is to purchase and install the Big Twin Screamin' Eagle manifold designed to go with it. But there's really no point in doing this on mildly modified motors. Again, the standard manifold is pretty hard to beat.

AFTERMARKET CARBS

The Who's Who of performance carbs: S&S, Mikuni, Edelbrock/Quicksilver, SU, Weber and all the rest can be, and have been, used to great effect on X engines. Thing is, there are dark sides to most all of them.

CARB THEORY 101

The basic principle of operation is still that of a discharge nozzle or "jet" dispensing liquid fuel into the carburetor's air stream. Here the atomized fuel is combined with the air to form a highly volatile mixture. This happens because the incoming air moves through a restriction in the carburetor's throat called the venturi. Air forced to move through a restriction will have greater speed and lower pressure. The fuel discharge jet is placed at the point in the carburetor's throat where the airflow goes from high pressure to low-pressure just beyond the apex, so that the fuel is pushed out of the jet and into the air stream that's moving through the carburetor's throat.

The fuel is pushed out of the jet because the fuel in the float bowl is at atmospheric air pressure of 14.7 psi, while the air pressure in the carburetor's throat is somewhat less. Thus, the fuel flows from the float bowl through the jet into the carburetor's throat.

So, if they all work the same basic way which type of carburetor is best? Wrong question. It is better to ask which carb best suits the riding you intend to do.

CARB TYPES-
Butterfly

S&S, RevTech, Keihins from 1976 through 1989, and Zenith/Bendix carburetor's are called "butterfly" type because they use a pivoting throttle plate to control the airflow through the carb's throat. Its hallmark is simplicity and manufacturers have spent many, many man-hours subtly honing its design to perfection. For good high rpm throttle response and sheer top end power they are tough acts to follow. Lately S&S and RevTech have added some secondary circuits and an accelerator pump to smooth out the carbure-

K&N makes more than just air filter elements. These complete air cleaners from K&N are machined from billet aluminum, come in flamed, milled or plain and fit most late model Sportsters. Biker's Choice

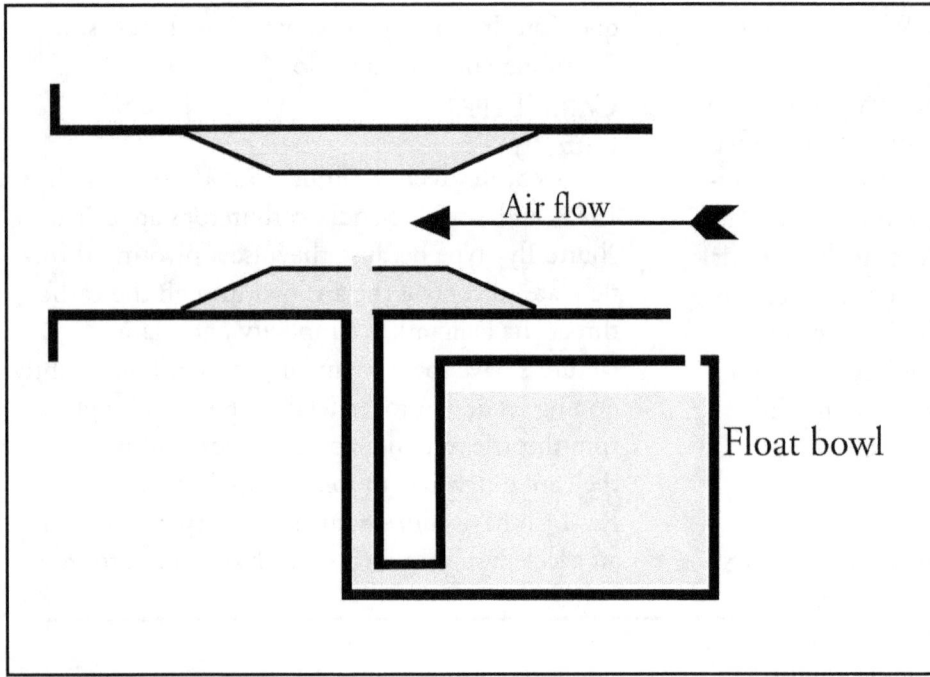

At the heart of every carburetor is a venturi, a restriction in the pipe. Air pressure within the venturi is reduced, so gas (under atmospheric pressure) flows to the venturi where it is atomized and mixed with air.

A CV carburetor uses a floating piston to create a variable venturi the size of which is determined by engine speed and load. Higher speeds create increased vacuum which works against the spring to open the venturi. As the piston moves up the tapered needle is pulled farther out of the orifice - providing more fuel.

tor's over-all response (and mask some of it's flaws). Namely, turbulence and "dead" flow spots in that obese throat as air passes over the throttle plate and the tip of the fuel spray bar. The lesson is clear, it's easiest to over-carburate with a butterfly carb. Getting top end rush can lead to low speed mush, all too easily. Once a butterfly carburetor has been correctly set it works well at the altitude it's been tuned for. The second biggest drawback to the butterfly carb is it's sensitivity to altitude.

Slide

Slide carburetors can produce the most power and have the smoothest transition from idle to full throttle. There's no butterfly in the way, and since the slide itself controls venturi size airspeed across the jet is sometimes ten times as fast as a butterfly carb of the same size. Because the slide is mounted at the apex of the venturi with the main jet needle attached to it a constant airspeed is maintained across the jet needle. That translates into fantastic part-throttle smoothness and excellent low speed throttle response, if you can get fuel to react fast enough to keep up. Which is, oddly, the biggest beef with slide carbs. Fuel just doesn't move as fast as air. Recognizing this, slide carb guys offer up a bewildering number of circuits with precision jets for both air and fuel. You get them jetted right and nothing's better. Get them wrong, you'll hate it. For example, the needle sizes and height increments in the slide amount to a seemingly endless number of combinations. Any adjustments must be done in a certain order. You start by dialing in the high speed circuit, then move to the mid-range, and finally low speed/idle. That can amount to hundreds of settings and nearly as many hours to get it just right. Tuners love 'em. Mechanics often don't.

CV (Constant Velocity)

The modern constant velocity carburetor is a hybrid carb using both a round, pivoting (butterfly) throttle plate and a vacuum-operated slide. The British invented the things and are quite fond of them, sticking as many as two or three on sports cars in the fifties and sixties. In fact, the version that Skinner's Union (*SU* to you and me) used on Jaguars has been adapted to Harleys for years now. Harley has used a Japanese counterpart from Keihin as O.E.M. since 1988 on the Sportster, and since 1990 on Big Twins.

The CV's trick is using a vacuum controlled slide to establish venturi size based on engine demand. Simply connecting a vacuum passage at the bottom of the air slide to a large chamber above it, and sealing the top of the air slide to the walls of the vacuum chamber makes this "self-regulating" magic possible. Open the throttle and vacuum increases in the carburetor's throat behind the air slide, sucking the slide up into the chamber above it. The higher the air slide rises the more the vacuum in the carb's throat decreases. The air slide stops moving when throat vacuum is equal to the vacuum in the chamber. Just the ticket for emission control. The CVs big drawback is that air must flow around two obstacles, the bottom of the air slide and the throttle plate, to get into the intake manifold. So throttle response isn't always crisp. This is one of the few weaknesses in the CV concept. Because the air slide reacts directly to the engine's vacuum, not your right wrist, it's not typically as quick on the throttle as the other types of carburetor's. That can be improved too, as we'll see.

Circuits

We've already learned the basics of carb function, but there's more to it than that. Call it the "fine print" on the carburation contract. All carburetor's have auxiliary circuits to help them get through times when they're not running on a fully warmed-up motor at wide open throttle. The quality and quantity of these circuits tends to relate to basic design characteristics. You're left wondering which of them are Band-Aids, and which are true enhancements.

At idle the throttle plate/valve or slide is nearly closed. Fuel is entering the carburetor's air stream from the idle mixture port, with the amount controlled by the idle mixture screw. If the motor had just been started and the enrichener/choke pulled out a rich air/fuel mixture would be created by reducing air, in the case of a choke, or adding fuel in the case of an enrichener, entering through it's

One thing that keeps S&S at the top of the game, is that they not only offer a good air cleaner and carburetor, but high performance manifolds to go along with them!

own special circuit. This mixture would be drawn up the emulsion tube from the float bowl.

At full throttle the air slide is all the way up and/or the butterfly flat as the horizon. On slide/CV carbs the jet needle's taper is at its smallest for maximum fuel flow out of the needle jet. Snapping the throttle open gets the accelerator pump shooting a stream of raw gasoline into the carburetor's throat through it's own discharge nozzle via a rubber diaphragm on the bottom of the float bowl. The level in the float bowl is controlled by a plastic float that opens and closes the needle valve.

At part throttle the slide/butterfly is somewhere between the two extremes of it's available movement. Now fuel is being sucked out of the main discharge nozzle, rising from the float bowl through the emulsion tube after passing through the main jet. As the fuel rises in the emulsion tube it's mixed with air that enters through the air bleed. The overall amount of fuel passing through the main jet is controlled by the jet's size and the size of the opening in the air bleed. *And it's here, between 1/4 and 3/4 throttle, that we spend most of our riding time.* It figures that this would be the trickiest area of tuning. And the range that pays the biggest dividends once it's tuned correctly.

Now we all know what the three metering ranges are. The low speed (idle to 1/4 throttle), the high speed (3/4 to wide open throttle) and the one we're here to learn more about: the midrange (1/4 to 3/4 throttle). This is *also* the main one the smog testing applies to. The "drive cycle" part of the emissions certification procedure simulates a "normal cruise". By definition this means about 95% of the operation of the motorcycle is at 1/8-1/4 throttle opening. Namely, 1800-2500rpm. Think about it for a minute (or check it out if you won't take my word for it) you can't legally ride a motorcycle constantly at much wider throttle openings. In order to get good "clean" numbers the carb must be jetted *inordinately* lean at *precisely* these engine speeds.

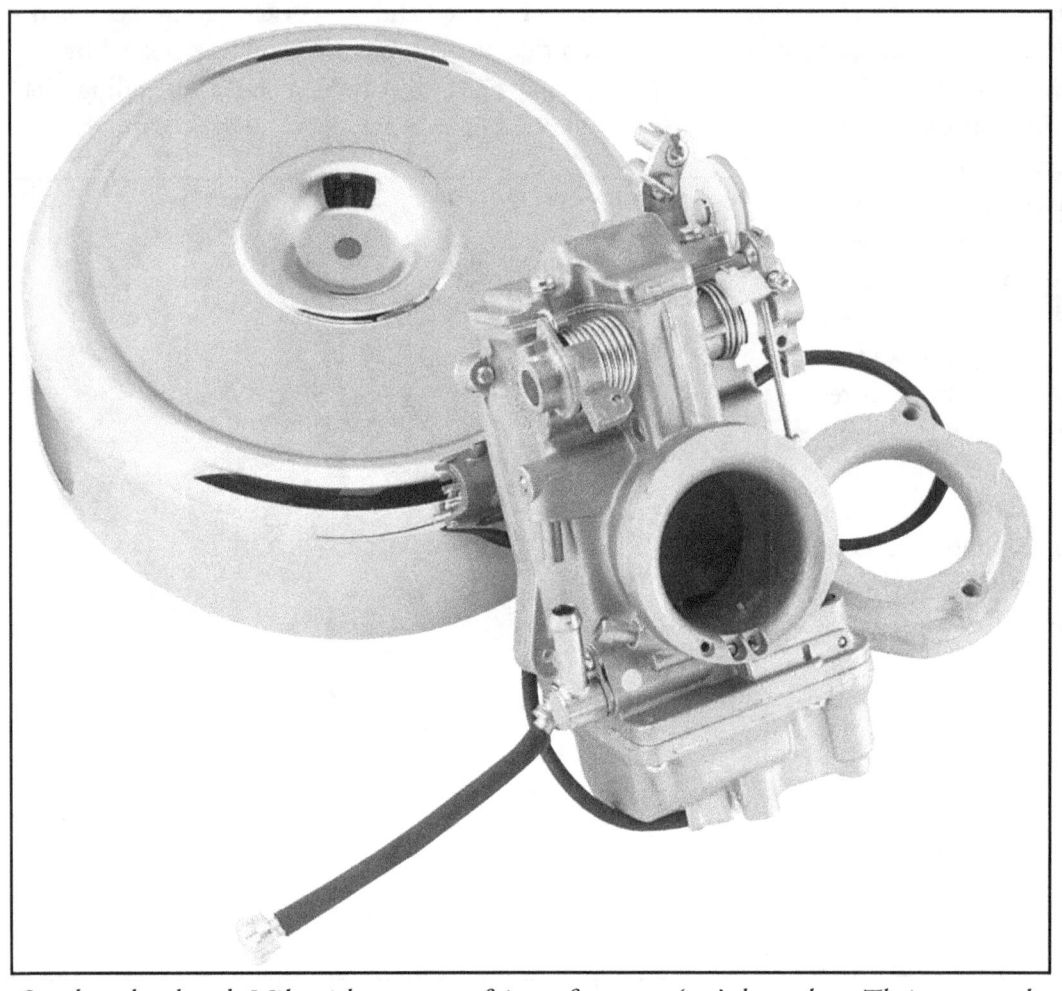

On the other hand, Mikuni has a pretty fair performance 'rep' themselves. Their approach is very sophisticated, and the opposite of S&S. Virtually every circuit can be re-jetted for both air and fuel flow. You can get one of these to work almost as precisely as fuel injection, excepting for the altitude thing.

TUNING

The CV is the carb that has the most flexibility as a performance street carb, not to mention the major advantage that it's already on most X motors. Since most of us will wind up with a CV we might as well start with the CV.

While it is fairly easy, though most often unnecessary, to swap a pilot jet or a main jet and "fix" those low speed and high speed circuits, it's another thing altogether to mess with the midrange. Due to the conspiracy designed to keep us from doing anything about it, it's no wonder tuning kits and replacement carbs are so popular.

The midrange circuit is made up of two parts, the needle jet (AKA: emulsion tube or spray bar) and the jet needle. The needle *jet* is staked into the carb body and was once offered as a one-size-fits-all replacement part by H-D. Can we make a wild guess as to why? Can we say "smog control"? Anyway, since the emissions standards have changed over the years and since there are lots of different models and countries and laws to deal with, the jet *needle*, in various tapers and lengths and such, can be bought.

In fact, there's a rather puzzling array of these little critters available. And what makes it so puzzling is, nobody, not the factory, not Keihin, *NOBODY* is willing and able to supply comprehensive data on these needles. In short, we are left with a partial solution to half the problem. We can buy a needle to tune with, but which one? Will that one be the right one for the needle jet in our particular carb? Is it safe to presume that if there have been changes to the needles over the years? And the jets have changed too? However, we are forced to treat the needle jet as a constant and devote our tuning time to the jet needles that are available (See Needle Chart).

For some reason the big overall winner in the empirical engine tests is the N65C, the infamous 1988 Sportster 1200 needle. This guy, in company with a 45 pilot jet, an "accessible" and properly adjusted mixture screw, and *no further changes*, performs near magic for the "lean staggers" on late models - in *exactly* the rpm range where we spend most of our saddle time. The needle and the low speed jet *combined* cost about 10 bucks. However, for those who prefer to spend more money and less time on a professionally engineered kit there are a variety of tuning and jet kits out there.

JET KITS

As you will see, some kits are "tuning" kits for race bikes while some are simple "bolt-ins" whose only *Raison D'être* is to fix a lean spot. In no particular order, here's a run down on some of the jet kits currently on the market, complete with certain insights into their suitability for your XL or Buell, whatever state of tune it's in. Can you guess which

If you like the idea of using a CV but feel the stock 40mm carb just isn't big enough, there's a 44mm Keihin available from Screamin' Eagle (shown here with a Big Twin manifold).

Needle Chart

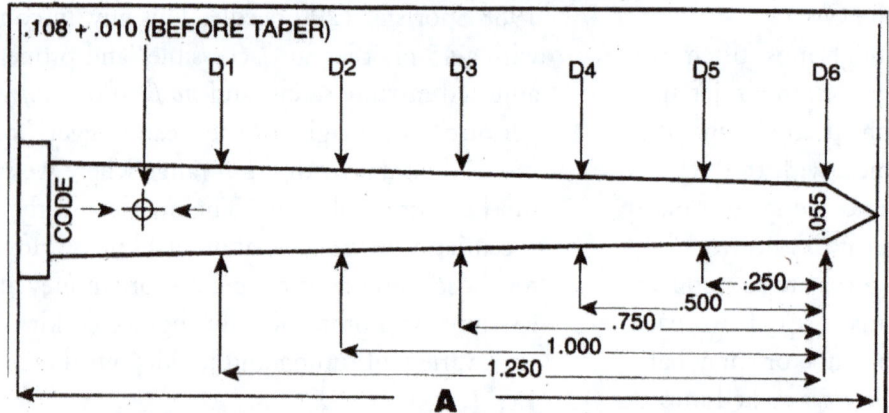

CV Carb Needles 1989-1994

Remember that code on your stock needle? Use that code to locate your needle on this chart. The chart shows the dimensions at different points on the needle. A smaller diameter dimension at a given point (relative to your existing needle) means a richer mixture *at that point* in the rpm range. A larger dimension means leaner. A longer overall length means that the main jet takes over higher in the rpm range. A shorter overall length means it takes over at a lower rpm. If you need a richer needle *at a certain point* in the rpm range, you should consider a needle whose dimensions are smaller only at that point. If you need to richen the *entire* midrange (approximately 1/4 through 3/4 throttle and/or 1500 through 4500 rpm) then choose a needle with a smaller diameter overall. Obviously, if you need to go leaner (rarely) then use a needle with a *larger* diameter. Change *only* in small increments. Do not make *radical* changes! (Note: Different micrometers may show slightly different measurements, so this is only a guide.)

H-D part #	Code	A	D1	D2	D3	D4	D5	D6
27182-92	N86B	2.233	.108	.099	.0895	.077	.072	.068
27183-92	N86Q	2.179	.108	.099	.088	.0785	.073	.0695
27184-92	N86F	2.250	.108	.100	.0865	.0785	.0745	.0685
27186-92	N86E	2.249	.108	.100	.0875	.0775	.073	.0685
27187-93	N65J	2.2675	.108	.098	.0885	.080	.071	.0635
27278-93	N86K	2.200	.108	.100	.058	.078	.0725	.0685
27279-93	N86J	2.2135	.108	.0865	.0875	.0785	.0735	.069
27280-93	N86P	2.198	.108	.099	.0865	.080	.073	.069
27091-88	N65A	2.255	.108	.0985	.0875	.0785	.068	.060
27092-88	N65B	2.2675	.108	.0975	.0875	.074	.066	.054
27094-88	N65C	2.266	.108	.0975	.0900	.081	.070	.063
27099-88	N65D	2.250	.108	.0975	.0895	.081	.0715	.064
27166-89	N72A	2.250	.108	.098	.083	.0765	.070	.067
27167-89	N72B	2.233	.108	.099	.087	.0775	.0705	066
27168-89	N72E	2.250	.108	.098	.0835	.078	.071	.065
27169-89	N72F	2.250	.108	.0995	.085	.077	.0715	.066
27175-90	N72R	2.267	.108	.0985	.0855	.077	.073	.068
27176-90	N72Y	2.250	.108	.099	.0885	.0775	.071	.067
27178-90	N72S	2.267	.108	.0975	.085	.076	.070	.067
27179-90	N72M	2.269	.108	.097	.0845	.074	.0705	.065

When you decide that re-jetting a CV is required; A) make sure it's really required, B) realize that if mileage goes to hell and horse power goes nowhere it wasn't required, and C) there are three parts to the jetting equation: Low speed (pilot) jet, high speed (main) jet, and the one everyone forgets, mid-range (needle) jet and its partner the jet *needle*. I cannot over emphasize the need to realize in which of the three areas you need to make modifications and make *one change at a time*. To aid in that endeavor here is a useful, but by no means complete, list of optional jetting for CV Keihins. This was *not* an easy list to compile as the Motor Company only provides part numbers, not sizes or information for this stuff.

This needle chart was assembled with great care from top secret sources and may self-destruct at any time.

one is right for you? If you can, most of the guesswork is over.

The Thunderslide kit from Dyno Jet.

The votes aren't in on this yet. It would appear the company is still developing this kit, even though it's been on the market for years. Like computer software, they keep sending out "updated" versions with subtle differences in design and installation. In fact, the instructions are marked accordingly to identify the version you are dealing with. In addition, the kits are for basically stock engines for both Big Twin and Sportster, but none specifically for Buell, yet. Empirically the correct Thunderslide kit works very well indeed on "uncorked" but not cammed-up Big Twins. Sportsters, and Buells are less a certainty. Bear in mind, these kits are simply *not built* to make horsepower, only to correct factory jetting and improve throttle response. Generally, that's exactly how it works out - within the parameters of the kit. However, using a kit designed for a near-stock Sporty may not do much good on a full-house Buell and vice-versa. Exhaust scavenging, cam timing, and air cleaner restrictions (or lack of) make major differences.

Dyno Jet kit —— without the slide.

Dyno Jet lists kits for both the S1 Lightning and the S2 Thunderbolt, as well as "regular" Harley kits. Buell kits are notably different than Harley versions, but again the point is to correct lean EPA jetting flaws in mildly uncorked motors. The only "race" kit offered is for 883's with disabled accelerator pumps. Here's a list of common applications:

- #8101 - is for California 883's & 1200's that came stock with no accelerator pump.
- #8102 - is for all Harleys with CV carbs, from '89 to '95.
- #8703 - is the 883 race kit.
- #8106 - S1 Lightning (presumably S3's as well) '96-on
- #8104 - S2 Thunderbolt '94-'95
- #27099-93R (Harley #) is the same as #8102
- #27045-97 (Harley #) is for CV carbs on '96 and later Hogs, not the same as #8106.

The carb bodies on '96 and later H-D's are slightly different than those used on earlier models. Mostly affecting accelerator pump passages which are designed to keep them from squirting any more than the absolute minimum fuel quantities necessary. They are the same bodies used on '96 and later Buell carbs, jetting excepted. Most of the catalog vendors for these kits, (Custom Chrome, Drag Specialties, etc.) do *not* make the distinction between '96 and later Harley carbs, but *Harley* does.

Looking down the throat of this QwikSilver carburetor pretty well explains why slide carbs are appreciated for their unrestricted "smooth-bore."

"Clone kits"

Be aware that the accuracy of the "knock off" needle tapers and needle jet drillings are not always accurate. Plus, too often these kits come with more choices than solutions, trying to kill all the birds with one rock. Choose the wrong needle out of the selection and you're nowhere, slow. Your particular bike may run like a striped-assed Magpie with one of these installed, but don't bet on it.

Factory Iron

This kit takes a slightly different tack in that it does *not* include a different needle jet. Rather, it treats that function as a constant and uses a different taper on the jet needle. The instructions also stress the need to hold that needle steady and useful tips on exactly how to do just that. Good advice for any tuner. Well made, the Factory Iron kit doesn't include a different spring either but that precious needle is made of titanium.

Yost Kit

Ah simplicity. This kit takes it pretty much right where it needs to go. Offering both jet needle and needle jet and not much else. But, judging from the empirical results and popularity it works.

Be extremely careful to correctly install any aftermarket CV "mod" kits, like the Yost Power Tube or Dyno Jet Kit. These kits tend to work or not in direct proportion to the care and attention to detail you lavish on them. Do NOT try to out guess these things, or mistakenly assume things like, "Gee Beaver, if modifying the slide spring a little works so well, then modifying it a whole bunch has gotta be better. Right?"

DIAL-IN

If you don't have access to a dyno for dial-in the next best thing is to find a deserted stretch of road, lay into the throttle and take note of how easily and quickly the engine pulls to redline. The engine should accelerate smoothly and quickly through all gears.

High speed

You can double check the main jet by quickly closing the throttle from wide open to 7/8 position when the engine's rpm is greater than 4500. If

When you choose an air cleaner, consider not just the style but how much capacity the filter has to move air to and through the carburetor.

the engine accelerates slightly the main jet is too lean. Go one size larger, but never more than one at a time. If the engine hesitates or misses slightly or feels sluggish and blubbers, the main is too rich and should be swapped for a smaller main jet. If the engine just slows a slight amount, the jetting is very close to correct. Another somewhat riskier trick involves flipping the enrichener on momentarily. You are adding fuel and if the scooter picks up and pulls harder it was running lean. If it bogs you were jetted too fat.

Mid-range

Hunting or surging at steady throttle openings from 2500rpm to 4500rpm, is a pretty fair indication of incorrect mid-range jetting. The trick is to figure out if the jetting is too rich or too lean. Snap the throttle open sharply. If the engine pops, cuts out, or backfires and won't pull hard, it's too lean. If the engine blubbers and farts it's too rich.

Low speed

Backfires through the carburetor above 1500 rpm indicates you should increase the size of your low speed jetting (pilot or intermediate jet) a notch, tweak the low speed mixture screw out 1/8-1/4 turn and try again. If the engine feels sluggish, sounds flat, blubbers or emits black smoke from the exhaust, turn the idle mixture adjustment screw in 1/4 turn or reduce the size of the low speed jetting.

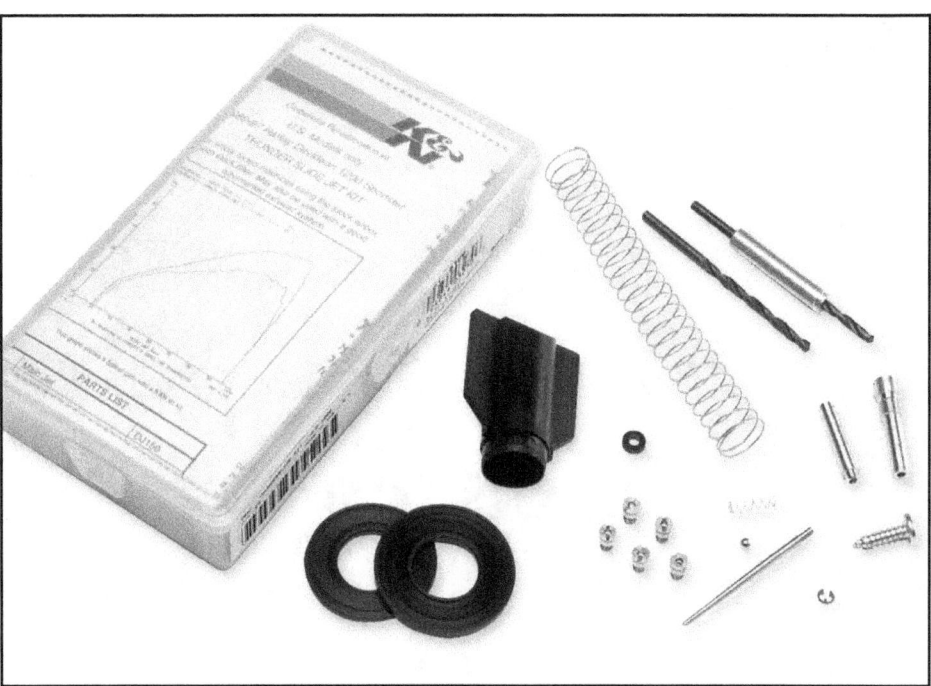

The K&N Thunderslide kit includes a redesigned slide (said to improve throttle response on the CV carb), as well as jets and a new tapered needle. Biker's Choice

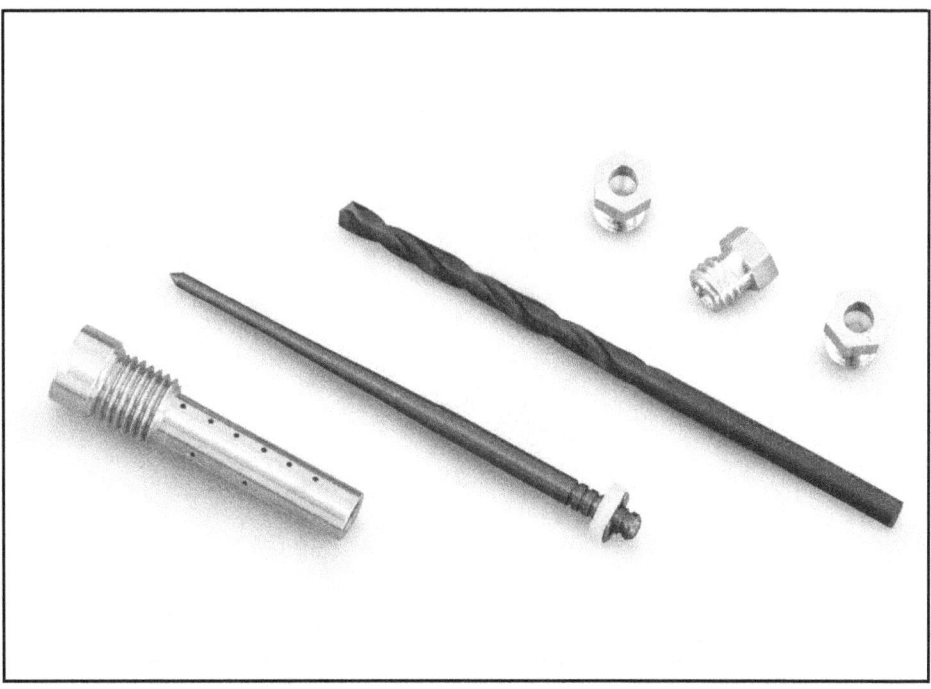

The Yost kit comes with the standard jets and a new needle, and their own emulsion tube designed to break the fuel up into smaller particles so it atomizes more easily once it hits the airstream. Biker's Choice

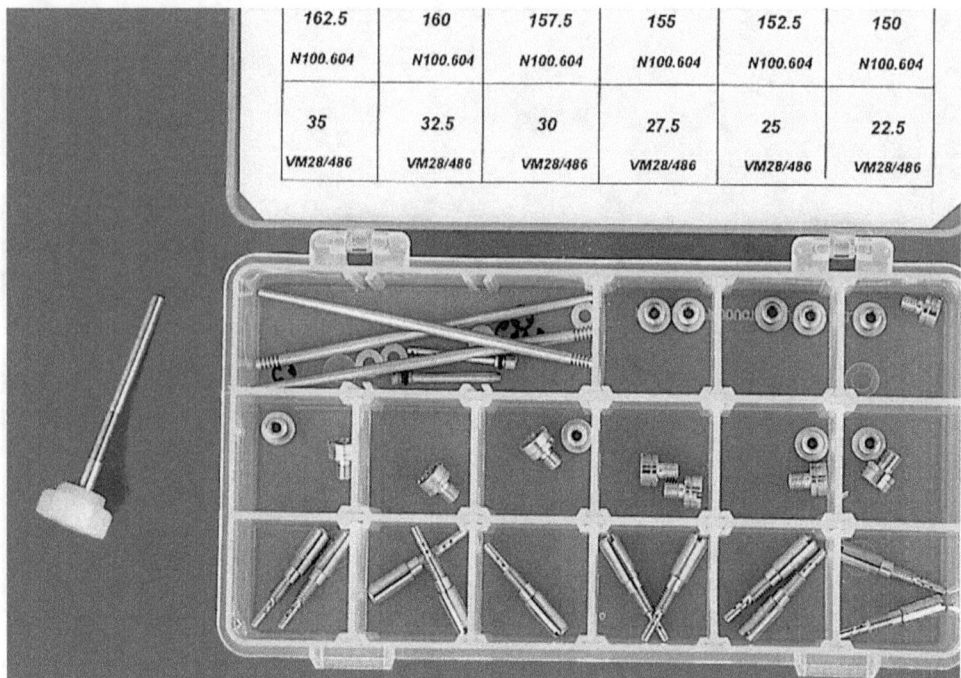

Mikuni makes this complete tuners kit, available for their slide carburetors.

This was probably the first true high performance air cleaner. It's still pretty hard to beat, based on the teardrop shape and the air-guide velocity dimple in the middle. The biggest drawback is the foam filter. Swap it for a deep K&N and this thing would likely still hold it's own with the new designs on a dyno test.

Mixture screw

First off you need to know that not all low speed adjustment screws work the same way. The rule of thumb is, if the screw lives on the air cleaner side of the float bowl it adjusts or meters air. If the screw lives between the float bowl and the engine, it adjusts fuel. Just like the stock CV for instance. Now that you know and after you've "accessed" it, what do you do with it?

Ignore all that 1 1/4 – 1 1/2 turn crap you may have heard regarding the "correct" adjustment for this important setting. With the engine at proper operating temperature and idle speed (900-1000rpm) turn the idle mixture screw inward (clockwise) SLOWLY until the motor starts to falter. Then back the mixture screw out *slowly*, 1/8 turn per adjustment and count five *slowly*, until the motor begins to pick up idle speed on its own and run smoothly. At this point, give the screw exactly 1/8 turn more and QUIT fiddling. Re-adjust the idle *speed* screw as necessary to maintain the rpm at about 900-1000rpm.

Altitude

At 10,000 feet, a 50 horsepower X motor is making a lousy 35. And, that's if the carb is jetted perfectly. For every 1000 foot increase in altitude, there is a three percent drop in power. Do the math. At sea level barometric air pressure is about 30 inches of mercury, or if you prefer, 15 pounds per square inch (psi). Up to an altitude of about 10,000 feet that pressure will drop about an inch for every 1,000 feet. So, at 6,000 feet you've got 24 inches of mercury and 20% less air available. The engine is 20% less powerful. End of story. The loss can be *more* than 20%, perhaps far more, if you don't jet roughly 20% leaner. Therefore, if the difference in flow between one jet and another is 5%, you'd need to drop to a jet three or four sizes smaller to restore the fuel/air balance. Less air, less fuel, same ratio.

The only carburetors with any kind of defense against running like crap without the re-jet are so called "altitude compensating" types. There are only two: The Edelbrock/Quicksilver and the stock CV. Think about that before you toss the stocker, especially if you plan on riding through the mountains.

Fuel Injection

Speaking of altitude compensation and precise metering let's take a quick tour of the basic pieces and processes in Buell's Dynamic Digital Fuel Injection.

- It's a "Closed Loop" design (more about that later).
- Each cylinder is individually controlled (call it single "gas" fire)
- Independent spark and fuel control (this one is obvious).
- Microprocessor based (equally obvious).
- Engine and air temperature compensated (meaning an oxygen sensor, more about that later as well)
- Sequential port injection (call this one "poop" on demand)
- Auto enrichment. That's automatic choke in car speak, but it adds gas rather than reduce air, so "choke" it ain't.
- Intelligent feedback. The system learns how you ride and what you've done to the motor, within reason. This is important as we'll soon see.
- Full diagnostic capability. Saves time, money and consternation. You don't have to guess what's wrong when, and *if*, it ever goes wrong.
- Complete engine management. Who needs management for partial engines anyway?
- Single sensor timing strategy. This means no grooves cut into the flywheels, ala Harley, and that it's possible to revert to a 'normal' electronic ignition if you ever go back to a carb.

Plus, we have a half a dozen sensors:

Throttle Position TPS. Telegraphs your punch.

Cam Position CPS. Where's that crank and how fast is it turning? Note: this is also the only sensor required to make the bike run. The rest have default "limp home" modes.

Intake Air Temperature IATS. Are you trolling through the desert or bombing through a blizzard? Note: this sensor lives and works in the Helmholz. You must, therefore, persuade it to move to any air cleaner you choose to run instead of the stock one.

At the heart of any CV carburetor is a floating piston with attached tapered needle. Piston (and needle) position are determined by the amount of vacuum pulling up against the spring.

41

That's right, this Buell is fuel injected, but not by the factory. A custom intake manifold must be made to make this happen, but it just might be worth it, since the thing runs so strong and crisp. You could do the same thing for a Sportster.

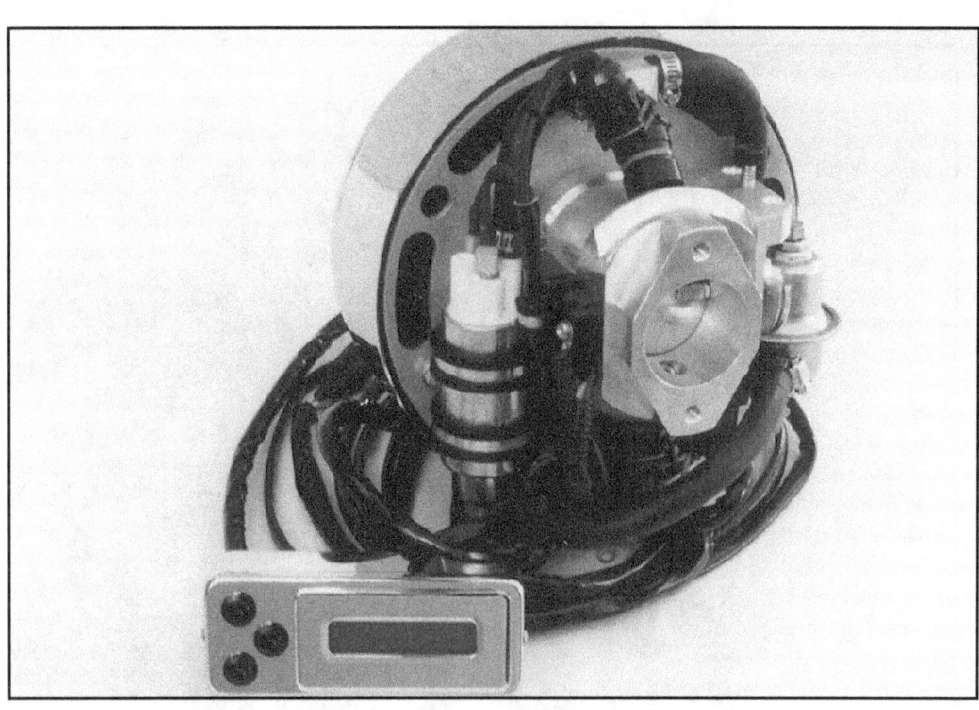

This is a better look at a Whitex fuel injection unit. Nearly all the components, including the fuel pump, are housed under the air cleaner for a neat, simple installation.

Engine Temperature ETS. Would that be with a cold motor or are you about to melt the beggar?

Oxygen O2. Is that mixture stoichiometrically correct for all the above? Note: this sensor grounds through the rear header pipe mounting. Keep your exhaust tight or else.

Bank Angle BAS. Should we shut the motor down for you now that you've fallen off?

And to manage all these sensors, we get the Brain, Electronic Control Unit or Module, making millions upon millions of decisions per second.

Even though Fuel Injection, all else equal, can produce as much as 8% more power it's really the functional increase in efficiency throughout the rev range that you can feel at the throttle, potentially far more precise than a carb. The system is a so-called "closed loop" design, yet open looped at both ends. Before describing this techno-babble term, suffice it to say what it really amounts to, among other things, is that the system is smart enough to figure out that you threw a pipe on the bike. Or an air cleaner kit or both and will compensate for it. At least to a degree, automatically.

In Automotive engineering terms, "closed loop" refers to the mode of operation whereby the ECU (Electronic Control Unit) monitors input from all sensors and trims fuel delivery and ignition timing "maps" to optimize engine performance. "Open loop" operation ignores most sensor input, so fuel delivery and timing are based on pre-programmed "table" parameters. In short, one system favors working to the orders of actual needs, the other to what should be needed.

That's where add-on aftermarket controls like the K&N Power Commander or the RevTech DFO come in. They allow you to override the system (within parameters of roughly 5-10%, built into the ECM) to clean up any little glitches in the factory settings and maps. For those who need to go deeper into the mystery new software-based technology allows re-mapping the ECM at core level. Actually, it's a little like a lobotomy for the brain. Since the factory uses proprietary codes the aftermarket approach is to wipe 90% out to create a clean slate. Then the program overwrites with a more performance-oriented baseline map that you can tailor to your needs.

AFTERMARKET EFI

As of this writing, there's really only one way to add fuel injection to an X engine. Whitek makes a self-contained unit that has all the necessary electronics hidden in the air cleaner. It has an advantage over factory efforts in at least two ways. First, it's a performance EFI system, not one that's primarily intended to comply with smog laws. Second, it has on-board, push-button adjustability. There are two drawbacks as well: Expense and the fact that it must be adapted to fit an X engine since it was designed for Big Twins.

But, don't worry because whether you like EFI or not, it is the future. And that means more sophisticated engine management. If things go like they have with the car guys, we'll wonder 10 years from now why we ever wanted a carburetor? If things go like the car guys, we'd *better* have an excellent aftermarket method of controlling it at the source, and I think we will. Then the responsibility is ours to learn how to use this technology for clean performance.

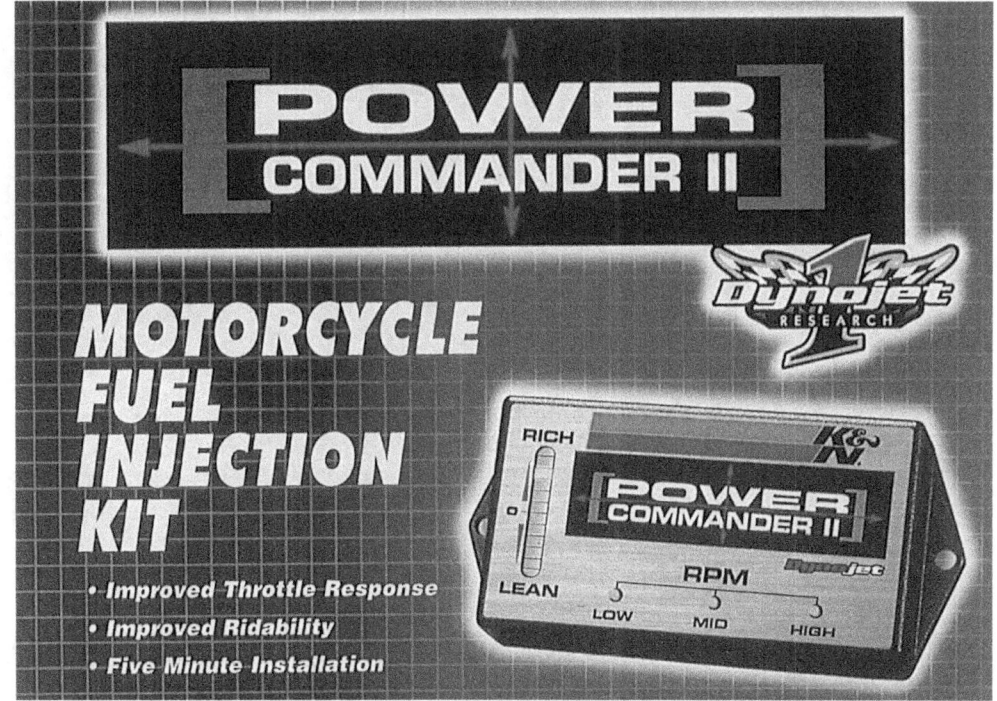

For factory EFI systems there are over ride systems like the Power Commander or Rev Tech Power DFO. But don't kid yourself, these only work within the ranges the factory mapping allows. That's just fine for most of us, since there's about 20% latitude, plus or minus, built into the amount of time the injectors operate.

Chapter Five

Ignition

How Best to Light The Fire

To knock the rust off an old saw, "It takes three things to make 'em run: spark, compression and fuel."

Everybody seems pretty conversant and comfortable with the latter two. But, with apologies to the Bard, the spark's the thing. Ignition systems always seem to create difficulties and controversy, real and imagined, and for good reason. It's ironic that the system most central to the happy banging and popping we hold so dear is the one we are least

The ignition you choose can be as simple as a dual fire coil triggered by a factory or aftermarket pickup, or as exotic as a dual-plug single-fire setup triggered by the latest offering from the aftermarket. What you need is a good, dependable spark with plenty of reserve - at just the right time.

likely to understand. Single fire, dual fire, battery and coil, magneto, inductive discharge, capacitive discharge. This s—t is complicated.

Ignition Types
Battery and coil

The battery and coil ignition, patented by a fella named Kettering way back in 1908, is simple and effective. Even though his patent drawing actually looks like something a drunken eight year old came up with. The stock ignition system on new H-Ds uses the same "inductive discharge" principle of operation, but without the contact points. Instead, we have the silicone chip to trigger our sparks. The major functional difference is that electronics don't require adjustment and maintenance. Only they do.

If they are to operate at optimum levels most aftermarket systems, single-fire or not, require a bit of tuning. The whole point of features like adjustable advance curves and rev limiters is to benefit by improving what is admittedly a less than optimum factory set up. Wow, a programmable, tunable, low maintenance, rapid rise, hot coil, solid state, multiple spark, single fire system just has to be the state of the art way to fire. Only maybe, just maybe, it's not.

Magneto

The much maligned Magneto is even older than the battery and coil, and not half bad as a high performance ignition, even today. Magnetos still have a lot of things going for them, but the first thing you should realize

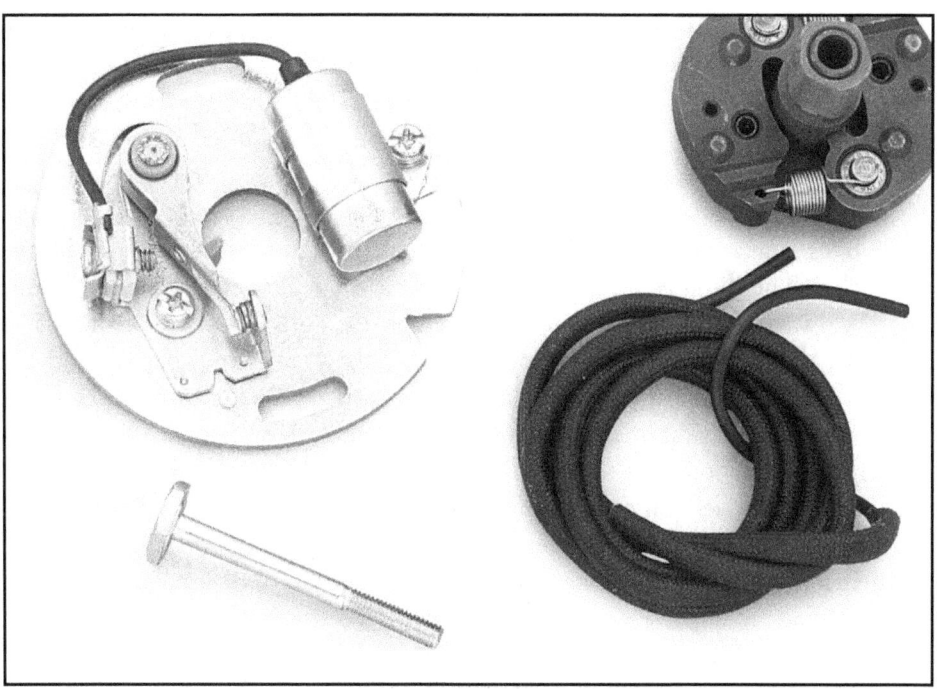

Despite the allure of a the simpler and easier-to-service points-type ignition, the system just doesn't hold a candle to any of the current factory or aftermarket ignitions - which provide more spark, easily adjustable curves and no maintenance.

Designed by Dave Perewitz, this coil bracket mounts between the cylinders and includes the ignition and starter switch. Shown are a pair of RevTech coils designed for dual-plug heads. CCI

45

is the fact they don't need a battery to work. Mags have rapid voltage rise, a good Mag can manage 30kv in 35 micros. No misfires, no fouling, thank you very much. By comparison, a battery and coil set up is painfully slow in the voltage rise race. It's been the standard for eons. It's simple and it does the job, as long as you don't mind the maintenance headaches. The thing is, most of us do.

As always, there's no free lunch here either in the sense that magnetos cost horsepower due to the fact they operate mechanically. The drag of those gears operating in mesh means as much as 3-4 horsepower lost to friction. The sheer weight of the things is a drawback as well. Since most magnetos weigh at least as much as a battery, some are notably heavier, so there's virtually no advantage to a magneto in the ballast department.

Cd Ignition
Then there's the system that theoretically should beat 'em all. Capacitive Discharge CD) technology, whether battery triggered or magneto style, has so much going for it, it can actually be a problem. Solid state, and with power and speed second to none, it should be the perfect ignition technology. But it's not. A CD ignition takes only a couple of microseconds to store enough energy to reach full voltage. This is so far below the "wet fouling" range of a spark plug that it becomes a non-issue. When it fires it's so fast that even if the plug was fouled it would spark. The problem is, this intensity and speed is so brief that even though the plug will fire there is no guarantee that the fuel /air mixture will burn. The spark duration of a CD ignition may only be 10% of the 0.5 -1.0 millisecond rate of a magneto or battery and coil. But with a combustion chamber three and a half inches across, or more on big-inch Harleys, this may not be enough time to get the mixture completely burned. That's why twin-plug conversions on H-Ds make some sense. Each flame has only half the distance to go in the length of time provided. That's also why using this technology, only adding the capability to do it several times to create a so-called "multiple spark" ignition, is the best answer yet if you can live with additional bulk. Voila, complete combustion. Only?

WHAT'S A COIL

The heart of all ignition systems is a high ratio transformer we call a coil. Like the name suggests, it is essentially a device made up of two sets of wire windings "coiled" around a core of soft iron. Put a current of a few amps at 14 volts through the primary winding (lets say about 400 turns) and you create an electromagnetic field. Now interrupt the current flowing through the primary windings and allow the magnetic field to collapse. The field collapses over the secondary winding (approximately 15000 turns of wire) and induces a current measured in only miliamps but with enough voltage to fire the spark plugs. One more time:14 volts times a step-up ratio of about 375:1, gives you 20,000 or more volts to fire the plug. Only you don't. Nothing is 100% efficient in the first place, and in the second place, this coil lives on a

Let's start where it all ends up, at the spark plug. Whether you're a fan of the latest tech or something like these Champions, it comes down to proper heat range, clean tips and proper gap. Biker's Choice

stock Harley and has to fire two plugs. Hmmmm? That means each plug has only half the available voltage to work with. Only it doesn't, always.

Electricity working as it does, like water, takes the path of least resistance to ground. Even if you are lucky enough to have two dead perfect spark plugs, new, properly gapped, and properly torqued in place, there's no guarantee that both cylinders are behaving exactly the same. If one is hotter or less mechanically sound than the other, the spark, like a mother vulture, will only feed the healthy one. And even a healthy cylinder takes nearly 15000-20000 volts to pop. That means the stock arrangement is only adequate.

Seriously, this is one of the main reasons why high output so-called single fire ignitions have the attraction they do. Each cylinder benefits from precise timing and all the available voltage from its own personal coil. Even if single fire is not something you want to mess with a tremendous improvement can be had by mounting a better (30,000- 40,000 volt) coil. Accel, H-D's Screamin' Eagle, Dyna, or any of a number of other high performers are available for duty.

As good as all the systems available are, and as many choices as we have, we should take a quick look at what the spark itself should ideally offer to its partners: compression and fuel. Face it, no matter what you have creating the spark, it's the spark plug that delivers it. Plugs

Good wires like these are worth as much as 2-3 horses on the dyno. Mostly, you want all the available voltage to travel through the wire and not bleed out. Cheap wires can be seen arcing to metal on cool, moist evenings, a nice light show but bad news for performance.

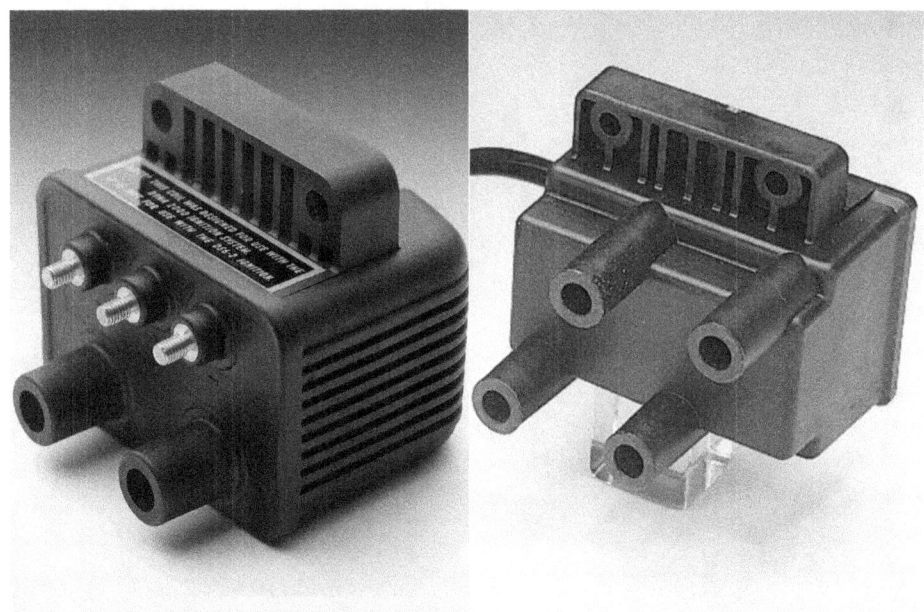

Ah the coil, lots of choices here. The priorities are, voltage to the plug, proper resistance values for the ignition system, easy mounting, small size and proof against water getting in and voltage leaking out (often from the wire towers). Coil on the left is for single-plug single-fire system while the one on the right is for a dual plug S-F system.

have their work cut out for them under the best of circumstances. And giant strides in metallurgy have made them so reliable we don't give them a second thought. Only maybe we should. From the surface gap racing plug to the split electrode (Splitfire) street plug, to the much maligned but damned clever Platinum tipped plug, there's enough technology in this simple device to enable us to screw up completely. Just remember, thread, reach, heat range and tip. And stay as close to what the factory says as possible. It'll be O.K.

And no, the heat range of a spark plug does not affect combustion temperature. All it does is determine the speed at which this temperature is removed from the combustion chamber. I think we've safely established that electrically speaking, speed and power are important factors in clean combustion. But, as true now as ever, timing is everything. Not just ignition timing, but the controlled rate of burn in the combustion chamber.

Tell you what, pretend you're a spark plug for just a minute. Here you are with your head poked into a dark room with a weird shape. You want to clearly see every nook and cranny, far and near, to make damn sure there aren't any gremlins hiding anywhere that can pour black gooey stuff all over you or stick a lit grenade up your nose before you see them coming. And, speaking of coming, the "floor" of this room is moving up toward you at what seems like the speed of sound. You only have a split second to reconnoiter, so you've got to light things up extensively and brightly. How do you do it? A flashbulb is probably too quick and too bright. A laser beam is too tightly focused. A match won't cut it. A smart spark plug would most likely snap on a searchlight like the ones you see at movie premieres and make a rapid but thorough sweep of the chamber (or room). In ignition parlance this approximates the "controlled burn" that is considered ideal.

To recap the objective: To ignite and burn (not explode) the fuel/air mixture in the combustion chamber, do it at exactly the right time, and do it completely, under all conditions, at any rpm. In order to do that, we need a few more components.

Sparkplugs

Preferably ones that won't foul easily, with a highly conductive electrode, featuring a gap that does not change or erode quickly. Possibly silver, platinum, or gold alloy. Automobile engines that advertise 100,000 mile of service before they need a tune-up use these kinds of sparkplugs, particularly platinum. No goofy little "noogee" that screws on to the top either. All they do is come loose and make misfires. No offense to any fan of the things, but split electrode plugs are largely a Band-Aid for a poor standard ignition system. Virtually all those who find an improvement in driveability with these plugs have a stock set-up. Virtually all those who can't tell the difference have an upgraded ignition system. Either way, don't kid yourself that sparkplugs make power, cause they can't. All they can do is allow the power made by all the other parts to get to the pavement unimpeded.

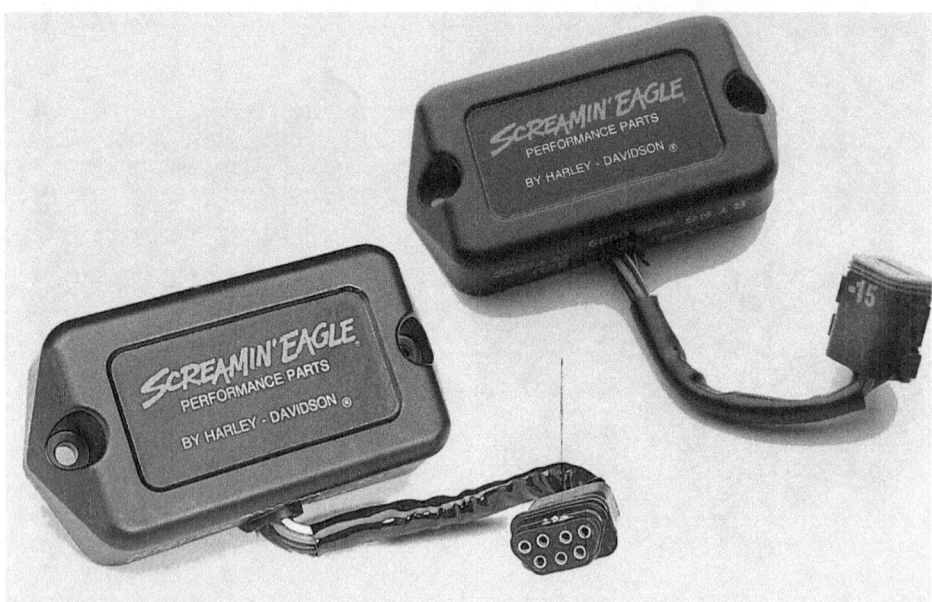

For 1986 thru 1997 models (except Sport 1200S) if you choose to retain the factory dual-fire system, an upgraded external ignition module, like the one on the left, is the way to go. There are 2 basic features you're after... a higher rev limit and a different initial advance curve. The curve should give a crisp "pull" without "pinging" and being able to reach a higher engine speed. On the right is the Deutsch style version designed to fit '94 - '97 machines.

COIL/SPARKPLUG WIRES

Certainly don't use a carbon core type. It is better to have a more durable and conductive core, with insulation that won't allow energy to bleed through the sheathing. We want molded, waterproof, non-arcing plug caps and well insulated coil boots, for the same reasons.

COIL(S)

30,000-40,000 volts or more. Waterproof encapsulation with coil towers that don't allow arcing from one to the other, and studs for primary wires that don't come loose. Once these criteria are met the smaller, lighter and easier to mount, the better.

TRIGGERING MECHANISM

Solid state Hall-effect type. Potted or encapsulated. Heat and vibration proof. Advance/retard controlled electronically or by vacuum, or a combination of both. Digital/adjustable timing for each individual combustion chamber.

IGNITION MODULE

A seriously smart electronic brain. Preferably one that automatically adjusts spark duration and/or frequency. Manually adjustable advance curves are the next best thing, assuming you can find the right curve for your particular engine's needs. Full advance at full throttle is a given, but part throttle operation is much more tricky. Too much advance at a given rpm can get you pinging, overheating, even a holed piston. Too little, and you're flogging a lethargic, 600lb slug. Worse, every engine seems to

Don't let H-D's habit of changing part numbers on these things confuse you - this OE Buell module turns out to be identical to a Sportster Screamin' Eagle module. The things to look for is the curve "code" (in this case "Q") and the rev limits... both clearly marked in white lettering on the module case.

So, if you find a module with a curve and rev limit you like but the plug is different... just use an adapter like the one on the left, or like the one on the right for pre-1990 models. The point is, you should focus on the capabilities of the module, not how to plug it in because there is a way.

49

As far a these capabilities are concerned, some will prefer to include adjustability, since what works for the set-up you have today, might not for what you plan in future, unless you can tweak the module, such as this one.

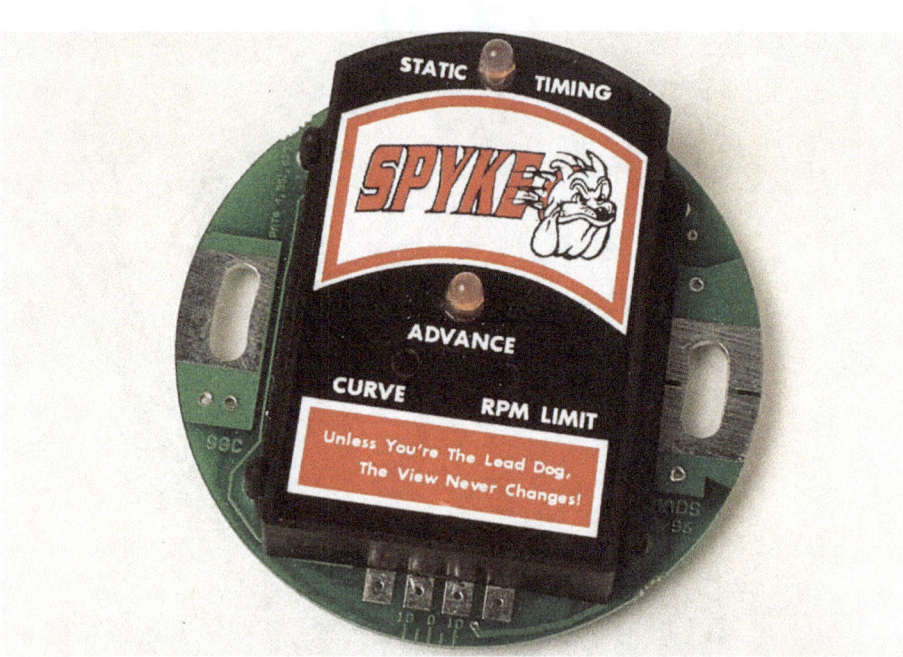

For some time the aftermarket has offered modules that fit entirely into the "cone" cavity, eliminating external modules altogether. The factory decided they could play this game too, so since 1998 that's been the OE set-up. There are plenty of potions for upgrades of this type as well! Whether a factory S E dual fire, the popular HI-4, or a single-fire, multiple-spark module like this one.

want something slightly different, something virtually unique.

ELECTRONIC SPEED

But, with no misfires, no fouling, thank you very much. To keep a spark plug happy the "juice" across the gap should hit 15kv in 40 microseconds, or less. By comparison, a battery and coil set up is painfully slow in the voltage rise race. Speeds on the order of 50-100 microseconds are about all you can get. Contrast this with a capacitive discharge ignition (CDI) which takes only a couple of microseconds to store enough energy for full voltage.

Now that we have touched on some of the more important ignition characteristics, lets examine the three common ways to combine them electronically: single fire, dual fire, and multiple fire.

THE SYSTEM

Dual-Fire: The H-D original is more formally known as V-fire III, and is still the factory's preferred method of making with the pops and bangs. It may or may not be yours. To its advantage are simplicity and reliability, and the many aftermarket and factory upgrades available. In standard trim an electric signal is sent from the pick up and reluctor, (also known as the sensor plate assembly and rotor) to a single dual-lead ignition coil. This roughly 20,000 volt coil promptly passes the dual-fire down both plug leads simultaneously to both cylinders. One theoretically needing the spark at precisely that moment, the other absolutely not needing any. Other than this wasted spark the primary performance flaw in the stock dual fire system is insufficient spark energy. The factory ignition with its relatively impotent coil averages 4-6% misfires at idle. How's it going to work at 6,000rpm? Upgrading to a 40,000 volt coil should be first priority. Second priority is to assure the proper spark curve and rev limit for your specific purpose. That may, or may not, mean changing the stock ignition module.

SINGLE-FIRE

The biggest performance advantage to a single-fire ignition probably is not the fact that each cylinder gets it's own individual spark, (from it's very own high voltage coil), as much as the ability to set the timing optimally for each cylinder. Treating each cylinder individually means good spark energy, elimination of the wasted spark, and inherently smoother operation from the two coils. This improves starting, offers crisper throttle response, and generates less vibration in most cases. Whether or not there is a power increase accompanying these benefits is subject to some debate. If there is you can bet it comes primarily from proper ignition timing. When we have seen horsepower show up on a dyno it usually stems from the simple ability to alter rear cylinder timing a few degrees, relative to and without affecting the front one. Impossible with the factory arrangement.

MULTIPLE FIRE

Okay, if offering its own increased spark energy to each cylinder makes sense, then what about custom tailoring spark requirements within the individual cylinders? That's the science inside Multiple Spark Discharge (MSD). You see, all the wonderful characteristics we've talked about so far kind of fall apart over one little issue, big bores. Most high performance ignitions, whether dual or single fire, are engineered to give a serious jolt at high engine speeds. Fine for racing, where quick rise time and laser intensity spark are so important. Part throttle behavior on a street bike is a different story, and one chapter in that story is the fluid dynamics that govern the flow of combustible mixture into the chamber. Mixture slows down to a relative crawl at lower rpms. It just sort of oozes in and with the spark happening so rapidly, the whole show can easily fizzle out before it can travel all the way across that wide t h r e e a n d a h a l f inches of piston. Add more bore and it's even more likely. This difference, between lighting the spark plug and lighting the mixture, is all the difference in the world. The hot rod guys have known this long enough to make dual plug heads, even on street bikes, a fairly common sight.

The theory behind that is to allow twice the spark, to travel half the distance, for more complete combustion. Good idea, as far as it goes, but not without drawbacks. Usually twin plug heads require an altered full advance timing to work best. Unfortunately, if you happen to lose one of your two plugs you might find a hole in your piston, quickly.

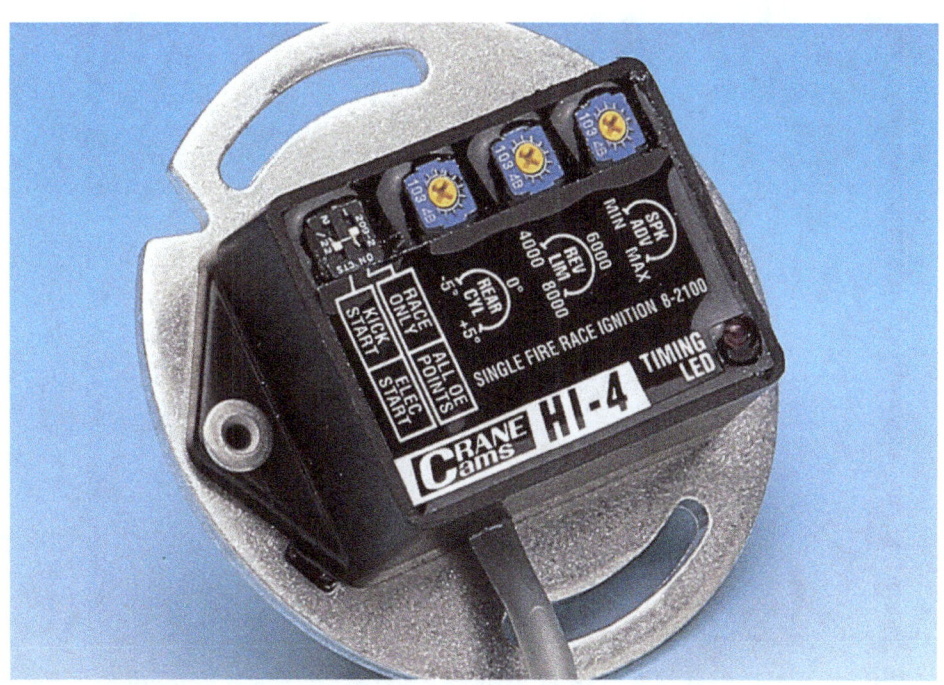

One of the most popular of the aftermarket all-in-one ignitions is this single-fire Crane HI 4. Allows adjustment of the curve as well as the rev limit. Even lets you set the timing of the rear cylinder ahead or behind the front slightly.

No such problems with multiple fire (MSD) set-ups. They address these issues correctly by using the time available at low rpm to send at least 2 or 3, and as many as 9 or 10 sparks into the chamber at idle, insuring a complete burn. As rpm rises flow speeds up, and the "window" of opportunity gets narrower and narrower. That's just dandy, because ignition is easier anyway at high rpm, and there's still plenty of time. The spark duration of a CD ignition may only be 10% of the 0.5 -1.0 millisecond rate of a magneto or battery-and-coil system. So, you still get a mega-hot jolt of multiple juice, even at redline.

Real World? Are you one who subscribes to the "Make mine a Genuine." philosophy, or do you just know in your heart there's got to be a better way? Do you need the kind of performance benefit each or any of these ignitions provide? Does the value of a particular system offset the expense? Are reliability and durability the real priority? Can you actually get one to fit your bike without bogus brackets, bungee cords and Band-Aids. That is, where and how do the coils mount? Where can you mount the module? You have to consider all the issues before choosing an ignition.

Once these questions have been answered it's easy to make a decision and select a design. May it light your fire and brighten your day for miles and smiles to come.

THE MODULES

OK, you're tired of hitting the rpm limit of the stock ignition module on your new Buell. Or maybe you'd like a little snappier response from that new Sportster? Heck, maybe you want both from either, or vice versa. Or, horror of horrors, you actually need a replacement for the original one that died an unheralded death just recently and you figure if you've got to spend the money, you want the best for your hard earned coin. Anyway, whatever your reasons you're shopping for ignition modules.

Factory ignition modules

You will usually save enough money on (O.E.M.) Screamin' Eagle modules to include a high quality ignition coil (for about $50-60.00) in the budget as part of the upgrade. Compared with the price of some aftermarket set ups it's a veritable bargain.

You may choose to stay with factory parts for one of two reasons. Value and/or availability. Or the fact that you don't necessarily see the big plus to getting anything fancier or 'Apres marquette'. Maybe both. Fine. We won't argue.

Given any good coil (Accel, Screamin' Eagle, Dyna, Crane, Nology, and others), the next thing is the magic module for a dandy dual fire.

The stock module retards timing at the rev limit, and advances initial timing toward full advance timing (the advance "curve") at a relatively slow rate.

Aside from the differences in the advance curve, there is the issue of timing at full advance. Traditionally, for XL's that retain a separate module,

For those who can't find what they need in the preset modules, adjustable or not, there's this--- a system that offers complete control over every aspect of ignition. All user programmable! This is for Buells but would likely work fine on Sportsters with external modules, presuming you don't adjust yourself into a blown motor! (This kind of stuff is not for neophytes.)

the unit that Joe Minton and others tuners prefer now is the 6500 rpm stock (J curve) module for a 1988-90 1200 XLH. Even this hot-shot, four-speed 1200 module may or may not be the ultimate for your particular Sportster. Although a stock 883 (G) curve is bit of a slug, with about 10 degrees advance at two grand and full advance four thousand rpm away, at least they usually don't "ping" like some 1200's do. Early 883-1200 conversions that were done with factory parts and a template for the combustion chamber re-work are even more prone to this behavior, especially if compression goes too much over stock levels.

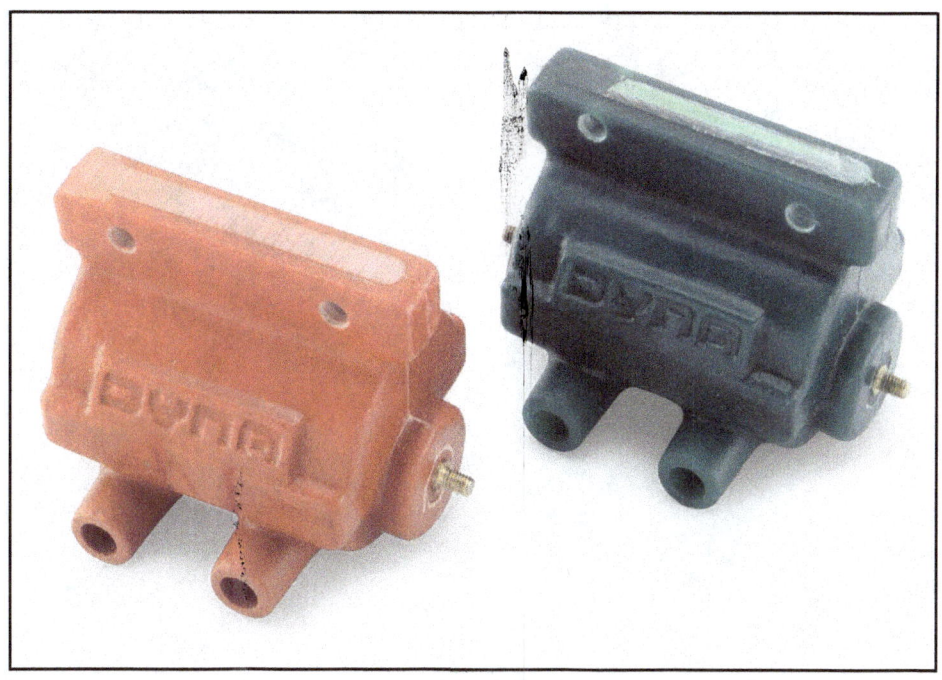

These OE style dual-fire coils (3 or 5 ohm) are an easy way to increase the output on the secondary side of your ignition system. Biker's Choice

Ignition Module Application Guide

Curve	Application	Comments
'Adjustable' (#32654-98)	'94 & later XL models	Four selectable curves and rev limits, dual or single fire capable. Deutsche (8-pin) connector.
'Adjustable' (#32655-98)	'93 & earlier XL models	Four selectable curves and rev limits, dual or single fire capable. Cannon (7-pin) connector. (*'90 & earlier models need #32408-90, or equivalent, wiring harness adapter)

Curve	Application	Comments
'G'	'86-87 883/1100 & '94-95	Lazy curve- "no-ping"
'H'	Screamin' Eagle '86-87	"Bath tub" heads
'J'	'88-90 1200	6500rpm limit
'K'	Screamin' Eagle Sportster	8000rpm or 6800rpm rev limit
'M'	'91-95 1200	6250rpm limit
'Q'	'96-97 1200	O.E. 6250rpm "Street legal" S.E.,6800rpm
'R'	'96-97 XL883	O.E. 6250rpm/883 "street legal" S.E.,6800rpm
?	98-on 1200	(32978-98A "in the cone" '98-on, 6800rpm) (32969-98 "in the cone" '98-on, 7500rpm)
?	98-on 883	(32979-98A "in the cone" '98-on, 6800rpm) (32971-98 "in the cone" '98-on, 7500rpm)

Designed for single-fire, dual-plug operation, these 3 ohm Dyna coils produce in excess of 30,000 volts. Biker's Choice

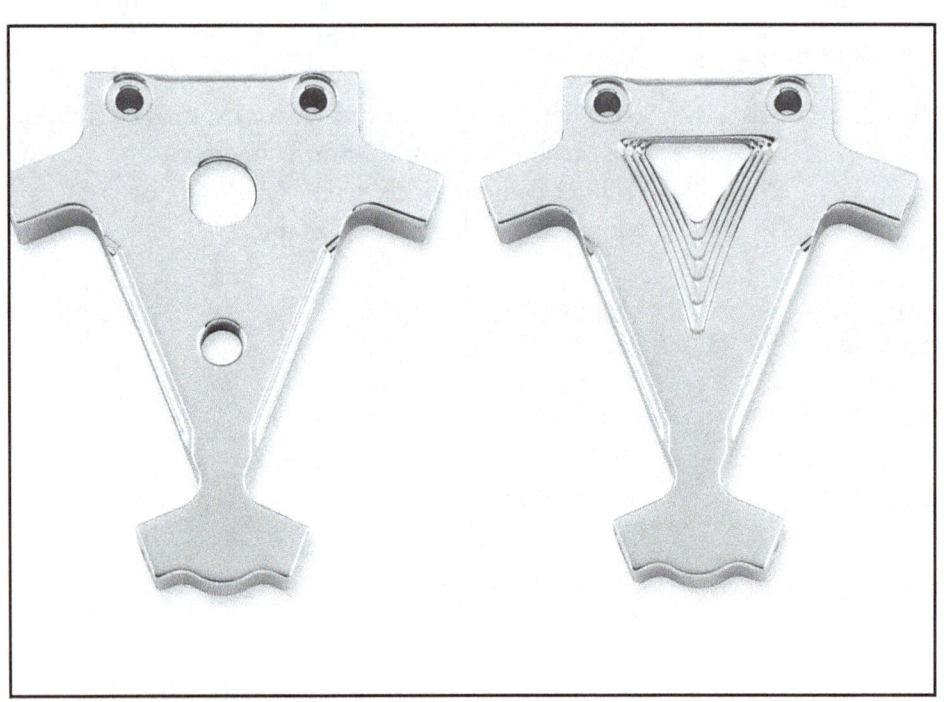

Chrome plated brackets like these offer a clean, sexy way to mount coils like those seen above. Biker's Choice

Conversions done with aftermarket pistons, or later factory conversions that eliminate the need to "cut the heads", are typically friendlier about pinging, but then you begin to see the need for module tuning.

A 1200 (J) box cranks in 20 degrees at 2000, and hits full boogie at 4200. The five-speed 1200 (M curve) brain is not the same, surprise. The (K curve) Screamin' Eagle number is different, yet. The factory used to sell yet another S.E. module especially for early 1986-87 XL's, with "bath tub" heads. You can get spoiled by this much choice; and, even though a points-type curve is the most aggressive of the bunch, that doesn't make it the best choice for your motor.

The factory has had plenty of time to think about its choices, and make up new ones, yet apparently they still haven't totally made up their mind about electronic ignition "brains." For instance, all the 1996 models have gone over to the (formerly International) H.D.I. modules. The reasoning behind this is a little vague, but the presumption is that it will improve emissions and driveability. It also allows the factory to "rationalize" its parts, using fewer numbers to do more jobs. And, bear this in mind as well, for the last few years the timing has been checked at "full advance" (35 degrees on a Big Twin, 40 on a 1200 XL, and 45 on 883s) at 1600 rpm. Today the new "International method" gets you 20 degrees advance at

1000 rpm, but it isn't fully advanced at 1600.

Thus indicating that the curve may be a little steeper initially but that it rolls in considerably slower than previously. Last but not least, the 1996 (HDI-type) curves are very definitely "mapped" differently, these new R, P, & Q maps are proprietary, and Harley's not talking. Remember not to get too caught up in the dark arts of specific advance curves because the simple truth is all they do for living is prevent detonation at engine speeds below 3000-3500rpm. If you have that problem, you need a curve that advances more slowly. If you don't have detonation difficulties but the engine revs like a tractor (slow) then you should benefit from a swap to a more aggressive curve, up to the point where detonation rears it ugly head again. That kind of makes a case for adjustable modules, doesn't it?

Aftermarket modules

The prime reasons to consider these are:

You can't find a factory unit with a curve and/or rev limit that works for your set up. You need a multiple spark capability and none of the factory modules offer that. You need the ability to set timing differently for each cylinder and the factory modules don't allow for that, either. Once that's been figured out there's no end to choices. So many that by the time you read this there will be even newer, better, more versatile and adaptable ignitions available. So it makes no sense to make specific recommendations. No one ignition is "best" overall, only for your specific application.

By now, hopefully you know what the system of your choice should offer, to best unlock the power you've built into your engine. So, I'll leave you with just one more ignition "point" to contemplate. Ignitions do not make horsepower, they simply let all the horsepower you put in, out.

Between the factory's Screamin' Eagle offerings and the immense output of the aftermarket, if you can't find what you're looking for in the ignition department, you just aren't looking hard enough.

Chapter Six

Charging & Starting

Hog Juice

Thanks to modern science and 100-some years of practice, The Motor Company actually has a pretty fair handle on the "reliability thing" as it romps through the first decade of its second century. But, like all that came before, and most everything that's liable to come after, it is not perfect. That actually suits most of us for a couple of reasons. For one, it gives the machines we love a dose of character "It's not a motorcycle, it's an adventure," as one wag put it. And two, it helps to keep our friendly local H-D

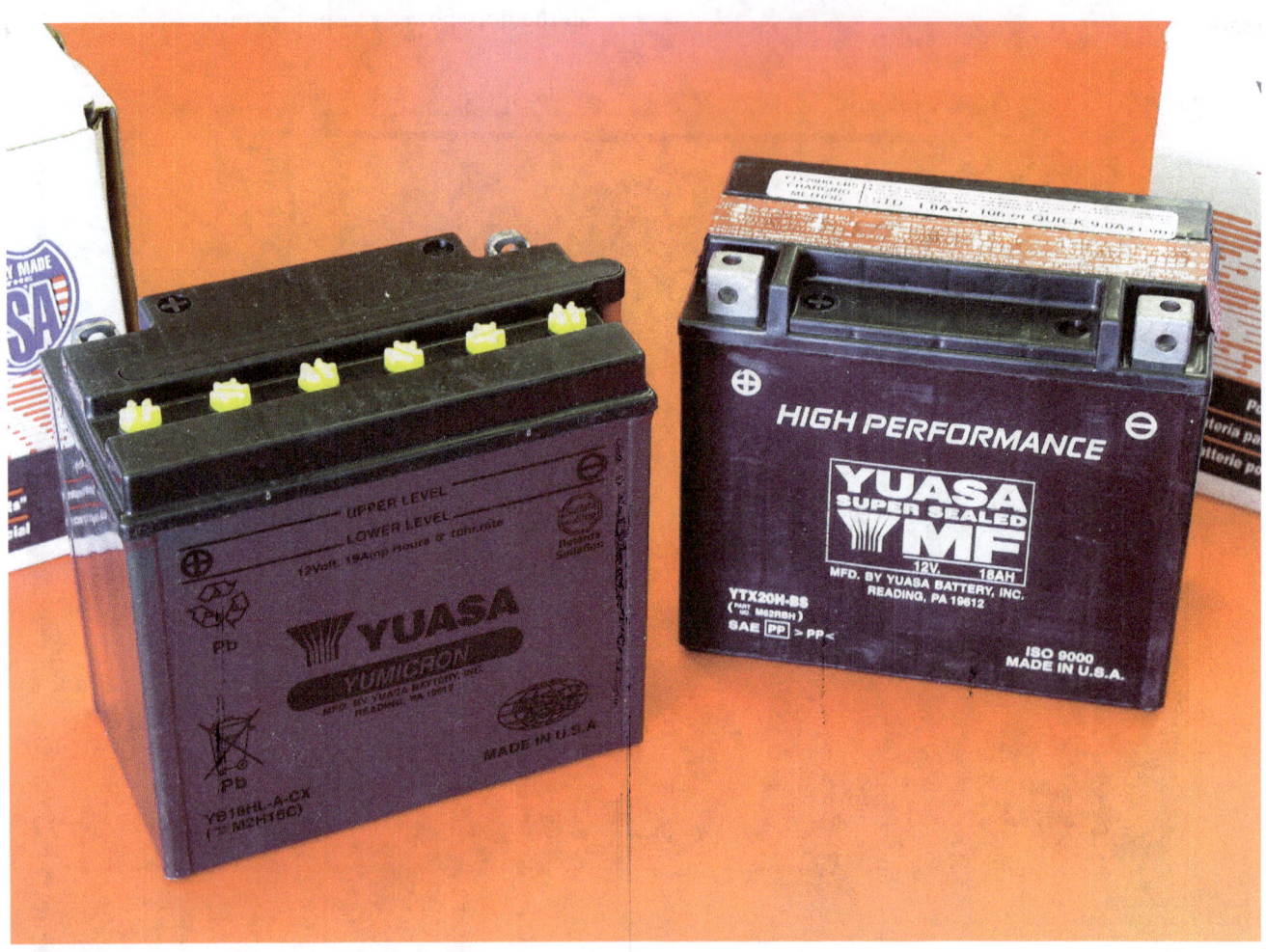

When it comes to starting big, high compression engines there is one component more important than all the rest, and that's the battery. Newer sealed designs put out more cranking amps than the traditional designs and may be the extra umph you need to crank that 99 inch X-motor.

56

shop in business. This is prima fascia evidence that at least three laws are still hard at work here. First, there's good ol' Murphy's Law. Then, the "Prado Principle" or the 80/20 law. Simply stated, 80% of the problems stem from 20% of the components. Last, but not least, the little known connection between Murphy and Prado - Duffy's Corollary - that basically guarantees you usually won't know which 20%. In spite of all this, there are a notorious few predicaments that are reasonably predictable and therefore preventable. Hopefully this will offer a brief overview of "Electrical Stuff" in the charging system, and a primer on how best to troubleshoot various problems.

Battery

Discovered accidentally by a guy who was trying to invent something else, 130 years ago. And they really haven't been able to improve them much since. By far the largest percentage of on road failures come down to a blown/dead battery. They are the heart of the electrical system, and it seems we spend an inordinate amount of time looking for a by-pass operation. Nobody likes to mess with them, so batteries usually suffer from neglect as much as heat and vibration, and take a "powder" on you when you least expect it. And yes, batteries are known to shake a cable loose given the slightest opportunity. This is why they invented star-type lock washers, right? Short hop

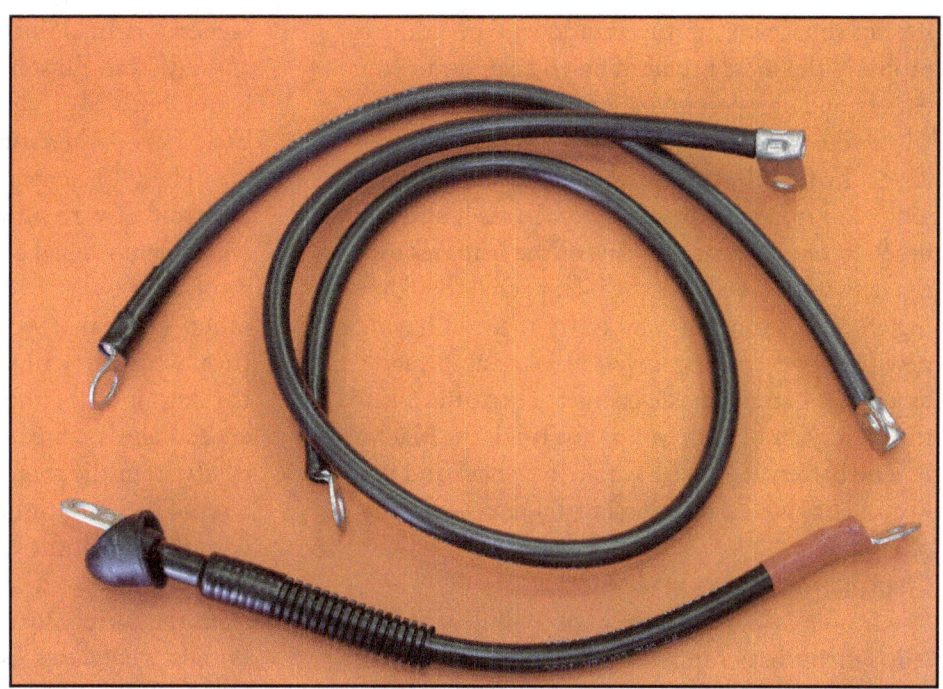

The best battery in the world can't crank that engine if the cables are undersized (which creates resistance in the circuit) or corroded. Always buy high quality battery cables.

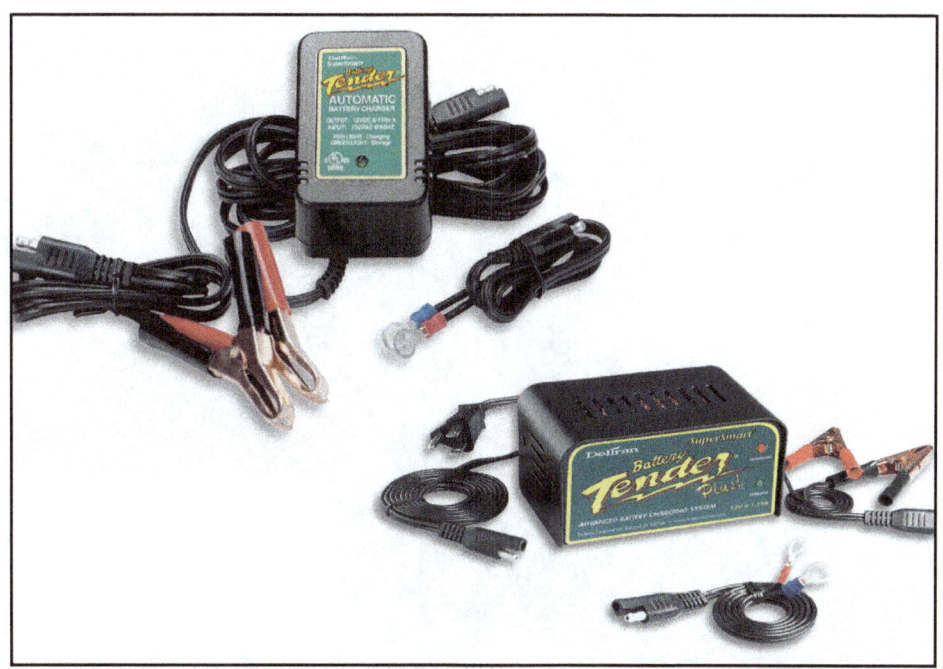

What we call trickle chargers can't be left connected to a battery because even with less than an amp of output they will eventually overcharge a battery. The only chargers that can be left connected are the smart chargers that actually control their own voltage.

startup-shutdown, startup-shutdown type riding is probably the most brutal thing you can do to your battery and an open invitation for it to rebel just when you need it most. Please – wet cell lovers check the fluid level regularly and particularly after a long hard ride on a long hot day. You can also lose as much as one percent, per day, of the batteries total capacity when you leave the bike parked. So, knowing all this, if you still want to try to avoid buying a new battery every year, invest in a low amperage taper-type battery trickle charger. Then attach it to the battery and (while you're not using the bike) use it. The battery will live a whole lot longer and you just might avoid a nasty accidental discovery or two, of your own.

CHARGING SYSTEMS

In some cases an entirely too rudimentary circuit/system that's supposed to keep "fire in the hole," run the lights and doodads, and mostly - keep the battery charged. To some degree the whole show is dependent on engine rpm to work. If that thought isn't enough to give you pause, try this - the battery has to help out when the engine idles, then get "paid back" as the motor speeds up. Over the years there have been three versions of charging systems, DC Generators (marginal concept at best, but thanks anyway, Tom Edison), AC Generators (better, much better, but still...), and (now we're talking, Mr. Tesla.) - the Alternator.

The DC Generator is essentially a rotating armature of wire surrounded by a set of field coils and a gizmo called a commutator, which is nothing more than two split rings that don't touch each other. The way it works is to instantly flip the electrical wave every time the armature makes one, so the output of the thing is (pretty much like you'd expect) always direct 12 volt current. To get the electricity from the rotating part to the parts that don't, a set of carbon brushes are used. Voila, a charged battery. Actually, it only stays charged if the system employs a "cut out" that disconnects the generator from the battery when the engine is not running. Because generators use brushes to mechanically transfer energy from the field to the armature and then on to the battery, the silly thing will work backward. When the engine isn't running the battery has more voltage than the generator, and without the cut out the battery will try to turn the generator into an electric starter. What a concept, crankin' over an iron Sportster with 11-1 compression, using the generator.

An AC Generator, not quite the same thing as an alternator, but most of us can't tell the difference and neither can the battery, is simply a magnet attached to the engine with a coil of wire right beside it. Fire up the motor and the magnet spins, making electricity in the coil. Ben Franklin knew about this stuff so it's nothing new, but he never got to honk a horn or work a brake light to see if it really worked. He also never had to figure out what was wrong when it didn't. It's primitive too, in that the lights are dim at idle, and without some control will blow bulbs and melt wires at high rpm. Stuff a battery in

In the days of old motorcycles kept the battery charged with a device called a generator, controlled by an electro-mechanical regulator. Generally, generators put out less power at a given rpm than an alternator while requiring more maintenance. Biker's Choice

the system and the dim lights issue usually goes away, but there's still a couple of problems. Remember, we're now dealing with alternating current, which changes direction every time the North and South poles of the magnet whip by the wire. No big deal to the bulbs or the horn, but the battery just hates this. One second there's power galore being stuffed into the battery, the next it's all sucked right back out. So to keep the battery happy and working we have to add a one way electrical valve, aka diode or rectifier. Makes you wonder why they don't call it a pacifier if it just has to keep the battery happy? In a balanced system the rectifier would pacify the battery. The trouble starts with a sustained high rpm ride or worse, a lack of battery maintenance. Either one leads to electrolyte boil off or evaporation and the battery starts to disconnect from the system. The bulbs, etc., are left to soak up all the excess voltage and they make lousy electrical sponges. Boiled battery, hot wires, blown bulbs - the system is out of balance. Obviously then rectifying is one thing, regulating is another.

A regulator, whether mechanical or solid state electronic, senses the battery voltage and adjusts the amount of power to the rotor accordingly. The faster the rotor turns, the more electricity comes out of the stator. Less power to the rotor = less magnetism = less stator output. Eventually the stator output drops so low the bike is running off the battery. When

Whether located behind the clutch hub or the engine drive sprocket, the modern alternator is made up of these three components, the stator (top left) where the power is actually generated, the rotor (which creates the magnetic field) and of course the regulator.

Batteries come in a wide range of sizes. for most Sportsters and Buells the size of the battery is fixed by the size of the battery box. Changing that box isn't an option. More power can only come from reading the ratings and buying the best.

59

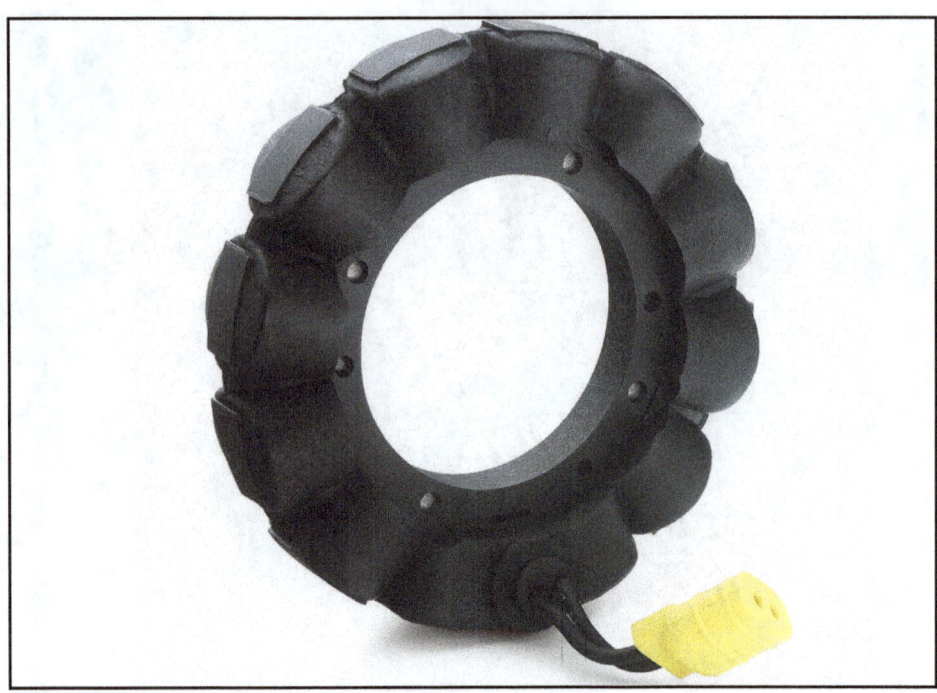

Stators come in molded and un-molded versions (this example is from Accel) rated by output. The plug needs to match the plug on the regulator. Biker's Choice

Like most parts of your motorcycle, regulators come in basic black, polished or chrome plated. Each regulator has three wires, two go to the stator and one runs to the battery or main breaker.

the voltage from the battery drops, the regulator sends more power to the rotor to get more magnetism and so on, and so on, as the cycle repeats itself.

All this good stuff applies to true alternators as well, with two major distinctions. First, all alternators rotating electromagnet, instead of a permanent fixed magnet are three phase. This means they have three coils of wire arranged sequentially at 120 degrees around the magnet. That makes them a bunch stronger, but no bigger than an AC Generator. Second, is that with an AC Generator you can have a dead battery (or no battery) and as long as you can push or "bump" start the bike – it will run. Alternators (at least automotive-style applications) must have some electricity, 'cause without it, there's no magnetism from the electromagnet, and you're walking.

TROUBLES

The stator, rotor (which together make alternating current) and regulator/rectifier (or Voltpack, in Harley-babble), which turns the alternating current into direct current, along with the battery - are the major players in the charging system, and they typically quit playing without telling you the game is over. The best idea is to have a way of knowing, in advance, whether everything is O.K., or not. A voltmeter/ammeter/idiot light –something - for Pete's sake, to keep you ahead of the game as you roll down the road. The potential for this sort of disabling electrical problem is there every time you ride, but no one seems to want to utilize a simple gauge as an early warning system. Yet, as rare as an oil pressure failure is on a Harley, I see flocks of folks out there with oil gauges bolted up to tell them about a system that doesn't screw up. The one that does, (A full 70-80% of the "stop you on the road" failures are electrical) people ignore, and almost everyone's out there "flying blind."

OK now that the rants over, what do you do when a problem occurs in the charging system? The first place to look is the aforementioned battery. It is the only component of the system lacking a designed life span. In other words, no one can tell exactly how long the thing should last. Too much depends on how it's maintained and used. Sportsters, with their hot oil bags in close proximity, and their solid mounted engines, present a pretty hostile environment to their batteries. How would you like it if you were right next to boiling hot oil and being shaken 3000 times a minute? So, whenever the lights go dim or mysterious misfires show up, let alone the embarrassing "ran fine 'till I shut it off and now it won't start" syndrome, check first for a weak and/or dead battery. To do this, you'll need a hydrometer, a voltmeter/multimeter, and (ideally) a load tester.

Once the battery is eliminated from contention as a source of problems you can put the hydrometer away, but keep the meters handy. You'll need them to check the rest of the system for bugs. For the record, the bugs usually consist of bad grounds, corroded connections, and chaffed or broken wires. Loose battery cables are number one on that list, by the way. Simple things to find and fix, just the same. Sometimes it's as simple as making dead sure the plug that connects the regulator/rectifier to the alternator in the crankcase is plugged in securely, and not corroded or suffering from hot-oil "rot". Occasionally, running a second or jumper ground to the voltpak will solve a problem or two. Sure, sometimes it's anything but that simple. Yet the vast majority of the time it's not beyond your ability to diagnose and repair. Nor is it typically a failure of one of the major components of the system.

In other words, always start with the simplest, cheapest thing it could possibly be and don't instantly assume a catastrophic failure of a major component has occurred. Electricity works just like water, in that it takes the path of least resistance and always flows downhill to ground. Try to paint a mental picture of this process when dealing with all your volts, amps and ohms. With luck, some common sense, a diagram or two, the Multimeter, and minimum tools, you can get it wired. If the little things in life don't matter (after you've checked them anyway) then it's time to move on to the medium-sized ones, like the last gadget or doodad that you added or spliced in for added performance or security. Meaning, that last thing you did is most frequently the first thing that goes wrong if it happens right after.

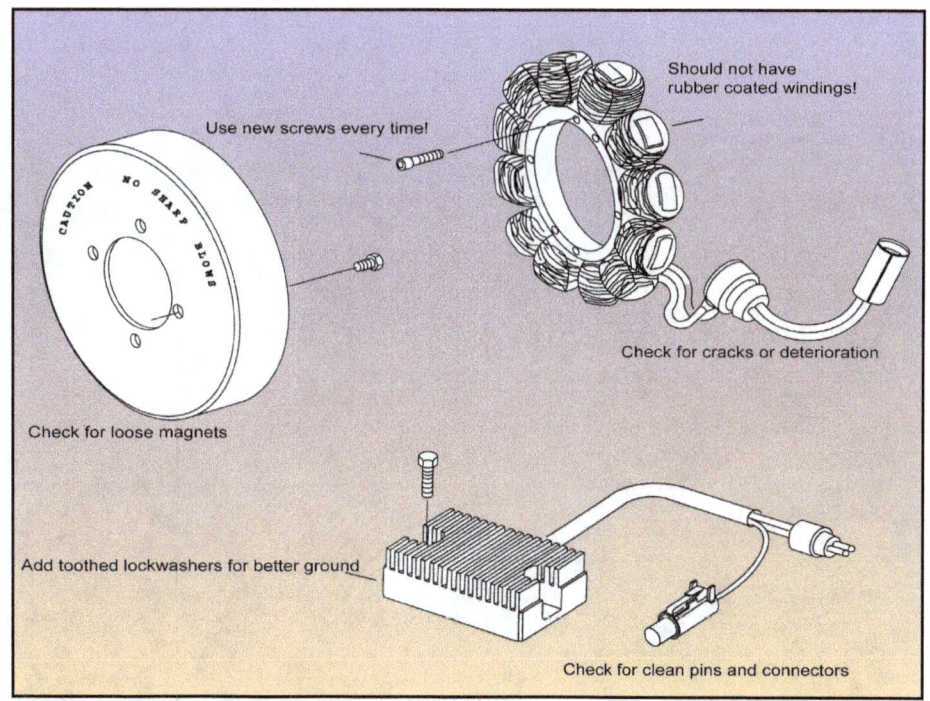

This is the basic program. The rotor and stator have it hardest. But the supporting players deserve all the help you can give. It does no good to have the best engine in the world and electrical problems. This just illustrates a few helpful hints to keep an important, overlooked system intact and operating at it's best.

61

Set the Multimeter to read milliamperes, and with the ignition switch turned off hook up to the hot (positive) side of the battery and connect solidly to ground. Then, check for current draw. No matter how much stuff you've added to the machine, (like a radar detector, for instance) you still never want more than 15 milliamps of draw. A no frills unit like a Sportster or Buell, should draw less than 3 milliamps. If the numbers for your bike under those conditions exceed the limits, start checking for bad components or shorts in them. Pull the suspect pieces off in sequence and re-test. While we're on that subject a check for voltage drop through any suspect component is a good idea.

The multimeter is set to read DC volts. The way it's connected its checking for voltage drops; in the connection between the battery terminal and the wire terminal, the connections between the terminal and wire at both ends of the wire, the connection between the switch terminal stud and the wire terminal at 'B', and the contact resistance of the switch. OK, if the voltmeter reads one volt DC or less the switch and input wires are fine. If it reads two volts or more you've found the rat. Now you have to trap it. Move the negative probe toward the positive battery connection - one connection at a time. Try the switch input stud 'B', and if the reading drops to one volt (or less) - Bingo. Replace the bad switch. If the reading is still two volts check the connector or the wire itself from 'B' back toward the battery until you trap the rat.

Alternator

Alternator equipped Sportsters have 23 amps to play with and EFI Buells have – well – more. Regardless of what you start with, you should have better than 3.5 amps left over. Put another way, if draw amounts to more than 19.5 amps total on your Sportster for instance, you've got a few too many electrical bells and whistles for the system to handle. Sadly, on older models, with only 19 or 22 amps available, it's pretty easy to overload the whole charging system. So think carefully about whether you really have to have that electric vest and the GPS, and the Fuzz buster, and ….

Suppose you've gotten this far and haven't found the gremlin. Hey, shut the beast off, and reset the multimeter for resistance. That's RX1 on the ohms scale. Now, unplug the regulator/rectifier from the Alternator. Touch the test leads to the sockets, or pins, as the case may be, individually, and test for continuity to ground. The answer you're looking for is zero. That's infinite ohms on the meter, by the way. Any other reading means the stator is grounded, which is electrical clap-trap for worthless, dead, and must be replaced. So much for grounded. If that ain't happening, then test for shorted. Same meter setting, only test from socket to socket (or pin to pin on older stators) looking for ohms. If you find any more than .012 of them, your stator is an ohm short of a charge - and

Designed by Arlen Ness, these regulators from Accel combine good looks with increased cooling area. Be sure to route the hot wire running to the battery carefully so it can't be pinched or chafed and short to the frame. Biker's Choice

must be trashed. A new one is the only cure for a bad case of the shorts. Sorry.

But, we still need to check the rotor. So, set the meter to AC volts, fire up the scoot and test across the sockets (or pins) and hope that you get 16-20 volts per 1000 rpm output. If so, all is well with the alternator and (especially if you ran a jumper ground to it) the rectifier/regulator is junk. Now as we all know, solid state rectifier/regulators cannot really be tested or repaired (at least not by you, me or the average bike shop), and unless it's just the rubber plug that's damaged, you may as well just pitch it.

The last thing to do is double check your homework. Whip the meter onto DC volts, hook it up to the battery, fire the bike and rev it a bit. Alternators should push anywhere from 13.5 to 14.8 DCV back into the battery. (A word of caution to the alternator mob - long rides in hot climates at a 14.8 volt charge rate will boil your battery dry.) All the wise guys who cut the yellow wire (you know who you are) so the headlight is not on all the time, need to be aware that the relatively high charging rate we're talking about here will also cut the life of the rectifier/regulator severely, since there are no longer lamps in the system to help use up current. A dry battery and an abused voltpak spell trouble for a charging system. Now you know.

If all else fails, remember this, the single most amazing thing about electricity - is that it works at all. So try to be patient. It can take what seems like forever to get something to operate properly at the speed of light.

STARTER MOTOR STUFF

Sportsters, since 1981, and all Buells, employ automotive-type compound starters. Meaning that the components which used to be separate, such as the starter clutch (Bendix, to us old-timers), and the solenoid, are incorporated into the body of the starter itself. These more compact compound starters offer an improvement in performance and reliability, but are more complex, therefore tougher to work on in the event that they need rebuilding or repair.

Unreliable they are not. However, with the trend to extra-huge displacement and high compression on Evo motored H-D's, the stock version of these starters can be strained to the limit. So it pays to keep them in top shape, and know a little bit about what to look for first if there's a problem.

If you experience a hard-start or no start condition, look at the simple and cheap possibilities first before you tear into the starter itself. You may discover that the wire that runs power into the starter has simply come unplugged. The next most likely candidate is low battery voltage. Slow cranking or a tendency for the starter to drag instead of spin rapidly, is the fault of a weak battery, far more frequently than the starter. Assuming of course, that you don't lay on the starter button for minutes at a time. Ten seconds is enough. If it won't start in that time, you need a tune up. That said, never underestimate the ability of the starter relay to cause grief, either. It seems the earlier relay used in the 90's era was subject to moisture contamination, and has since been re-designed. If all you get when you hit the button is silence, you need a relay. If you get a rapid clicking

For checking out your charging circuit, not to mention a thousand other electrical maladies, a multi-meter like that shown here is a very handy tool to have. Biker's Choice

sound, but nothing else, then it's okay and the problem is downstream of the relay.

If you have removed the starter for any reason, and have trouble getting the thing to crank without binding or freewheeling once it's re-installed, double check the amount and method of torque you used when you bolted it back in. Nine times out of ten, you'll discover the mounting bolts are both too tight causing the body to distort and bind. Or one bolt is snug and the other is way too loose, allowing the starter to cock when it engages the ring gear and bind or free-wheel, or both, on alternate occasions. A back and forth technique, tightening first one mounting bolt then the other, and being very cautious of over-torquing, is best to avoid this kind of problem.

If you've checked everything else, then you may actually have a starter motor problem.

STOCK STARTERS-

P/N 31390-86 was factory original from 1986 to 1990 on all Evo XL models, but from 1991 to 1994 only on 883s. You can get parts to rebuild them, but the factory offered up a subtle clue as to their suitability for big inch motors. They don't sell that starter as a replacement assembly. Only the newer style (P/N 31390-91A), original on 1200 Sportsters, is sold as a replacement for 883s and 1200's alike.

In other words, the original 883 1986 version probably won't survive a high compression 1200 conversion, let alone a hopped up, or big-inch application. The -91A will most likely work because it's made for a 1200 in the first place. If not, we'll get into so-called "hi-torque" alternatives in a minute. The most likely culprit in a starter problem is the starter clutch. If the symptom you have when you try to start your bike is a high pitched "whirring" or whining sound and the starter free-wheels rather than engaging, chances are you need to replace it.

Once on the bench, a series of quick (3-5 seconds each) tests can be performed to see what the most likely problem is. The first is the solenoid pull-in test, done by grounding the threaded post and the starter housing with two test leads from the battery negative terminal. Then touch another lead from the positive battery terminal to the plug-in terminal on the starter. The splined shaft on the end of the starter should jump out smartly. If not you need a new solenoid. The second test is simple. With all the leads connected the same way, move the lead connected to the threaded post from the negative battery terminal to the positive battery terminal. Just touch it for a couple of seconds and if the splined shaft remains extended, all's well. If not, again the solenoid needs to be replaced. Test three is to leave everything as it was for test two, then remove the lead from the plug-in terminal on the starter. The shaft should snap back into its hole. Now you see it, now you don't.

If everything has checked out after all three solenoid tests, you need to tear the starter down, it has a bad starter clutch. You'll need the new starter clutch

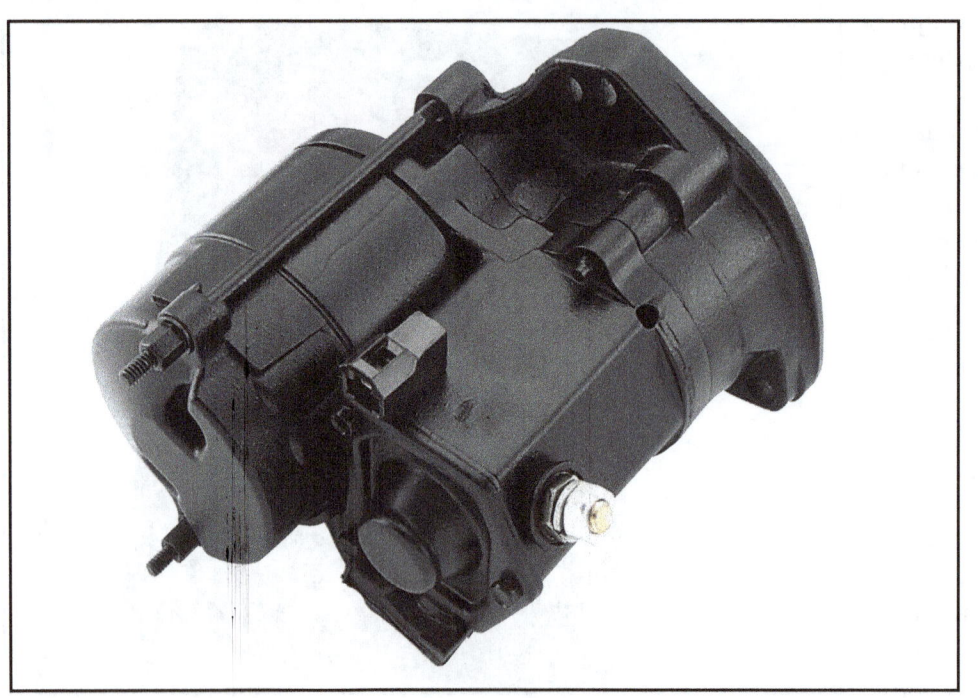

Starters come in standard and high torque models from both the factory and the aftermarket. Upgrading from an 883 to a high compression 1200 may mean upgrading the starter as well. Biker's Choice

and a starter repair kit for your model starter. (see chart.) The starter comes apart in two sub-sections. From the sub-sections, carefully withdraw any parts you need to inspect or replace. Pay particular attention to the small plastic cage that holds several steel rollers. It should be free from cracks or deformities and greasy. Same with the rollers. Once the new starter clutch is installed, if all else checks out okay, you can re-assemble and re-install the starter and hook up the battery.

All this helps for sure, but even in top shape the relatively puny factory starter motor has it's work cut out for it, pushing two pistons measuring 3.5-inch or more up the bore of a long(er) stroke motor, especially if the oil is thick and cold, the cables cruddy or cracked, and the battery old and tired. The situation goes from barely tolerable to down right dubious when you've gone to all the time and trouble to build an extra large displacement, high performance engine with cranking pressure up around 200 psi, and can't count on starting it reliably. Basically, if you have an engine with that much more power, you need a motor with more power too. A starter motor, that is.

Lord knows there's no shortage of the things available. But how do you know which one you'll need? There's plenty of confusion with some manufacturers rating the starters in kilowatts (kW), some in plain old horses (mostly between 1.4 and 2.6) and still others boasting more about reduction ratios, ranging from 1.44 to 1.9-1.

Some basic guidelines, would amount to something like this:
• 1.2 kW starters: fine for most bikes up to 80-in.
• 1.4 kW starters: work for engines up to 96-in.
• 1.6 kW starters: up to 100-inch torque monsters.
• 2.0 kw rating are usually only required for problem children, starter killers that truth be told, often have plenty of other issues that properly addressed would eliminate the need for starters that draw so many amps they become a problem unto themselves.

A QUICK TIP OR TWO:

Horsepower is a rather antiquated English rating system, that in modern electrical parlance amounts to 746 watts. So a stock H-D starter with it's 1 1/2 horsepower rating is essentially a 1000 watt or 1.0 kW unit, in case this helps you.

A starter should not draw much more than 10-15 amps when you use it If it does you'll have problems with batteries rated at 18-20 amps, so-called cold-cranking amps notwithstanding. In an automotive circuit, current is calculated like this example: 10 (amps) x 12 (volts) = 120 watts. You simply cannot sustain huge loads on the system for any length of time. That's where the idea of reduction gears comes in. Same draw, more work done mechanically. Remember that when you pick out a hi-torque starter. You may be better off with a starter that has a lower power rating, but is "geared up" for the job, hence is less hard on the electrical system.

APPLICATION CHART

Sportsters
• 1986-90 (all models) Starter assembly #31390-86
      Solenoid kit #31605-90
      Starter clutch #31567-81
1991-1994 (883 only) uses 31390-86 variation, but replacement assembly is 1200- style
      Solenoid kit #31605-90
      Starter clutch #31567-81
• 1991-on 1200 (and replacement starter for 883)
    Starter Assembly #31390-91A
    Solenoid kit #31603-91
    Starter clutch #31663-90

Note: the pinion gear is part of the assembly on Sportster starters, complete with cast-in collar. Big Twin starters do not have the pinion gear as part of the assembly. This is the principle visual difference between Sportster and Big Twin versions of these starters.

Chapter Seven

Gearing

Making The Most Of Available Power

Odd as it may seem now, there was once a time when, except for XR racers, Harley riders were pretty much stuck with whatever the factory liked for gear ratios. Not any more. If you can't find what you want for external gearing choices, you'll sure be able to manage it internally, or with some combination of the two. With the advent of 6-speed overdrives and multiple choice first and top gears, it's actually to the point where it borders on overkill.

Chain drive may seem like an antiquated way to transmit power, but it sure makes it easy to change final drive ratios with an almost endless range of possible front and rear sprockets.

High Speed or Low

As is, you could smoke the typical Big Twin clear up to the point where Sporty's run out of 'leg' and into the shakes. H-D sells a lot of Big Twins for this simple reason, they will pull away from Sportsters at high (read illegal) speeds. Leaving the age old argument of, "which really is the better scooter overall" out of it for now, think about the potential solution.

Change the gearing. You could swap the rear pulley (and belt) to the so called International 55-tooth on the rear. You could swap front pulleys up or down size wise. You could switch to chain drive and get gearing options not available with belt drive. Or, you could switch to a Baker 6-speed if you can afford it, and get the best of both worlds, through the gears acceleration and effortless, vibration-less high speed cruising.

The trouble is, purveyors of all this good gearing stuff have a tendency to couch common sense information in technical jargon, cryptic numbers and marketing buzzwords. Close ratio, 0.86 top gear, 3.21 first gear, and other nearly meaningless terms. Meaningless, that is, when used out of context. So, what is the context?

Well for most of us, it probably amounts to knowing how many fewer revolutions per minute our engines would turn with "such & such" a top ratio change. But it could also be how much faster we could go at the same rpm, after a change. Some even want to know things like, how much will my acceleration or my fuel mileage improve? Everybody has their own motives for altering gear ratios, but not everybody knows what the results of a given change might be.

An Extra Gear

By adding a sixth (overdrive) gear to a typical five-speed gearset, you can drop your engine speed at 75mph by over 500rpm, from 3648rpm to 3137rpm. A Big Twin with 3.15 overall gearing is spinning 3398rpm at the same road speed. Now ramp the Sporty up to 95mph. That moves the XL engine to 4634rpm with the stock fifth gear. But with a .86 ratio on sixth gear the rpm drops 14%, just like it did at 75mph. Only this time, it's 3986rpm. Meaning that at road speeds that used to make the Sportster a bad jack-hammer from engine vibration, it's still on the cusp of smooth. The Big Twin at 95mph is turning 4381rpm, actually spinning its engine tighter than the Sportster. Two things about that; one, Big Twins tend to have some form of vibration control these days, which isn't on the Sportster's spec sheet. Two, with an overdrive the XL's rpm advantage just gets better the faster it goes.

At 120mph in overdrive, for instance, the Sporty is spinning just over 5000rpm, the Big Twin over 5500rpm. Top speed? Hard to say, because that isn't JUST about gearing. Suppose it's 140mph for the sake of the discussion. At that speed, the stock top gear on the XL would put the engine in the shrapnel zone at 6830rpm. The Big Twin would have to hit 6500rpm, also well into the upper limit of its engine health. Overdriven however, the Sporty turns a relatively sedate and safe 5873rpm, and once again well below the Big Twin revs at the same speed. Wanna

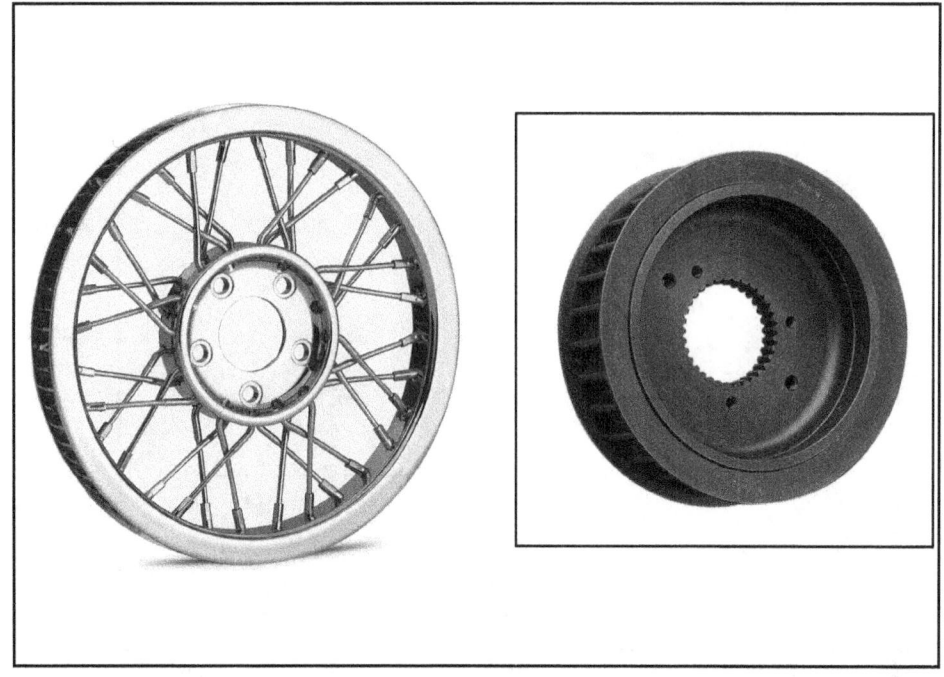

You can likewise change the final drive ratio on belt-drive bikes with available rear wheel and transmission pulleys. Biker's Choice

run with the big dogs dirt bike fans? This is one way it's done. Gives you the same performance through the gears, too.

To top it off, there are also options for the bottom gear. You see, since 883's and 1200's share an identical first gear ratio, it's easy to conclude that the ratio was chosen by the factory to favor the possibility of an under-powered 883 trying to haul two portly passengers uphill from a dead stop. It's not that far off of the concept of the old "granny" gear a feature for decades of trucks that actually worked for a living, and had to get heavy loads under way.

A 1200 Sporty or Buell suffers from this choice. It already has plenty of power for leaving lights with alacrity, but when you wind it up in first, then shift to second, the rpm drops 27% when you start to pull that cog. So if you were at 6000rpm when you shifted, second would engage at 4394rpm. Not the best choice for the drag strip, since the engine isn't pulling as hard as it could to move you forward. Switch to a first gear ratio slightly closer to second and the engine stays in the meaty part of the powerband. So instead of a 2.73 first, suppose you install the optional 2.61. Suddenly the 6000rpm first to second drop is only 22%, to 5280rpm. The flip side, in case drag racing isn't a motivator for you, is that in those sticky situation like a series of tight, slow, wet hairpin turns, where stock second is so high you're lugging and first is just too low for comfort, the close ratio first comes to the rescue again. It has less radical behavior upon downshifting and more speed available in low gear.

There's also the idea that by getting internal ratios where you want them you free up some potential options for external ratio changes.

JUST CHANGE THE PULLEYS

Which brings me to the other, cheaper, option. 883's have 27/61 pulley counts, 1200's come with 29/61 as standard. Suppose you leave the gearbox internals alone, simply put that 55-tooth rear pulley, 29-tooth front, and matching belt on the back. Now you wind up with a 3.03 drive ratio, considerably taller than the 1200's stock 3.63:1. At 70mph, suddenly the Sport that spun about 3500rpm before, drops to right near 3000rpm. Since that's an even larger reduction (.83) than the overdrive sixth gear option, you might think it's the way to go. For some, it might be. For the hard core performance fan, I doubt it. You see, they still want to run away from Big Twins and other bikes with sport cruising pretensions. Not that you couldn't after a pulley change like this, but it would take a hell of a lot more engine work. That's because with external changes like this pulley, that same reduction applies to every gear in the transmission not just top gear. 17% for example, drop across the box, means first gear begins to act like second, second like third, and so on. Taking off from a stop isn't as brisk and every gap between gears stretches out that same 17%. Put another way, to get the acceleration performance back that was given up by this gearing change, would require at least 17% more power from the engine. There are trade-offs in every performance modification. At least with gearing changes you can tell up front what to expect after the fact.

GET OUT THE CALCULATOR

But regardless of your choice or method of tailoring your ratios, don't use old-fashioned "rule of thumb" guesswork. Better to grab a pocket calculator and do the math before you do the gears and pulleys without proper knowledge of what to expect from the changes.

Shown is an aluminum rear sprocket designed from Sportsters only, and a range of possible transmission sprockets. Transmission sprockets can often be ordered with an offset if you're converting to a wider rear tire. Biker's Choice

Trans Ratios (In Each Gear) **X** Stock overall (or "final") Ratio = "Intermediate" Ratio

Examples of Intermediate Ratios:

Gear	(86) 87-90	91-94	95-0n (HCR)	
1st	(2.52) 2.29 X 3.98 = (10.03) 9.12	2.78 X 3.63 = 10.09	2.69 X 3.63 = 9.76	
2nd	(1.83) 1.66 X 3.98 = (7.28) 6.59	2.03 X 3.63 = 7.37	1.97 X 3.63 = 7.15	
3rd	(1.38) 1.25 X 3.98 = (5.49) 4.98	1.49 X 3.63 = 5.41	1.43 X 3.63 = 4.72	
4th		1.00 X 3.98 = 3.98	1.22 X 3.63 = 4.43	1.18 X 3.63 = 4.28
5th			1.00 X 3.63 = 3.63	1.00 X 3.63 = 3.63

Gear	H-D 95-0n STOCK/% Change	Andrews S Ratio/% Change	Andrews Y Ratio/%Change
1st	2.69	2.368	2.026
2nd	1.97 = 26.8%	1.876 = 21%	1.670 = 17%
3rd	1.43 = 27.4%	1.489 = 21%	1.364 = 18%
4th	1.18 = 17.5%	1.216 = 18%	1.158 = 18%
5th	1.00 = 15.3%	1.000 = 15%	1.000 = 14%
(Optional) 6th		0.89 X 3.63 = 3.23	11% Change (Overdrive)
(Optional) 6th		0.86 X 3.63 = 3.12	14% Change (Tall Overdrive)

Overdrive RPM differences

MPH	rpm in 5th	RPM in (.86) 6th	RPM Drop
65	3162	2719	433
70	3405	2928	447
75	3648	3137	511
80	3891	3346	545

Some XL/Buell Internal Gear Ratios Combinations:

	91-94	95-up w/HCR*	XL6	XL6 w/HCR	XL6 'S'	XL6 'S' w/HCR*
1st	2.78	2.69	2.61	2.52	2.37	2.29
2nd	2.03	1.97	2.03	1.96	1.88	1.81
3rd	1.49	1.43	1.49	1.44	1.49	1.44
4th	1.22	1.18	1.22	1.18	1.22	1.18
5th	1.0	1.0	1.0	1.0	1.0	1.0
6th	———	———	.89	.86	.89	.86

*HCR refers to the 5th gear pair (main gear pair) that is standard O.E. equipment from 95-up.

XL/Buell Secondary Pulley Ratios (5-Speed)

Front	Rear 55-Tooth	Rear 61-tooth
26-tooth (Aftermarket)	2.12 Ratio	2.35 Ratio
27 (H-D OEM)	2.03 Ratio	2.26 Ratio
28 (Aftermarket)	1.96 Ratio	2.18 Ratio
29 (H-D OEM)	1.90 Ratio	2.10 Ratio

To find RPM at a given speed: Mph X Final Ratio X 366 / Rear Wheel Diameter

To find MPH at a given rpm: Rpm X Rear Wheel Dia. / Final Ratio X 366

XL/Buell Secondary (Drive) Chain Ratios

Front	Rear 46-Tooth	Rear 47-Tooth	Rear 48-Tooth	Rear 49-tooth
21-tooth	2.19 Ratio	2.24 Ratio	2.29 Ratio	2.33 Ratio
22-tooth	2.09 Ratio	2.14 Ratio	2.18 Ratio	2.23 Ratio
23-tooth	2.00 Ratio	2.04 Ratio	2.09 Ratio	2.13 Ratio

*Primary x Secondary = Overall ratios:
*Engine sprocket Rear sprocket
*Clutch sprocket x Trans sprocket
Four-speed Sportsters - 1.74 primary ratio. Stock five –speed Sportsters and Buell's - 1.60 primary ratio.)

These are some good examples of why it's important to know what to expect from a gearing modification. But you don't have to take my word for any of it. Now you can figure it out yourself for any combination.

Or, for the really lazy, the math impaired, and/or those who don't own, and/or can't operate a pocket calculator, but do surf the web: http://www.cunnington1.freeserve.co.uk/gearing_v12.xls

Chapter Eight

Valvetrain

Up & Down and 'Round & 'Round

There are a few things you should definitely come to terms with when contemplating upgrades to the valve train:
• Mass moves slowly and loads up everything. Remember this when you start thinking you need manhole-sized valves and sewer sized ports to have a hot-rod head.
• Velocity matters more than sheer volume.

You cannot defy the laws of physics, especially where a push rod design that predates your granddaddy's dating is concerned.

Let me see if I can put this another way. The

The valvegear you use will depend on the cam, the heads, the intended use for the engine, and your own opinion and budget. No matter what you buy, all the parts need to work together to help you achieve your goals.

lightest valves and pushrods money can buy are a better investment than some jumbo poppets that weigh more than a super-sized McDonalds meal. Not only because it helps relieve strain on the valvetrain, but because it lets the engine hit the redline quicker. Think about this for minute. It's really the poor man's lightened flywheels. I can tell you that a proper exhaust with decent scavenging, coupled with good cam choice and a light valve train can make more than a second difference in the time it takes to hit 6500rpm on a dyno. Why is this important? Well, take two otherwise identical 80hp engines and screw the throttle to the stop. The one that revs quicker wins every time. Using a computer analogy, its about "access time". The quick revver can get to its 80-ponies, or any part of them, faster. So it is faster.

The second player in this dynamic-duo is port velocity, which starts with intake valve opening. You'd do well to realize that valve shape and size have almost as much importance as port shape in this game. The age old habit of stuffing the biggest valve possible in the hole is asking for a huge dent in the bottom end power for a negligible gain at redline and not much below it. Particularly if the shape of the valve, in detail, is ignored in favor of the size. Another way to look at that scenario is that you could have peak dyno power that exceeds your buddy's X motor hop-up by 10-15% and still lose to him in the real world if that other engine makes good bottom end and midrange power and revs quicker.

The best of both worlds, this hydraulic lifter is designed to "turn into a solid" above 5600 rpm. JIMS

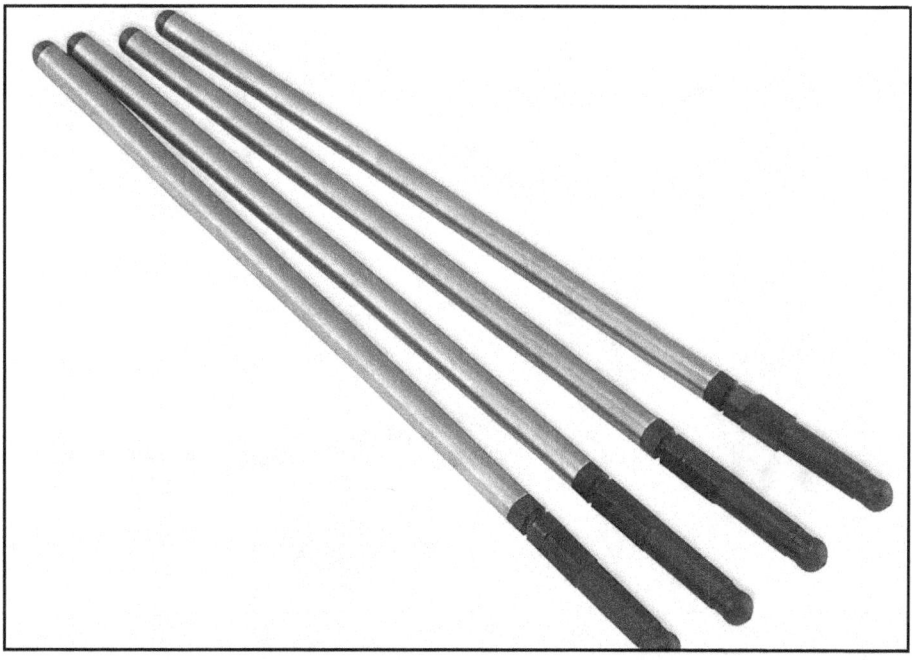

Pushrods need to be chosen with an eye toward weight as well as stiffness – to minimize the need for heavy valve springs and avoid valve float. Biker's Choice

Which leads to physics lessons galore. Hey, we don't make up these rules, we must simply learn to play by them. Friendly fantasies don't cut it, and one of the hardest to disabuse ourselves of is that X engines like engine speeds much higher than 6,500rpm. Quite the contrary. They are not happy at 6500 and will not survive at sustained engine speeds much above 7,000. Building engines that ignore these facts is a waste of time and money and a certain failure waiting to happen, if used as prescribed.

All this preamble is a way of saying be realistic in your expectations and you won't be disappointed, you'll be rewarded. The challenge of Sportster/Buell engine building is to know where the edge is and play as close to it as you can. This is lesson one. And Hey, for a change we can start this new job at the top.

There is a reason for the term "valve train". The functions of each part are so interconnected it's best to look at them as parts of a whole rather than individually. Rocker arms oddly enough are one of the most overlooked areas for performance improvement. Stock arms are plenty strong and will work fine for a surprising array of competition situations. Roller rockers have definite advantages, they reduce nasty side wiping on the valve stems and cut friction, thus increasing reliability and offering fractionally more power, especially with really lumpy cams. But once again, if you get out the scale before you get out your wallet, you usually find light weight is not a feature of roller rockers.

Which presents us with another series of decisions. Do we want durability and longevity for a street motor with a possible friction reduction bonus in the quick rev department? Or, as racers, shall we consider a lot more work and employing either type of rocker arm, stock or roller, lighten the dog-crap outta them? Funny, that store-bought ultra-light rockers aren't on most radar screens for H-D high performance. There's a pretty good reason for that actually, since doing it right would probably look more like titanium materials than lightening existing parts.

Grinding away on computer designed arms is a short cut to failure of the part, so undertake this approach carefully, if at all. The other way, using a scale to select the lightest arms and matching the weights, regardless of which type you choose to use, might drive the parts man nuts. But it's likely to get you the best balance of components for superior performance.

Valves are often sold in "kits" with keepers and springs. You still have to be sure the springs meet the specs recommended by the cam manufacturer.

Since you know by now that you want the lightest, strongest valves and rockers you can get (ignoring size for the moment), you might as well hold that thought when you're picking out pushrods too. No one seems to advertise the weight of a full set of these things, adjusting nuts and all. But there are differences. It's worth noting that ounces on a scale can turn into hundreds of pounds, even tons of pressure at 6000rpm. It is also known that chrome moly pushrods are several times stiffer than those made from lighter aluminum. Time to stop and think again. What are the trade-offs? Street motors that will never see the extreme limits of engine speed and do not have cams with radical profiles, will be better served with the strongest, lightest aluminum rods, rather than heavy moly rods, marketing hype notwithstanding.

For drag race or roadrace applications where most of the action will be closer to redline than idle throughout the event, you should consider the moly route. And those double adjustable pushrods, sold primarily on the "convenience" of extra adjusting nuts (and all the associated weight and complexity that goes along for the ride), are likely to be both too flexible and too heavy to be of any advantage. (Save the money for a tube of elbow grease instead).

Tappets are the next step in the chain. Stockers work fine for 90% of the jobs you'll ever ask that engine to do, given one caveat. Cams with unforgiving ramp profiles. Once upon a time, that tidbit meant that solid tappets were the only way to deal with cams that gnarly. Not anymore. Screamin' Eagle and JIM'S big-axle tappets will handle shock loads from fast ramps far better than the standard offering. Plus, this designed-in improvement can be coupled with so-called "hydro-solid" characteristics. Simply put, these tappets function exactly as normal hydraulic units at lower engine speeds where there's plenty of time to follow bumpstick contours, practically regardless of that contour. They then revert to behavior that mimics old fashioned solid lifters at high speeds. Meaning they won't pump up or aerate and lose contact with the profile of the cam at revs above 5600 or so. This upgrade can be worth several horsepower "on top," all by itself. But again, it pays to think of this as part of the entire "train", as a system, and as compatible as possible.

We saved springs for last. The advice here is keep the rates as soft as possible - dare I say "light"? Sounds great to tell the boys you've got some kinda maniac, mega-stiff drag race coils stuffed in there, but they'll have the last laugh if you cream the valvetrain every 20,000 miles. Check with the cam maker to find out what sort of seat pressure and travel to coil bind they recommend for the grind du jour you fancy. Then shop around. Plenty of cam peddlers don't offer the right springs themselves. So you might have to consult a valve spring builder. The point is, some square ramped, mega-lift drag race profiles, pounding on springs that pound right back, is not only a classic case of the immovable object/irresistible force thing, it's counter productive. All you need is a spring that will not bounce at revolutions you intend to use, with the cam you've chosen.

Valves sizes for Evolution 'X' engines.

	Intake	Exhaust
883	1.585	1.35
1100	1.84	1.615
1200	1.715	1.48
Buell S1W	1.81	1.58

There's some insight to be gained by realizing that the S1W valves in S1W heads, with S1W port shapes make more power than any of the others if you also use S1W pistons. What is not so easy to figure is that any of the others can be improved significantly without changing the size of the valves.

Shape is just as important. The shape of choice for valves has been the "Penny on a stick" profile. Fine when the basic criteria is just to keep as much material out of the way of the air flow as possible. But, besides how much, there's a where and how issue to be addressed in modern air flow measurement. Totally flat backs on intakes tend to let incoming mixture pack up behind the head. Intakes with "waisted" stems and somewhat tulip-shaped, semi-flat backs hollowed out on the face to save weight, will typically out perform the stock shape. These are fairly traditional shapes.

Where traditional shapes tend to fall short is on the exhaust side of the equation. Without getting into complexity and explanations beyond need for our purposes, let's just leave it at this:

An exhaust valve with a smooth radius from a flat, even mildly convex face to seat area, and a very shallow sort of "W" cross-sectional head to stem shape, sure ought to help.

Valve sizes have been shuffled a lot for various X engine applications. However, bigger isn't always better. Matching valve size to port flow is the best way to get the best from them. If you opt for the biggest valves you would be well advised to get the lightest ones as well.

Chapter Nine

Camshafts

Pick The Right Bumpstick

Could it be that until the resurgence of performance planning for the venerable XL motor (thanks to Buell), nobody really cared about camshaft grinds? I mean there is no end of choice for cams in the Big Twin orbit, probably hundreds of grinds out there by now. But XL/Buell bumpsticks? That's been a totally different story until lately. Even now the list is a scant couple of dozen choices and not all of those are suitable for banging around on a street machine. Still, it's high time someone gathered all the low

Unique in all motorcycledom, no other engine in production uses four separate camshafts to activate four pushrods leading to four valves, in two cylinders. Yet this allows cam grinders almost infinite latitude in giving each valve exactly what it needs.

down on lift and timing and duration, and overlap, and such.

GRIND GRID

The accompanying charts represent the critical stuff for all "known" and popular grinds for 5-speed Buells and Sportsters. If any are missing, they must be new or non-entities – sorry. Accuracy, or lack of, is to be regarded with healthy skepticism for at least three reasons.

One: A simple typo can make a liar out of anybody. Plus the fact that some of these grinds can be considered as "subject to change without notice" in the interest of even further refinements. The factory has even changed part numbers regarding O.E. cams for 2000 and later models.

Two: These specs have a certain level of "close enough for the girls we date" to them. Some are older references, possibly from second or even third hand sources. One or two are supposed to be secret, so why should they tell us the truth? Fact is, some cams are changed in detail (a hair more lift, a degree on the intake timing and so on) simply to avoid being identical to the competition.

Three: No cam specification can be totally trusted until it's been degreed. None of these have had that honor, it's left up to you, and that is as it should be. Just the same, most of this data is on the money.

Okay, now that the CYA part is covered, we can move on to the second thing that's exposed for discussion here. That is, rather than blind guessing about the best choice for your needs – use software

Details about grind numbers can usually be found right about where the stock cam on the left and the Sifton 231 on the right are stamped. If the numbers alone don't tell the whole story take a look at the difference in the lobes.

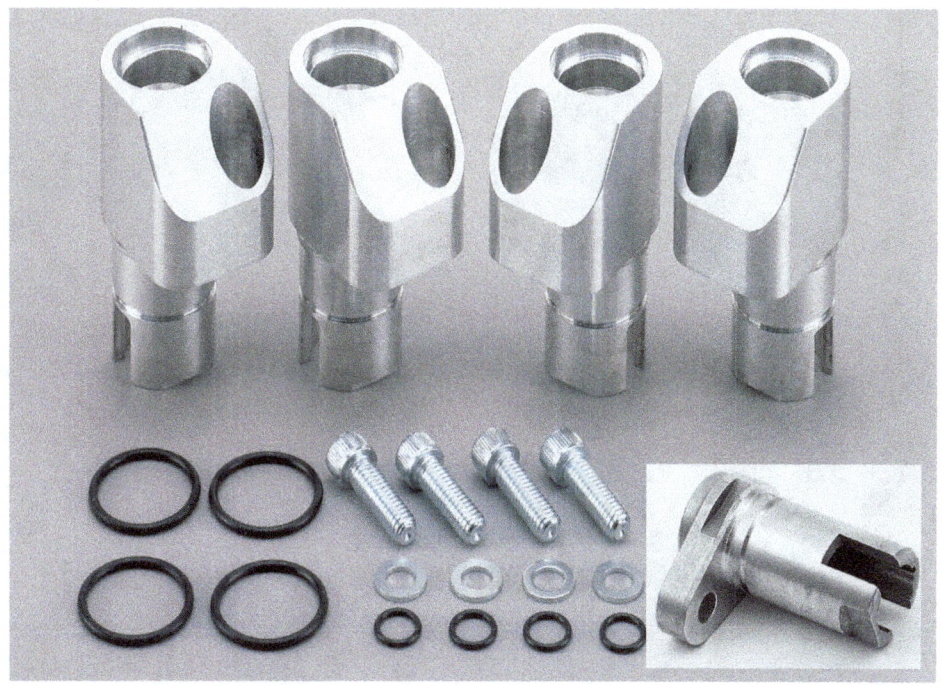

The inset picture shows something 5-speed Sportsters and Buells will never have, tappet blocks. These do need to be checked for wear during cam replacements. The billet lifter blocks are from S&S designed for their Super Stock crankcases though they can be used on 4-speed cases as well.

"predictions". Don't misunderstand, this is not a total cop-out. There are some cam selections that can be relied on as the "right" choice for 80-90% of us, 80-90% of the time. And, we'll talk more about some of those. It's just that a good engine simulation program is a damn sight better than simply asking ten people and getting ten opinions.

THINK FAST

These predictive programs can literally do complete engine "builds" in advance for you, from the ground up – head flow, bore and stroke combinations, the works. In other words, they can do more than function as a simple cam selector or video entertainment during winters and other non-riding situations. But for the purpose of cam selection alone, they are sensational. You will be able to quickly see the difference between one contender and another. Worth every penny and every minute of time you can devote to them.

Obviously, predictive software also has it's limits. Mostly, either it doesn't calculate torque all that accurately, or every dyno in the country is optimistic. (Just figure it is because there was nothing nearly as efficient as the Buell exhaust out there when the program was written.) Most software is not that far off for Sportster output, but blows it when it comes to Buells. As a rule of thumb, you can add nearly 20 percent to the torque numbers predicted and be close to dyno-verifiable truth for Buells.

Horsepower estimates on the other hand, are tantalizingly accurate, usually within 3-5 percent of what it is going to show on a dyno pull. That's very useful for comparing one potential cam choice with another similar option, before you part with your hard earned.

Speaking of hard earned – there is no one magic cam grind out there. In fact when you compare apples with apples, most are so close it comes down to which one you can get a better deal on. The problem is, too often apples are not compared with apples, more like pineapples or other types of hand grenades. For that reason it's best to view the listings in the chart as falling into rough (really rough) categories.

"Bolt-in" is supposed to be just that, but like everything else mechanical, there are issues. Usually involving valve springs and upgraded push rods and tappets and such. Pure bolt-in cams would not require such things, even if they are recommended.

"Beyond Bolt-In", means the upgraded springs and what-not are pretty much a given if you want the most power and reliability out of that grind. It's also the level at which "modified" can take on a whole new meaning. Typically, headwork. In some cases this means grinding clearance for lift in the cam cavity, and a host of other necessities. It means more work and expense. Both at the outset of the installation, and at the culmination, if you screw up. The guys who build these cams know from whence they speak, so if you doubt, drop a dime and ask 'em. You'll be glad you did.

Assembly lube is the topic of some debate. Some believe motor oil is fine, others prefer something a little heavier like this Torco product. Either way, Don't try dry. Installation of radical cams means checking clearances inside the cam chest and a thorough cleaning after any grinding is done.

"Big-Inch" cams are the problem children, at least where Buells, and software, are concerned. For instance, Andrews #9 grind should be used in larger displacement engines, but isn't always. It still seems to work. Some others in this category wouldn't if you took the same chance. And there's the definition of big-inch to assay. Many of these grinds are for strokers, not big bores. And some would work for both. That's a real consideration with a Buell – or Super Street Sportster scenario. Sure it's nice to build a 96-inch torque monster, but it ain't so nice to rebuild it when you miss a shift and blow it up at seven grand. Or, wear out the valve train every 15-20,000 miles because of aggressive cam profiles.

At last count, there were at least three affordable resources for engine simulations. Engine Analyzer 3.0 is the most expensive, but possibly more helpful than the others in that it can also point out basic limitations and potential errors in your "cyber engine" design before you find them the hard way. It's also a program for all engines, not specifically Harley or even motorcycle.

Dyno 2000 is the latest iteration of what most people used to call "desktop dyno", but it's come along way. Along with EA3.0, it too offers drop down menus for all the variables, in many instances specific options are already on the menus, and you can build your own cam profiles, head flow charts and more. Or let the computer suggest the best options (begin to see how this might be of value?). The last is Accelerator 3, and the only one that's Harley specific. This program, in addition to being invaluable for engine building, has gearing programs and can be linked to real dynamometer files – to keep things totally honest. Any of the three will give the most credible results. None cost more than a couple hundred bucks. You can find out more about where to get these programs in the Sources section of this book.

Or, for an even ROUGHER guide – check this chart.

Selection Performance Tendency	CAMS From 220° to 240° Duration @ .053"	CAMS From 240° to 260° Duration @ .053"	CAMS From 260° to 288° Duration @ .053"
Idle Quality	Smooth, stock-like idle. Moderate intake manifold vacuum. Somewhat sensitive to altitude, jetting, and ignition advance	Slightly lopey idle. Lower manifold vacuum. More sensitive to altitude, jetting, and ignition advance	Rough to very rough idle. Very low manifold vacuum. Very sensitive to altitude, jetting, and ignition advance
Power Band	Excellent mid-range throttle from 2,000 to 5,000 rpm.	Excellent top end power from 2,200 to 6,000 rpm.	Best power typically from 3,200 to 7,000 rpm or more.
Torque Band	Max torque typically from 2,500 to 5,000 rpm.	Max torque typically from 2,500 to 6,000 rpm.	Max torque typically from 3,500 to 7,000 rpm or more.
Cylinder Heads	Stock with good 3 angle valve job, to slightly modified cylinder heads.	Some race preparation necessary, typically valvetrain, porting and matching.	Fully race prepared cylinder heads, with valvetrain up-grades typically mandatory.
Compression	Stock to Increased compression ratio typically not to exceed 10:1	Increased compression between 10. and 11.0:1	Increased compression between 10.75 and 12.5:1
Carburetion	Re-jetted stock and moderately increase cfm rating with high flow air cleaner	Increase cfm rating with high flow air cleaner and larger carb	Maximum increase in cfm rating with fully race-prepped high flow carb and air cleaner
Valve Springs	Stock to 20-25% stiffer.	Stock to 30-35% stiffer w/ light, strong retainers	Set to lift and ramps – ranges from slightly stiffer than stock to almost twice the stiffness

The reality check is to be honest with yourself about how you intend to use the cam of choice. Some lend themselves far better to the kind of three to five rpm "grind" that are useful 90% of the time. They may not give that extra 5-ponies on top for bragging rights, but if you'd rather use the power available than talk about it, such a cam set might be the way to go. Others who spend a lot of throttle time at higher engine speeds, where the extra power of a proper profile for that use, would find a more radical grind invaluable. If the bike is run for pink slips or trophies too. Then you gotta have all that can be had, damn the poor low rpm performance. In short, oftentimes the nature of bike and rider makes as much difference as the intended use.

And, Just So You Know

Buell's lend themselves better (relatively) to high-rpm work for other designed in reasons too. By comparison, Sportsters, with their solid mounted engines, turn into jack hammers at redline so they need, and can better use, the grunt down low. Buells are lighter machines and blessed with vibration isolation so top-end horsepower can be unleashed with impunity. This is about the rider more than the machine, but that's as big a factor in proper cam choice as any. Where and what kind of power you want is your decision, but you ignore the realities at your own risk.

For instance, even stock displacement 883's hit piston speeds of 4500 feet-per-minute at 7000rpm. That's grenade territory if you stay that wound up very long. Might be a nice place to visit, but you simply can't live there. And the average stroker shouldn't-wouldn't-couldn't even visit.

There's a simple formula to calculate piston speed, so figure it out for yourself: Stroke times RPM divided by 6. It's also pretty much a given that 4000 feet per minute is the safe sustainable limit for piston speed.

So with a stroke of 3.81 inches, the formula tells you real quickly that buying a cam that peaks at 6250, is about right for the real world. Not surprisingly the factory cam, and ignition rev limit, recognize this and are set for just this limit. Anything over that shortens both engine life and the mechanical fuse.

But have fun selecting your stick anyway, and whatever you do, don't let the selection "grind" on you. You aren't stuck with any particular choice. One of the beautiful things about cam changes on X engines is they can be accomplished in two or three hours. So it's not like you can't experiment in the real world.

Camshafts

Pointers: engine breathing is a function of engine size, exhaust system efficiency, intake and exhaust port flow characteristics, intake manifold design and carburetor size. Typically, long-stroke, large-displacement engines tend to produce high velocities and usually require a cam profile with high lift and long duration. Scooters with real mufflers and "non-tuned" exhaust systems create exhaust back pressure that affects (destroys?) the scavenging effect. These machines usually require camshafts with less overlap. Or in alternative terms, a larger lobe-center-angle. But, lift, timing and duration aren't necessarily the most important specs – regardless of engine layout.

A couple of general (if not downright vague) tips might help: With all else being equal the cam with the lowest lobe center numbers will feel least "cammy". The overlap in non-big-inch motors is another indicator of peaky power, lots of overlap leans towards top end power.

Duration numbers can also tell many stories but if there's a large variance between intake and exhaust (Sifton's Stingray, for instance) it's usually for a specific purpose. The Stingray let's 883s and 1200 conversions using small intake valves take a deeper, longer breath. If the duration is longer on the exhaust side that generally helps poorly flowing stock ports exhale longer and helps the engine run cooler.

Remember those nifty adjustable ignition advance curves available in some modules? You'll need this feature most, in inverse proportion to cam timing variations from factory spec. Long duration, especially on the intake side, without compensating with a compression increase virtually guarantees you'll need to change the advance curve. You'll need more initially. For instance, if off-idle to 3500rpm worked with stock cams at 8-degrees initial advance, you may need anywhere from 10-16 degrees with "long" cam timing to get decent low speed response. Conversely, if you've over done it somehow, to the point where preignition or detonation are a problem, you'll need to reduce initial timing and slow the curve to prevent engine damage. There's a direct relationship between cam timing and ignition advance curve timing. Outfits like Snap-On, Sun-Pro, even Equus (available from Summit Racing) offer so-called "dial back" timing lights. Some even feature digital readouts of both engine rpm and advance, simultaneously. I'd say dial-in with a dial back, is going to save you lots of time, aggravation and piston crowns, when used properly.

Manufacturer	Cam Grind	Intake Open BTDC	Intake Close ABDC	Exhaust Open BBDC	Exhaust Close ATDC	Intake Duration	Exhaust Duration	Overlap	Intake Lobe Center	Exhaust Lobe Center	Lobe Sep. Angle	Intake Lift	Exhaust Lift	Intake Lift TDC	Exhaust Lift TDC	RPM Low	RPM High	Min. CID	Notes
HD Stock	D (88-91)	2	41	41	2	223	223	4	110	110	109.5	0.458	0.458	0.094	0.094				Bolt-in
Andrews	V2 / N2	22	38	46	18	240	244	40	98	104	101.0	0.465	0.440	0.180	0.155	2000	6000		Bolt-in
Andrews	V4 / N4	30	46	52	24	256	256	54	98	104	101.0	0.490	0.490	0.216	0.189	2500	6500		Bolt-in
Andrews	V8 / N8	32	44	55	28	256	263	60	96	104	99.8	0.490	0.490	0.226	0.212	2000	6000		Bolt-in
Andrews	V6 / N6	34	50	56	28	264	264	62	98	104	101.0	0.490	0.490	0.241	0.212	2500	6500		Bolt-in
Andrews	V9 / N9	33	53	53	33	266	266	66	100	100	100.0	0.555	0.555	0.240	0.240		6000	80	
Andrews	V80 / N80	32	60	66	30	272	276	62	104	108	106.0	0.600	0.600	0.264	0.244		6500	61	
Andrews	BV / NV	35	59	59	35	274	274	70	102	102	102.0	0.590	0.590	0.260	0.260	2000	6000	88	
Andrews	V83 / N83	32	64	70	30	276	280	62	106	110	108.0	0.630	0.630	0.267	0.248		6500	80	
Andrews	V87 / N87	34	70	76	32	284	288	66	108	112	110.0	0.670	0.670	0.283	0.269		6500	100	
Edelbrock	1742 / 1743	18	42	46	22	240	248	40	102	102	102.0	0.590	0.590	0.166	0.192				
Hurricane (XB9R/S)	XB606	34	50	61	23	264	264	57	98	109	103.5	0.606	0.606	0.240	0.200		7800		Buell Firebolt
Red Shift	567V2	23	48	53	18	251	251	41	103	108	105.0	0.575	0.575	0.204	0.162				
Red Shift	531V2	28	51	60	19	259	259	47	102	111	106.0	0.525	0.525	0.195	0.195				
Red Shift	573V2	23	56	63	17	259	260	40	107	113	109.8	0.580	0.580	0.213	0.162				
Red Shift	585V2	21	58	66	13	259	259	34	109	117	112.5	0.580	0.580	0.190	0.140				
Red Shift	643V2	27	61	70	18	268	268	45	107	116	111.5	0.645	0.645	0.224	0.165				
Red Shift	625V2	32	58	62	29	270	271	61	103	107	104.8	0.625	0.625	0.250	0.228				
Red Shift	623V2	31	62	67	26	273	273	57	106	111	108.0	0.623	0.623	0.268	0.221				
Red Shift	670V2	40	58	62	29	278	271	69	99	107	102.8	0.655	0.655	0.270	0.243				
Red Shift	785V2	27	71	77	19	278	276	46	112	119	115.5	0.785	0.785	0.240	0.180				
Red Shift	729V2	34	65	71	28	279	279	62	106	112	108.5	0.725	0.725	0.278	0.228				
Red Shift	723V2	38	62	74	24	280	278	62	102	115	108.5	0.715	0.715	0.320	0.210				
S&S	500	34	50	56	28	264	264	62	98	104	101.0	0.500	0.500	0.241	0.212	3500	6500		
S&S	555	33	53	53	33	266	266	66	100	100	100.0	0.555	0.555	0.241	0.241	2500	6500		
Screaming Eagle	Bolt-In	28	48	52	24	256	256	52	100	104	102.0	0.497	0.497	0.211	0.191	2500	6000		Buell O.E. (except S2)
Screaming Eagle	Hi-Performance	26	50	55	30	256	265	56	102	103	102.3	0.536	0.536	0.211	0.191	2000	6500		Bolt-in
Sifton	Stingray	28	42	50	20	250	250	48	97	105	101.0	0.480	0.480	0.190	0.180				NLA
Sifton	Evader	28	44	50	22	252	252	50	98	104	101.0	0.515	0.515	0.200	0.180	3000	6500		NLA
Sifton	Manta	30	48	50	28	258	258	58	99	101	100.0	0.540	0.540	0.250	0.250	3000	6500	80	NLA

Valve Timing and Cam Events: A Poppets Progress Primer

No doubt, one of the most important factors that governs power output for a given engine combination is valve timing. Without proper valve opening and closing "events", even the best engine, the most efficient cylinder heads, or cutting edge induction and exhaust systems, will be no less than wasted. Take the attitude that "this cam picked up two tenths for my buddy so-and-so" at your own risk.

The fact is, with a relatively few choices, Prado's Principle, or the 80/20 Rule is in effect. Meaning, 20% of the known "popular" performers wind up being used in 80% of the hop –ups. Or looked at the other way, there are really only 20% of us that ever use other than 80% of the aftermarket grinds out there. Or even worry about these things.

For the 20% who care to delve deeper, on the other hand, the plain truth is that even small differences in such things as carburetor, capacity, compression, exhaust tuning, or gearing changes can have profound effects on what the proper valve timing should be.

Figuring that a certain cam profile works okay in a boatload of given applications is one of the most common rookie mistakes made when selecting cams.

In other words, one size may fit most, but definitely does not fit all.

To realize why, we need to understand some basics of camshaft timing, and exactly why valve events occur when they do. Starting with the exhaust opening point.

As the piston is being pushed down the bore by force exerted by the rapidly expanding fuel and air mixture that's being burned in the combustion chamber, it heads for bottom dead center. At this point in the cycle, the mixture has exerted most of the energy available from its combustion, and the amount of torque applied to the crankshaft is reduced by a combination of less available thermal energy and the reduction in leverage the connecting rod has on the crankshaft.

Now, the exhaust valve cracks open. Suddenly there's considerable difference in pressure between the exhaust gases in the header and the combustion gases still trapped in the cylinder. This pressure rise across the exhaust valve starts the flow of exhaust gases out the exhaust port and into the head pipe.

When the piston hits Bottom Dead Center BDC and begins its travel back up the bore, the pressure difference between the gases still in the combustion chamber and the exhaust header effectively reaches equilibrium.

Next, it's time to pump the remaining gases out of the cylinder as the piston travels up. As the piston nears Top Dead Center (TDC), the exhaust valve begins to close, reducing the cross sectional area or "window" that escaping exhaust gases must pass through to exit the combustion chamber. This increases the velocity of the exhaust gas and its inertia.

Many manufacturers offer cams as a kit, with springs and retainers in steel (or a lighter material). You will still have to check some clearances and installed pressures, as recommended by the instruction sheet that accompanies the kit. S&S

As the exhaust valve is closing, the intake valve simultaneously begins to open. ZAP - a low pressure area in the combustion chamber, which exerts force on the intake charge to help begin drawing in fresh charge, even though the piston hasn't reached TDC yet. As the piston passes through TDC and starts back down the cylinder bore the exhaust valve finally closes, while the intake valve continues to open.

The piston must now suck on the intake charge in order to draw it into the cylinder. As the piston approaches bottom dead center, the intake charge gains velocity, and inertia. Once it passes through BDC and begins the compression stroke the intake valve begins to close. But, mixture is still streaming steadily into the cylinder because of its inertia. As the piston gains speed the velocity of the piston and the velocity of the incoming mixture equalizes and the intake valve closes completely.

The piston now works on the trapped intake charge to compress it. At some point before TDC the spark plug ignites this mixture. The piston now does an enormous amount of work to force its way that last little bit up the bore and pass through TDC. As soon as the crankshaft has swung through TDC, the burning mixture expands and forces the piston down the bore and the cycle starts all over again.

The important thing to be learned here, is that one camshaft timing event has a most definite effect on the remaining three. For instance, if the exhaust valve opens too early, power is lost and blown out the exhaust. Of course there'd be less pumping work required to evacuate the cylinder after the piston passed BDC, and less exhaust inertia at TDC because of the decreased mass of exhaust gas available at the end of the exhaust stroke. This leads to less force exerted on the incoming intake charge, with a decreased amount of total cylinder fill because of the inefficiency of the overlap period. Other changes in valve timing have similar effects.

The single most important valve timing event is the intake closing event. The reason is that there is only X amount of time, in any engine, let alone an X engine, to complete any process within the engine at a given engine speed. And, as speed either increases or decreases, there's a corresponding increase or decrease in time available for properly filling the cylinder. So for increasing engine speed the intake valve must close later because there's less time for cylinder fill. The trade-off is that closing the intake valve at a later point in the cycle hurts low end performance because there's not enough charge velocity to maintain the inertia needed to fill the cylinder. Reversion stuffs some charge back into the intake manifold at low engine speeds, which results in a lower "signal" across the carburetor. Poor idle and throttle response follow shortly.

Conversely, earlier intake closing means the engine will have good idle characteristics and tremendous low speed throttle response and torque. But as engine speeds rise, the valve closes before cylinder fill is complete. Zing - a decrease in power at nose bleed engine speeds.

Plus, if a given cylinder head has a large cross-

Charts like these are often used to provide a graphic representation of any particular cam grind. This makes it easier to understand the term overlap and fact that the intake valve (for example) opens before the pistons actually hits TDC and while the exhaust valve is still open.

sectional area (fat port), the low speed velocity suffers, so a camshaft profile that closes the intake valve early is useless. If the valve closes early with this cylinder head layout, cylinder fill won't be worth diddley at lower engine speeds because of the inefficiency of the ports and cylinder fill at high engine speeds will suck because of camshaft selection. An engine like this will never produce acceptable power at any speed because of the mismatch in camshaft and cylinder head selection.

Conversely, if you try heads with a relatively small cross-sectional area, with dandy low speed velocity, and a cam is used that has a late intake closing point, then the engine won't produce high speed power. The velocity through dinky ports gets so high that the flow through the head effectively chokes, even with an exceedingly radical camshaft.

The point at which both the intake and exhaust valves are simultaneously open, is the "overlap" point. Overlap has an effect on how broad or peaky the powerband is for a given engine set up. During overlap, the exhaust valve is closing and the intake valve is just beginning to open. If cylinder fill at high speeds is going to be worth squat, then overlap must be used to advantage; that is, the valves must be simultaneously open for a greater amount of time to allow max draw on the incoming charge at high rpm.

The trouble is, big overlap tends to have sour effects on idle quality and low speed engine performance because of the lack of intake and exhaust gas velocity. There isn't much inertia, there is lot's of intake charge contamination with exhaust residue left from the previous cycle. Greater intake charge heating and greatly reduced burn rate, all leading to crappy power at low speeds. And lots of overlap combined with huge ports is even worse.

Exhaust design has a big affect on camshaft profile too. Stock head pipe size maintains exhaust gas velocity pretty well, so less overlap is required to produce the same efficiency as a fat pipe. Obviously, cylinder heads with good intake-to-exhaust flow ratios need less exhaust duration to achieve the same power as a head with a poor intake/exhaust flow ratio. Poor flow ratios mean the exhaust valve needs to open earlier to maximize blowdown and scavenge exhaust gases.

The key element in all of these scenarios is the same: time. Bottom line, the amount of time necessary to complete a given process governs exactly when that process should begin or end.

Forced induction, including turbos, Nitrous and superchargers) is a whole new ball game, but the basic rules that govern camshaft profile selections don't change. At least not if you play this game to win. Two main factors influence parameters in a forced induction application, fuel burn rate and increased air/fuel volume. In a nitrous oxide application, the burn rate of the fuel is actually changed by the chemical composition of the NOS. The extra oxygen means the fuel burns a bunch quicker than in a naturally aspirated engine. So the power gain happens in a much shorter period of time than normal. That's why NOS has such a kick when you finally let the

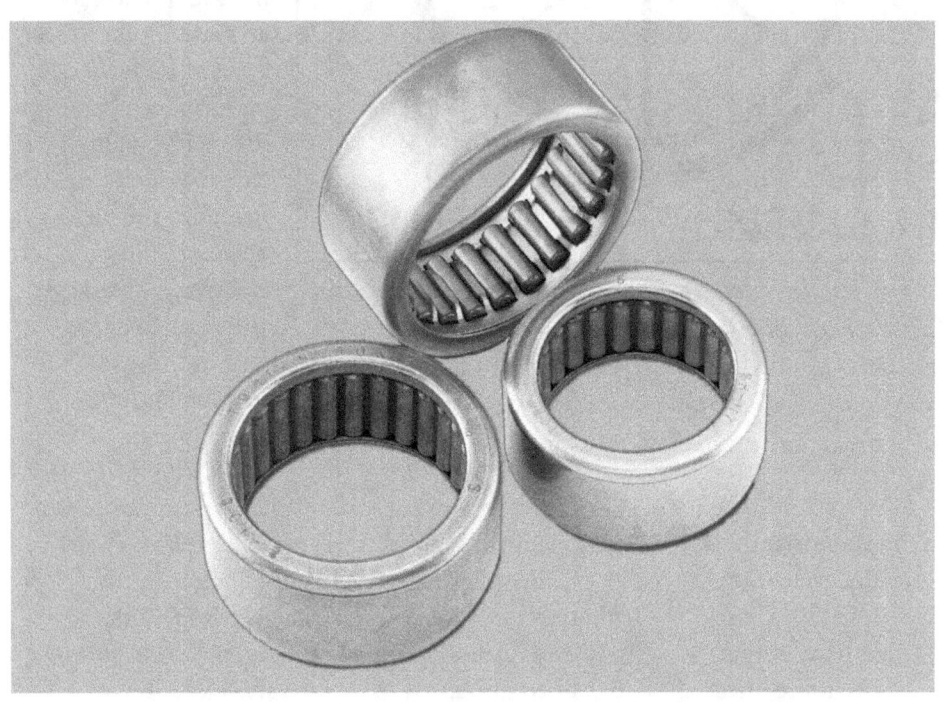

It's always a good idea to check and probably replace the cam bearings when installing a camshaft. Be sure to use the bearings with the maximum number of rollers for maximum support and long bearing life. Biker's Choice

"squeeze" out of the bottle. Therefore, there's no benefit to opening the exhaust valve later in the cycle. In reality, opening the exhaust valve later reduces power output because of an increase in the volume of exhaust gases that must be purged from the cylinder. Late exhaust valve opening also means greater pumping losses to evacuate the cylinder. Also, because of the decreased efficiency of the blowdown process, much greater amounts of residual gases have to be scavenged during the overlap period. If there's too much to get rid of then there's reversion back into the intake tract. That could make fuel, air, and nitrous oxide in the intake manifold ignite, BAM. That's why typical nitrous oxide cams have a wider lobe separation angle (less overlap) than naturally aspirated cams do. By moving the exhaust opening event to a point earlier in the cycle and minimizing overlap, the separation angle increases.

Blown applications are similar to NOS in some respects, but because the burn rate of the gasoline is not chemically changed, there are differences. For instance, the exhaust valve closing may actually need to be delayed by a few degrees, relative to a nitrous cam. Since the fuel is still burning as the piston descends the bore it would be a shame to open the exhaust valve too early and blow useful power straight out the exhaust port. Of course reversion (or spit back) would be a pretty fair impairment to power too. Blown alcohol engines have even more bizarre needs, since alcohol burns much slower than gas. The energy available in alcohol is roughly half that of gasoline as well, which means that roughly double the volume is needed to make the same power. So the intake lobe needs more duration to deliver the proper amount. Exhaust closing would likewise need to be considerably later than that of a gas cam grind, since the burn rate is so much slower.

Turbocharger motors are completely different than any of the above. There's a unique variable called exhaust backpressure. Overlap relies on that pressure differential across the exhaust valve to properly scavenge the cylinder. With a turbo, backpressure in the exhaust is almost always higher than in the intake manifold. Meaning, overlap has to be cut way back to avoid reversion. Also, since the charge volume is higher than normal, and the burn rate is slow, exhaust opening needs to be delayed a bit. So most turbo cams have short duration, little overlap, and wide lobe separation angles. Max effort turbo motors usually sport solid roller cams and high lift ratio rocker arms as part of the arsenal.

Now that we know a little something about camshaft timing events and their specific applications, the 20% of us that aren't happy with 80% of the available cams on the market might just be able to get ourselves in the zone for determining camshaft requirements for given combinations. And/or predict changes needed to improve combinations we currently have.

Cam and pinion gears can be checked for size using the pins shown here (in an effort to ensure a smooth mesh between the gears) but most mechanics work by feel.

Chapter Ten

Heads

Heads Up Reference for X Engines

What is the deal here, anyway? Evolution Big Twin Harley engines had the same cylinder head design since their inception in 1984. Twin Cams have four already, if you include the Screamin' Eagle variants. X- series Evo engines, Sportster and Buell, on the other hand, have a total of six variations, at least (at present). And that's not counting aftermarket designs, or the unique new redesigned XB9 Buell.

When the Evo X engine appeared in late 1985

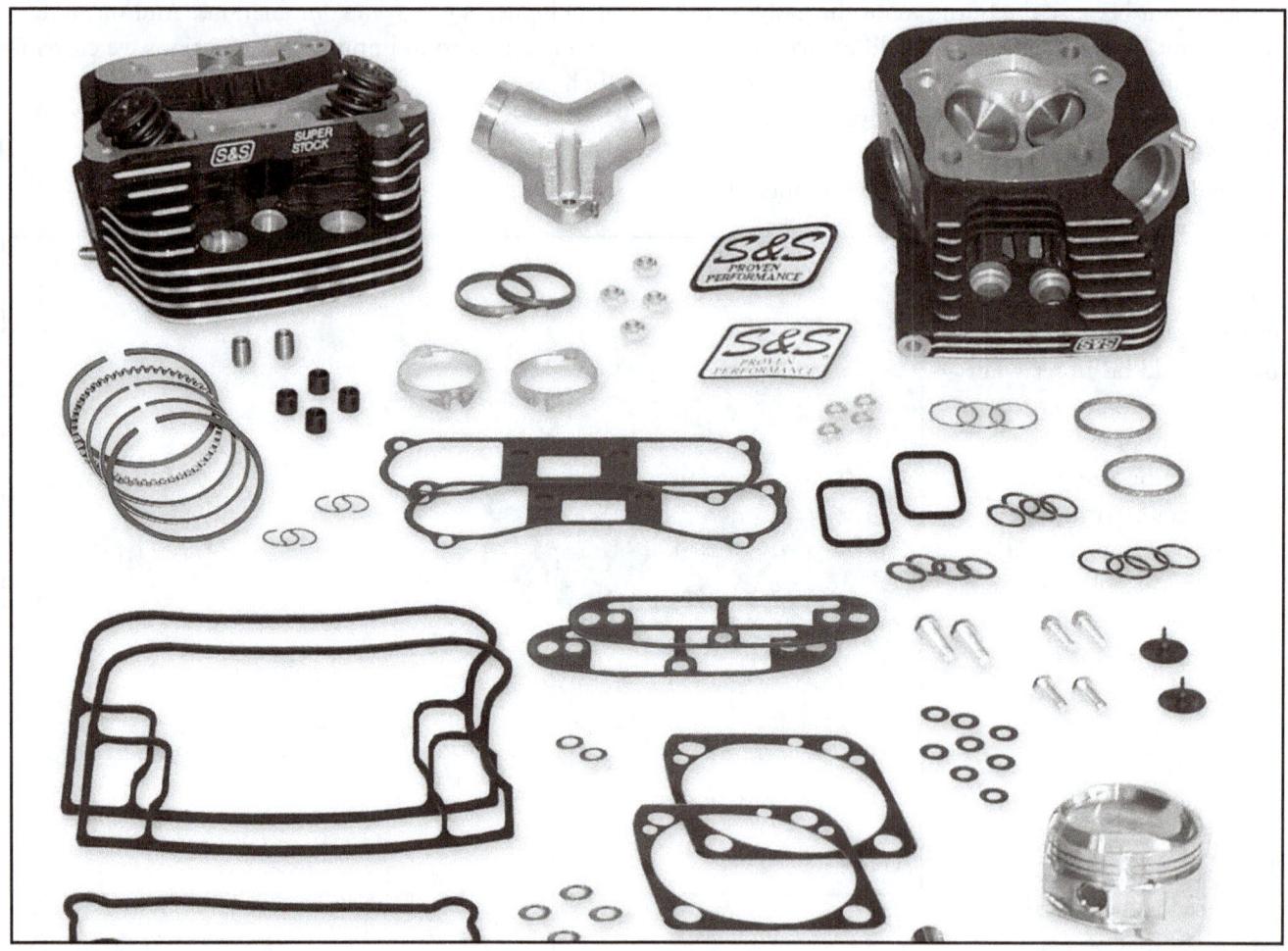

By buying the heads as part of a kit, like this example from S&S, you are assured that the head and piston shapes are complimentary. These kits are available for both 3-1/2 and 3-5/8 inch bore sizes.

as an '86 model, it was 883cc displacement. Rather than mimic the D-shaped combustion chamber of its big brother, it took a different path to efficiency. Blessed with a shorter stroke and a bore 1/2" smaller than the 1340 engine, it had different needs. As the engine has grown and its performance potential increased the heads have changed as well, as we'll soon see.

Head history-

1) The original sand cast head design for 883s used a relatively small, tight chamber with a squish band incorporated in the layout to prevent detonation and increase swirl with smaller valves, and a chamber shape that, for lack of a better term, was "semi-hemi", it surprisingly turned out roughly 80% as much power on 3/5ths the size. Pretty impressive. Not long after it's introduction, somewhere in the 1987 model run, the 883 got a different, die cast, head casting with subtle changes to chamber and ports. Most folks agree that it slowed them down, too. 1986 model 883's are considered the best runners of the small-bore bunch.

2) Could be that part of the reason for the casting change in mid-stride was that 883s had a sibling forthcoming, in the form of the 1100 Sportster. Same stroke, bigger bore, (but not a full 3 1/2-inches yet) and completely different combustion cham-

Here we see the family resemblance between the 883 head and the S1 Lightning version. The S1 benefits from a squish band, necessary for larger bore, and larger valves.

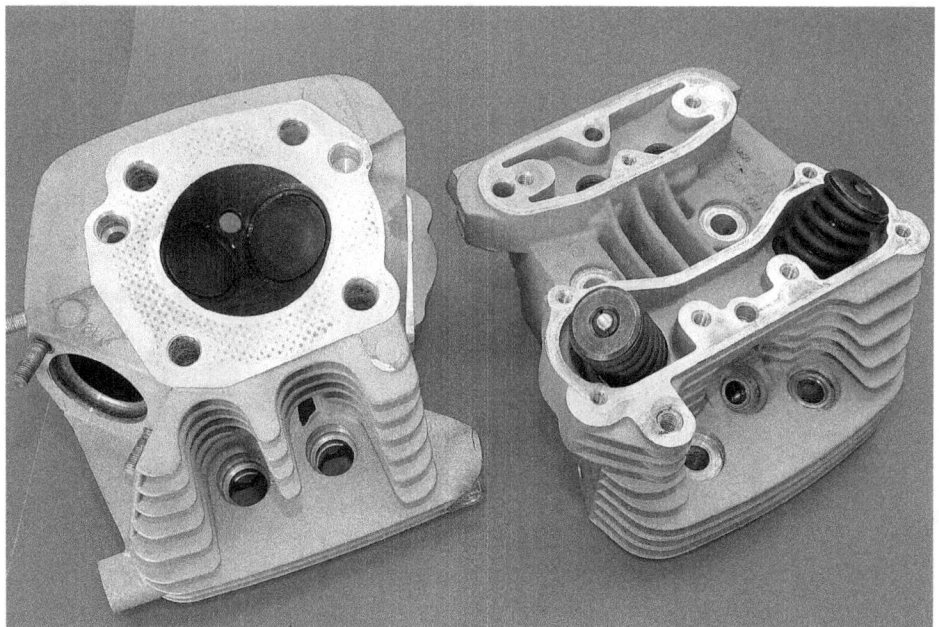

These are stock 883 heads, fresh off a motor undergoing conversion to 1200 status. When converting using factory flat-top pistons, H-D recommends grinding the chamber – they'd rather have more volume in the head to reduce compression than leave the pressure and control detonation. Most 1200 conversions using the little 883 valves have more bottom end and mid-range than "born" 1200s, must be due to velocity through the ports at lower speeds.

bers. If you didn't know better you'd swear that the factory had Jerry Branch design these critters. There were the familiar bathtub chambers so near and dear to Jerry's heart, and lo and behold - 1340 sized valves. The intake and exhaust valves were identical in head diameter to the 80" motor, and the notion was with a tight chamber and big valves the 1100 would be a rocket ship. The design didn't do too badly, but for some reason or other H-D wasn't satisfied. After a short production run the 1100 got its 3 1/2" bore, and yet another set of heads and became the 1200.

3) 1988 and later 1200 XL heads are nearly hemispherical. The factory took a tack in a totally different direction with this design, using smaller valves and a very open chamber. One suspects that The Motor Co, took a page from Ford here. Ford had tried a closed-chamber head much like the 1100's in the 1986 Mustang 5.0 V8, for that one model year only, and the 5.0 cognoscenti ruled it a low-powered, albeit clean burning mistake. The very next year, and from then on, Ford was back to open chamber heads. Could it be that Harley discovered the same situation existed with its own 1100 heads?

Whatever the motivation, the open-chambered 1200 heads are still with us, on base 1200 Sportsters.

4) Not so on Buells with the exception of the S2. As soon as Buell had access to H-D's deep pockets out popped the S1 Lightning head. Surprisingly, these heads harkened back to the 883s basic chamber shapes which tightened up the chamber for increased mechanical compression, and featured an extended squish band to accommodate the larger bore, while also keeping detonation out of the picture. As anyone who's ever ridden a Lightning will attest, it helped a bunch. The Lightning heads are largely responsible for putting the "sport" back in Sportsters.

5) Introduced in 1997 the XL1200S was The Motor Company's response to Buells. Granted, it's still a far more traditional machine. It at least let hard-core Harley buyers know that the factory still had a trick or two up its sleeve where the granddaddy of Superbikes was concerned. It was good when it appeared and it got better. In 1998 we saw yet another iteration of the Sport 1200, this time utilizing S1-style heads with a twist, in the form of threads offering an extra sparkplug hole.

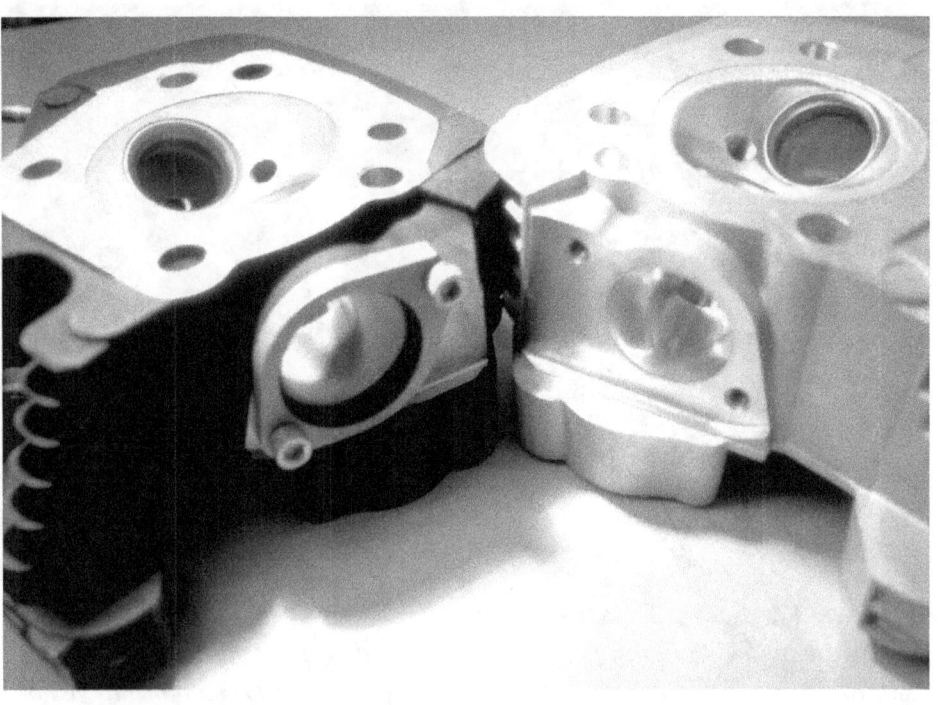

Naked 1200 Sporty head on the left, T-storm on the right. Aside form the obvious differences in the combustion chamber shapes, slightly larger valve sizes, more efficient port diameters, un-shrouded and shortened guides, and careful attention to subtleties in all areas of power production, the two heads are almost the same.

Twin plug heads are not a new idea to performance freaks. In fact, two sparkplugs per cylinder dates back to the dawn of automotive engineering. Then it was a useful trick to help overcome reliability deficiencies in primitive ignitions. Once ignitions ignited regularly, the hod-rodders and racers found it helped power, particularly where high domed pistons shrouded the incoming charge. By the 1930's everybody from Maserati GP cars to Muroc Dry Lake racers had played with the more the merrier sparkplug concept. It wasn't, and isn't, without drawbacks. Usually, to get the best power from a twin plug engine the timing must be altered. No problem with that, unless and until one the plugs fouls, or simply quits for some reason. Then, the very real prospect of engine damage arises because of the altered timing and its attendant pre-ignition/detonation potential. Still, in so many words, to get a clean burn across a big bore it has its uses. Clean burn, is the operative term and the main use that H-D finds for twin plug S1 head's on the 1200 Sport.

Another feature of the '98 1200S model is cams with more overlap and more aggressive timing than stock 1200 bumpsticks. This means more unburned hydro-carbons, kids. The EPA frowns on that kind of thing these days, so unless Harley was willing to use Big Twin-type catalytic mufflers on Sportsters, (and it wasn't), twin sparkplugs were a way out. Hence the performance benefits of 1200S heads, while they may exist, are likely secondary to the task of providing low emissions with hotter cams.

Something to think about. It works so well, that H-D basically used the Buell design, added the 1200S option of twin spark plugs, plus a few minor tweaks and added it to the roster of Screamin' Eagle parts.

6) Meanwhile the boys at Buell weren't done giving head(s) yet. Content with pursuing their secondary roll as "Skunk Works" for H-D performance, as well as motorcycle manufacturer, they've developed yet another set of heads. These are the Thunderstorm/White Lightning version. And, it's right here that we find a departure in concept from all the other incarnations of X heads.

White Lightning of the distilled variety is generally kept in a jar, or at least a container it won't eat right through. Mechanical White Lightning also needs a container of its own. The head provides the lid, the cylinder forms walls, and the piston the base, and basis, of this new power bottle. Unlike the other heads, Thunderstorm heads need pop up pistons to work as designed. Not massively domed but noticeably more proud than the flat tops of yore.

The system works like this: The heads bring bigger valves, re-contoured ports and un-shrouded guides to the party. The pistons make back the losses of trapped volume in the combustion chamber, that accompany the improved head configuration. At 10-1 mechanical compression, it's a zero-sum game relative to regular S1 heads. However, it's a quantum improvement over S1 heads when it comes to performance. Make no mistake, the Thunderstorm beats the Lightning, like the Lightning beats the Thunder Bolt, like the Thunderbolt beats the Sportster 1200.

With each incremental improvement in design, and there will be more in the future, our favorite four strokes - suck, squeeze bang and blow – better. To give us more BOOM and ZOOM. Let it go to your head.

Spring selection is only half the job. There are plenty of opportunities to mess up by "slapping" the springs and retainers into the heads. Time taken to double check shimming, spacing, coil bind, seat pressures and so on, pays off! These two heads come from the factory with different spring rates, top collars and shimming, even though both heads can run either cam that comes "native" to it.

Two Valves -Too Big

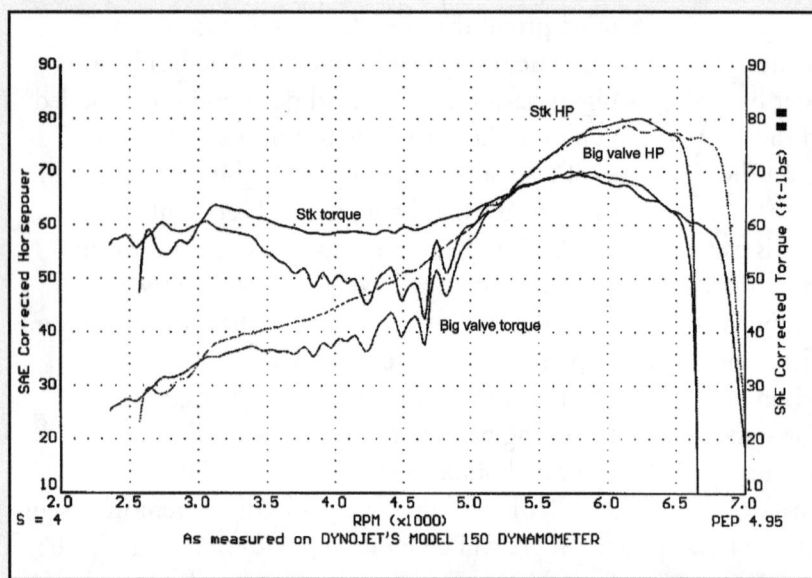

Chart 1. This is what happens when you throw BIGGER (and heavier) valves at an engine, without any additional modifications. The mid-range is actually worse than stock in terms of both torque and horsepower, with peak power essentially the same as stock.

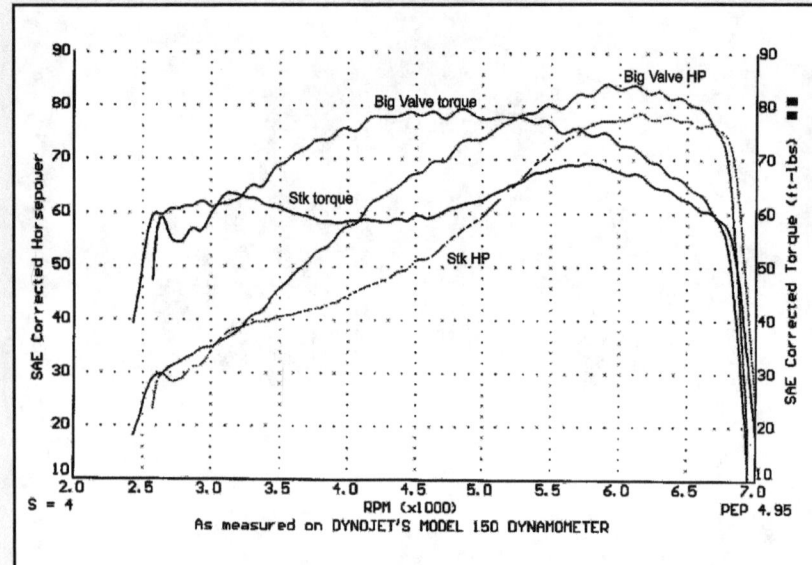

Chart 2. By integrating the big-valve heads with a Buell race pipe and a correctly jetted carburetor the power, both torque and horsepower, finally show nice smooth increases over stock.

It's an American tradition; "Bigger is better". Right? "Nothing succeeds like excess." "If a whole lot is good, way too much is great!" "Size does matter." I could go on.

Truth is, a cryptic comment from the boys at North American Sport Bike (NASB) about preparation for Lightning Series race bikes lead to an experiment I'd like to share. Here's the comment: "It is recommended that larger intake valves and seats be installed (#18023-86 for the valve and # 18020-83 for the intake seat)."

Huh? What the Bejezuz does *this* mean? Buell themselves put big valves in a Buell S1W "White Lightning" (also referred to as Thunderstorm) heads and here the race guys are saying to do it again - only more so. Turns out, these numbers refer to the stock parts of a 1986 1100 Sportster. So far so good.

XL1100 engines also use a bigger *exhaust* valve and seat. The 1100 heads have a completely different combustion chamber shape, and the Factory only tried it that way for one year, but since when does that dissuade one from trying something truly off the wall?

The theory is that not all of us are going to rush right out and drop the requisite denaro for a Thunderstorm top end anyway. The question: could the same benefit accrue for less money, by installing 1100 valves in a standard, open-chambered 1200 Sportster head? Swapping valves and seats, labor included, costs less than new heads. If it works, it's a viable alternative, isn't it? The short answer is - maybe.

CHART ONE

In the Hot-Rod tradition of the great V8, it is almost axiomatic that a bigger valve, especially intake valve, will increase flow and thus power.

Two Valves - Too Big

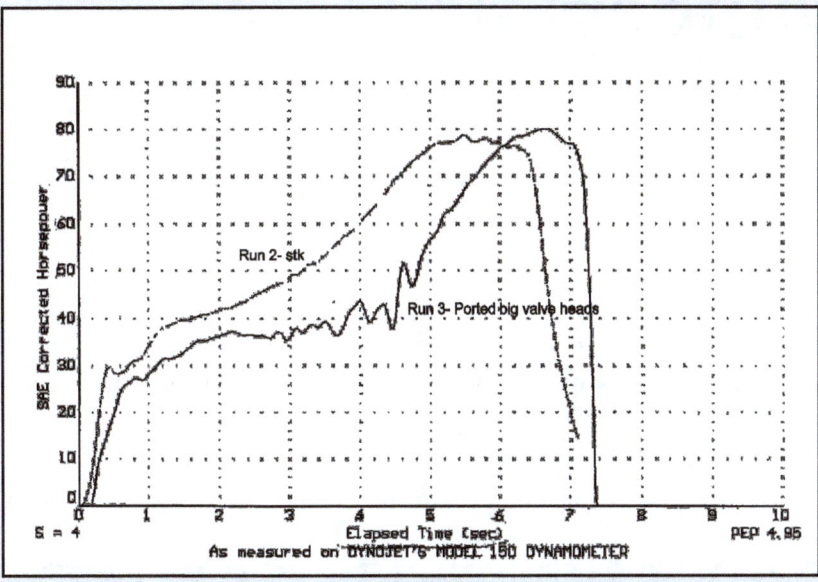

Chart 3 This chart and the one below are testing the same engine combinations seen on the other page, but for time-to-rpm, not just for horsepower and torque. Note that once again the stock engine took less time to achieve nearly the same power as the big-valve engine.

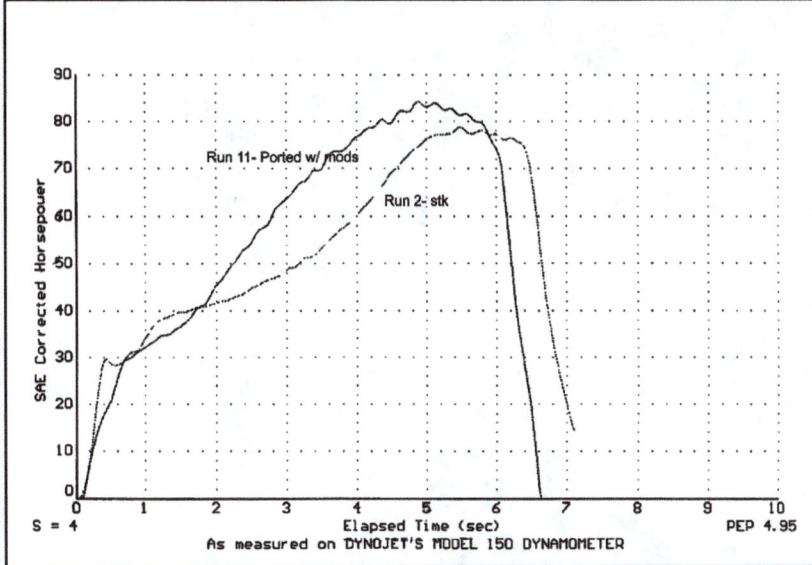

Chart 4. By creating an entire, integrated package of improvements the engine not only makes more power as compared to stock, it takes less time to reach that power (and rpm).

Makes sense. A bigger valve's circumference means more area for flow the minute the valve moves off its seat.

Apparently there's more to it than that, as you can see by examining the chart at the top of page 88. That dyno chart examines exactly what happens to horsepower and torque when a stock engine is equipped with big-valve heads and nothing else.

Chart Two

Chart number 2 at the bottom of page 88 shows the increases we hoped to achieve with the big valves come when those modifications are combined with other well-thought mods. Namely the pipe and re-jetted carb.

Chart Three and Four

Chart numbers 3 and 4 look at the same issue from a very different perspective, that of time. Again, the stock engine makes nearly the same power - in less time, than that same engine with big valves. The chart shows the same sucky mid-range too, as compared with stock.

With chart 4 you can see that the addition of the competition exhaust and properly jetted carburetor, to the "big-valve" engine leads to better power, achieved in less time.

The Moral of the Story

First, there is no magic bullet. Good power comes from a combination of parts, all working together to make good useful power throughout the rpm range.

Second, there's more than horsepower and torque to consider when hopping up an engine. Think about time as well.

Chapter Eleven

Pistons & Cylinders

Dished, Domed or Flat

It's hard to talk about pistons without talking about their role in determining the compression ratio, or their partner in crime, the cylinder. This chapter contains discussions of all three, along with a look at Volumetric Efficiency(V.E.), and a separate section on the various ways in which an 883 Sportster can be converted to 1200 or even 1250cc.

Let's start with this much – there are three things that create and affect what we glibly refer to

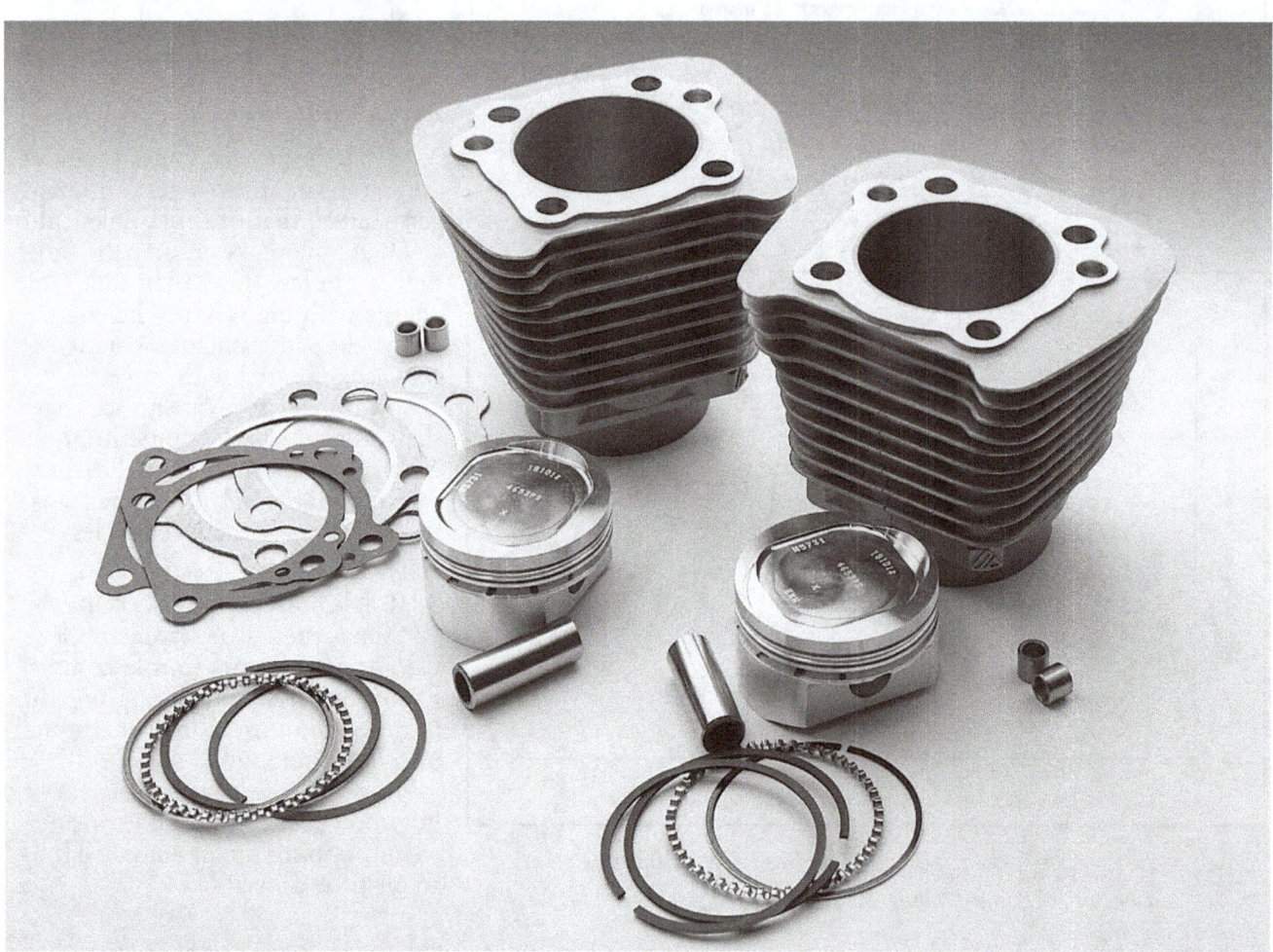

There are 1200 kits and there are 1200 kits! This one is all about a painless swap with stock 883 heads, hence the dished pistons. But, there are pistons and there are pistons.

as the combustion chamber. They are the cylinder head, the valves, and the piston. All of them can be changed or modified to affect how much pressure is available from this chamber. In this case if time is money, pressure is power.

The camshaft variables that affect compression are typically increased duration and/or overlap. More of these mean the chamber isn't closed as long, therefore more of that precious pressure can leak out. So most of the time, if you add much of these two elements in your hop-up you need to increase what's commonly referred to as nominal compression ratio. The time honored way to do this has been to take some meat off the gasket surface of the heads or mill them a few thousandths in other words.

Let's save some time with this part of the concept, shall we? Stock mechanical compression on Sportsters with standard cylinder heads is 9.0-1. Here is how much you need to take off the surface to get to some common higher ratios with the original equipment manufacturer flat top pistons:

    10.0-1 = .053"
    10.5-1 = .0672
    11.0-1 = .095
    11.5-1 =.114

The formula for any old ratio you might choose that isn't shown is stroke (3.81" is

Piston selection can be a science unto itself. More often than not these choices should "center" mostly on head configurations, much as the 883 conversion does. With open chambered 1200 heads, squish chambered Buell heads, the classic "bathtub", hemi's and many more... there's plenty of reason to make a proper choice. The end results will mirror the success of those efforts.

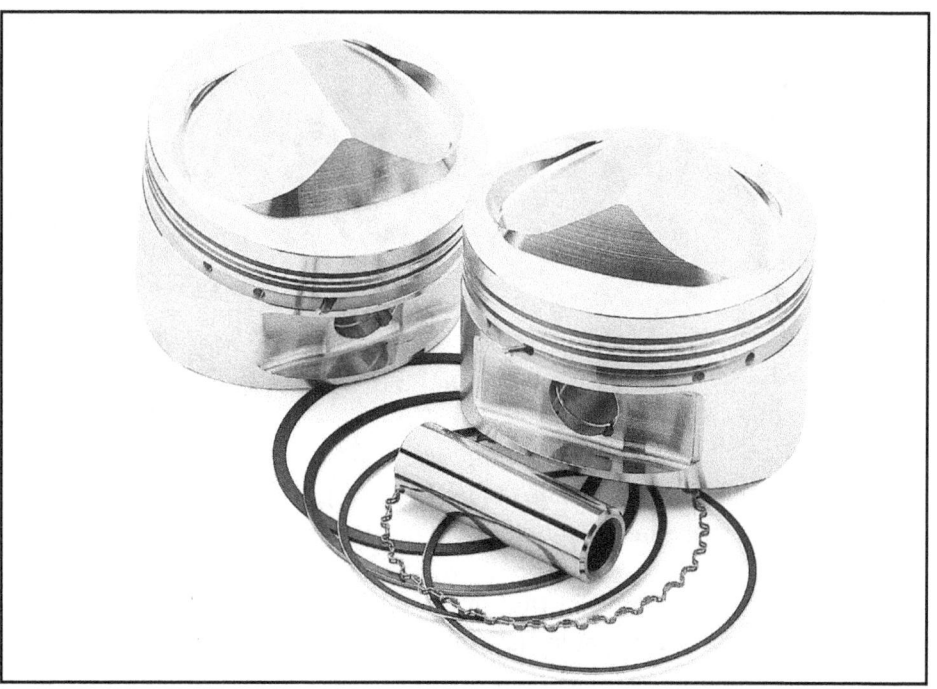

These JE pop-ups look as though they would work well with big valves and an open chamber. There are plenty more variations where this came form too. So take your time making a selection.

standard for all X motors except the Firebolt) times stock ratio minus 1, minus desired ratio minus 1. Just don't forget to factor in gasket crush.

Here's an example of a 1200 XL going from 9.0 to 10.25-1 compression.
3.81 x (1/9.0-1 minus 1/10.25-1) = amount to mill.
3.81 x (1/8 - 1/9.25)
3.81 x (.125 - .108)
3.81 x (.017)
.065" milled = 10.25:1 mechanical compression ratio

Now think about it for minute – the milling process, if you do nothing else, makes the chamber volume smaller. So you've got pressure at the expense of volume. That means you won't necessarily make more power. You'll need to increase flow as well as pressure to compensate for the loss of volume. Often, besides the camshaft bit we discussed, that means bigger valves - the addition of which usually adds volume to the chamber, negating some of the advantages of milling in the first place. Could turn into a vicious cycle.

It's not as bad as it sounds. Most of the time milled heads work fine, which is why folks have done it all this time. But there's another, maybe better, way to think about it.

UP, DOWN AND FLAT OUT

Take the 883, as an example. It comes with flat top pistons and relatively small valves. Yet simply by increasing the diameter of an equally flat piston, to say to the size of a 1200 (a measly half an inch), you bump mechanical compression up too high. So, to get chamber pressure back in the ball park, 10-1, most 1200 conversions these days employ dished pistons with concave bowls cut into the crowns.

Stock 1200 XLs also use flat top pistons, but with an open chamber head designed to arrive at a mechanical compression ratio of 9.0-1. The VE may only be 65-75%, though.

A SHORT DISCUSSION OF VE

The name of the game in engine building is or should be, increasing volumetric efficiency. Volumetric Efficiency in a 4-stroke engine is the relationship between the quantity of intake air and the piston displacement. In other words, VE = the ratio between the charge that actually enters the cylinder and the amount that could enter under ideal conditions. An engine would have 100% volumetric efficiency if, at atmospheric pressure and normal temperature, an amount of air exactly equal to piston displacement could be drawn into the cylinder. Practically impossible to achieve in naturally aspirated engines, (no super-

S&S offers what appears to be a combination of flat, dished and pop-up, all in one piston. Obviously it's purpose-built for a specific combination of head, cam and compression, all in the interest of good VE. S&S

charger or turbo) because the ports through which the air must flow offer resistance.

On the other hand, Buell 1200s, with less volume in their "squish band" chamber than a stock XL1200 head, simply stay with flat top pistons to get its increase to a 10-1 ratio. Still, it's a dead certainty that the VE on a 10-1 Buell is slightly better than a 10-1 Sporty, all else being equal.

Lastly, there's the Buell Thunderstorm engine, with bigger valves and a 10% larger squish chamber which must use pistons with a slight pop-up crown, to get compression back up to it's advertised 10.0-1. The same ratio as lesser Buell engines. And both these Buell layouts can, and do use the same cams, whether stock Sportster grinds, (S2 and M2) or the S.E./Lightning version (S1, S1W, S3 and X1). The VE of this combination is superior to any of the other factory configurations, by a lot more than a mere "point" in mechanical compression would indicate.

The point is – the piston is not only a major player in determining compression, it can be one of the deciding factors in increased Volumetric Efficiency as well.

Still, with all this juggling we are left with three basic types of factory pistons to consider dished, flat and domed (or pop-up). Along with many detailed aftermarket variations, when you play with compression via piston swaps. But what exactly is compression in the first place?

NOTHIN' BUT THE "TRUE"

The true compression ratio (CR) of any engine at a specific RPM and throttle opening isn't mechanical. It is dynamic. You can calculate Dynamic CR via this simple equation.

Dynamic CR = static CR x VE

So let's say we have a static CR of 10:1, and because we have the cam timing, pipe set up, and intake pretty close to perfect for our intended hop-up, the VE is pushing 90% at 6000 RPM. The dynamic CR of this particular engine would be. D= 10 x .9 or 9:1 dynamic CR.

Perhaps an even simpler way to measure this is to take an actual reading, in pounds per square inch, of the engine in question. Commonly called a compression test, this reading along with its partner the leak down test can supply valuable indicators of the engine's general health and help determine volumetric efficiency, i.e. power output. Most healthy street Harleys require an optimum cranking compression pressure of 170-175 pounds. Racing requires higher readings of course, but much over 200psi means there an imminent problems in there somewhere, for anything with a license plate.

Why is this important? Because it's the state of tune we're concerned with. What is important for power and efficiency is finding how hot we get the mixture during compression. That is not defined by either mechanical CR or VE. It is the combination of the two. So what does that mean?

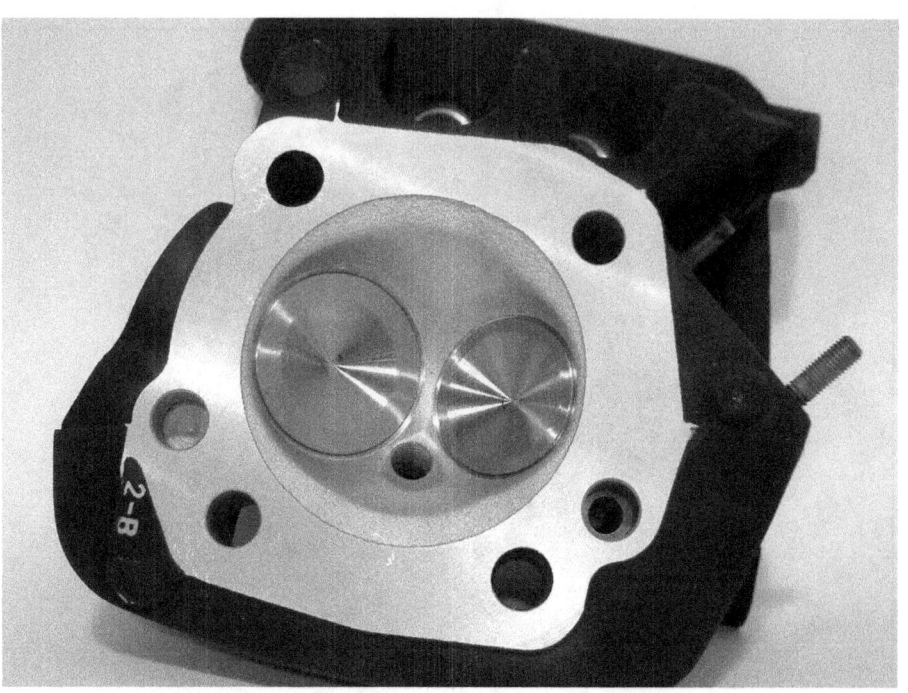

Use of these stage 2 Millennium Technologies Thunderstorm heads requires the use of the correct piston, not just for the correct compression ratio but for the best flow and burn.

Here's the deal. Keeping in mind that mechanical compression ratio alone doesn't always lead to detonation, poor mixture quality is often the enemy of efficiency, volumetric or otherwise. By improving the homogenization of the incoming mixture prior to and during combustion it is possible to increase flame speed, hence volumetric efficiency.

The later the point of ignition, the less pressure against the piston's motion approaching TDC on the compression stroke. If negative work is reduced, the net amount of pressure applied to the piston is increased. Better burning means less spark timing. This is a good thing for VE and easier on the piston to boot.

This mixture motion, or turbulence, is the front edge of study these days by some of the finest engine designers and builders in the business. One major facet of mixture motion is the layout of, or modification to, piston crowns.

Tumble and Swirl

You get all this good turbulence from swirl and tumble. Motion along the plane of inlet flow generally describes swirl. It can be the same direction as mixture flow, or the opposite direction. In other words, positive or negative. Tumble is like a slinky headed downstairs - essentially an end-over-end flow perpendicular to the swirl.

The Crowning glory

A piston's crown can affect both swirl and tumble. A flat-top piston influences swirl more than tumble, because there's nothing but a flat, broad surface with a couple of small valve cut-outs to set off the swirl. But you can add tapered ramps and/or strategically placed texturing or dimples. All affect swirl, improve quench, and aid combustion efficiency.

Pop-ups or domes on the crown, or shapes built into the cylinder heads, can shoot the flame front more toward the exhaust valve at the same time they increase compression ratio. Get too crazy with it, though, and all you'll get is a glorified roadblock to flame propagation and inefficient burn. Not to mention no power and all kinds of detonation from excessively lean spots in certain parts of the chamber. Excessive swirl can also cause fuel droplets flung out of the mixture, which screws up in-cylinder air/fuel ratios.

Like swirl, tumble can either aid combustion or reduce net VE and create torque losses. A double-edged sword, like everything else about engine building.

Take it from the top

If the engine you're tuning likes spark advance, does not live up to torque-output expectations, requires more fuel than you think necessary, and is detonation-prone, it's a good idea to examine your piston crowns. Uniformity of color is certainly one area to consider. This is not easy, but a uniform burn-residue color across the face of the piston crown is the bull's eye. Variations point to screwy

S&S offers a variety of kits designed to bump the displacement to 1200cc (or more). Kits use flat-top pistons and require modification to the stock combustion chamber. S&S

air/fuel ratios that existed during the burning. Dark areas are fuel-rich burns, lighter patterns mean air-rich mixtures. No color usually indicates a lack of combustion (unless the engines too new to leave any residue). Could also show fuel wash, which can prevent complete combustion, usually not a happy thing for the rings either.

Each, and all, of these symptoms indicate poor mixture quality whether lean, rich or a smattering of both. And you can see it on the crown. Scrutinizing the tops of the pistons is also a quick method of determining whether you have different mixture properties in different cylinders. Adjusting individual cylinder spark timing helps, but unless or until you are able to equalize the burn between the barrels, you're still dealing with unequal and un-optimized power. So spend some time reading the piston tops, it's just another tool for seeing what your engine is trying to show you.

BARREL ROLL

Curious that the least changed part in an X engine is, of all things, the piston. That's right, in an evolution engine in which virtually every piece has been changed or modified since it's 1986 debut, the piston is pretty much the same, with the exception of the Teflon-type coating added to the skirt. The cylinder, by number, has only been changed twice in all that time as well. In Harley-speak, the last digits in a part number indicate the year the part was designed, or in some cases, re-designed. The piston, new coat and all, is now a teenager at 17 years of age. In tech terms, that's more like Methuselah, but so far there's been no need to re design it. As for the cylinder, it's been revised only one time since 1986 -unless it's a black cylinder. The black wrinkle bit showed up as paint, then became powder coat, hence the painted/powder-coated barrel gets it's own number nomenclature. Same part, so far, so good. Obviously The Motor Company has not found fault with the basic layout of these two partners in crime. Still, that doesn't mean we won't, individually, on rare occasions.

There are a few things that can go wrong. Mainly because the hole isn't really round.

An egg-shaped bore makes life hell for pistons and rings, especially rings. A fair hint that this is a player, if everything else looks okay at tear down, would be un-even wear on the ring. Harley (Hastings) piston rings, at least the top two, can tell quite a story if you know how to read them. One chapter of that story goes like this: a dull grayish silver is the normal appearance of fresh, out of the wrapper rings. On the outside, working edge that is. Broken-in properly the little rascal's outside edges begin to look like bright shiny chrome about half way up from the bottom. The top still looks dull silver. While it's kind of neat to think that Harley engines do their own chrome-plating as a part time job, it's not so fun to realize that by the time that "chrome" goes all the way

Despite the fact that these are nearly identical pistons, one stock flat-top and one Thunderstorm, it shouldn't be assumed that one is a direct replacement for the other.

from top to bottom on the ring's edge it's shot, worn out.

If the barrel goes out of round the ring will be shiny in say, one third of it's circumference, while leaving maybe 2/3rds dull. Or, could be it'll show shiny from top to bottom in spots, but look new in other spots. Either way it's not sealing and not good. It's a squeeze play, running one portion of the ring too hard against the cylinder wall, and the rest not hard enough, if at all. Usually, there are more or less corresponding scrubbings on the piston as well, but it's not a certainty.

If it's possible to have an oval hole in the barrel, it's also possible that the bore is not straight. H-D takes great pains to avoid that pitfall. For proof you have to look no further than the recommended method of clamping the cylinders in torque plates for re-boring. Almost all the barrel's resistance to shape shifting comes from this clamping. You can take a fresh cylinder assembly, which comes with its own matched piston, set it upside down on a bench or table, lightly oil the bore, stick the ringless piston in half way, and squeeze the cylinder flange with your hand and watch the piston drop. What has happened is that your squeezing efforts change the shape of the unclamped barrel. In service, clamped under a properly torqued head and into the crankcase, this doesn't happen. Neither does it happen if you use torque plates to bore a new oversize hole. The plates, and/or engine studs, preload and pre-stress the cylinder, so it will grow and contract concentrically, as it runs. The likelihood of a crooked hole is directly tied to the effort expended in proper torquing/pre-loading of the cylinder, not to mention the boring process.

Harley-Davidson has had a few problems with the liner separating from the cylinder. If it happens on virginal engines, untouched by human hands and errors, The Motor Company may accuse you of abuse and over-heating which means this is not a warrantable offense. Never mind that once you can get a .005" feeler gauge betwixt liner and fins, you own an alloy flower pot, not a usable Harley barrel. In some cases this condition can be pronounced enough to allow the liner to stand proud of the head gasket surface, so badly that head gaskets will blow constantly. Maybe it's finally time to re-design the cylinders and pistons after all? Or maybe, warped and twisted as we may be, we just have to stay cool?

Barrels Of Fun with Aftermarket 1200 Cylinders

Here's an idea. A cylinder that stays cylindrical. Surely you've heard this is important to a piston trying to make its way through life. As mentioned, the factory cylinder doesn't always help out all that much. An off-the-record suspicion amounts to the notion that the genuine spiny-lock barrels, the factory offering on Sporty/Buell and Big Twin alike, were being cranked out at full capacity on machinery past its best, as

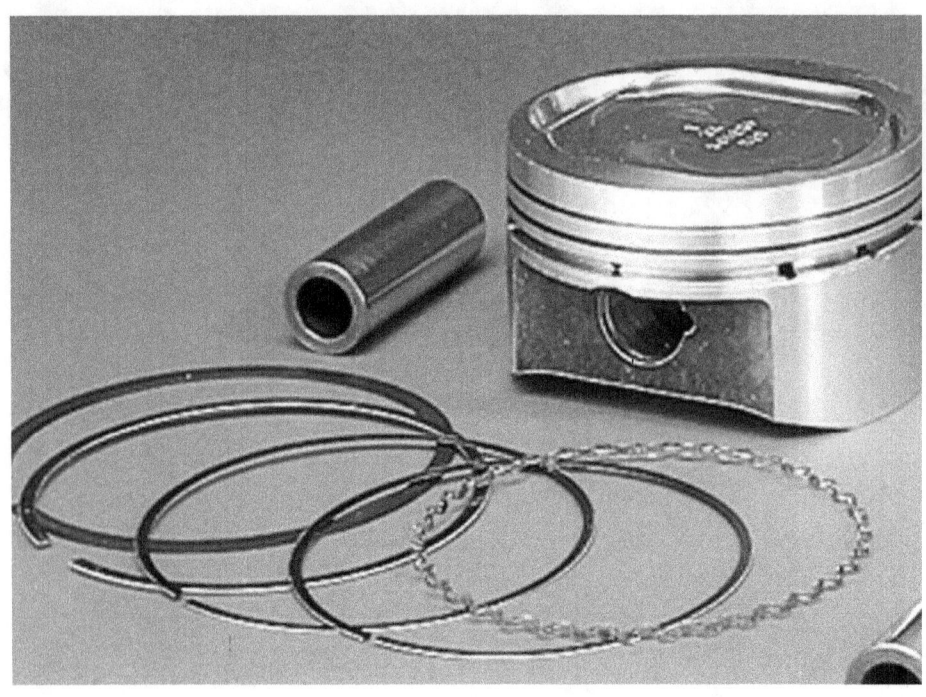

Nearly all conversion pistons come with the pin and a complete set of piston rings.

recently as 1999. Though much improved of late, many a factory unit is anything but cylindrical.

These negative propensities were not lost on American Air-cooled Cylinders. AAC, you see, has been a purveyor of fancy racing cylinders to the partisans of another air-cooled performance legend, Porsche. Years of experience with those little rear-engined slot cars has shown just about every conceivable weakness of air-cooled cylinders under severe stress. So, AAC wasn't too impressed when introduced to Harley cylinders. In the end, American Air-Cooled Cylinders cooked up an uncookable solution.

AAC's Harley-Davidson and Buell nickel-silicon-carbide coated alloy barrels promise to be indifferent to the levels of abuse that tweak the stockers into uselessness. At least Don Tilley (holder of many National Championship racing titles with Harleys and Buells) thinks so. He's been using them with great success for a while now, and if Tilley likes them, they're pretty good units. He doesn't race Buells with junk parts and that's why he wins.

An advantage of the linerless barrel (on right) is the extra surface available where the cylinder base meets the case. Uniform torque will spread the load across this area like the base of a pyramid.

What's different about American Air-Cooled Cylinders? Well, for openers there's no steel liner. There's no distortion. There's less piston friction. And that adds up to more power and more consistent power at max temperatures and rpm. Would you believe an average increase of 5.8hp, with highs as high as eleven?

Look at it like this: 883s have about five pounds of ugly fat in the form of a half-inch thick cylinder liner. Traps heat like a fur coat in the tropics. Cut the half-inch out, and the thinner 1200 liner is no longer trapped, it's totally free to warp the liner and/or the cylinder. Steel expands and contracts at a rate quite different from aluminum, to mention nothing of the differences in expansion volume. During initial starts the piston absorbs the combustion heat faster than the not-quite-up-to-speed (or size) liner. Knowing what the research says about cold start wear and tear in the first place, is it much of a stretch to realize you're asking for partial cold seizure under these conditions? Now, turn that scenario 180-degrees around. You've just shut the bike off after a hard run on a cool night, the liner cools faster than the piston or the alloy part of the cylinder. Bingo. Hot-cold partial seizing. Keep it up over time and the barrel begins to destroy itself, liner pulls away from aluminum. Blam! Since AAC barrels are liner-less, heat transfer is a lot more uniform and quicker. Coupled with the fact that AAC barrels are made of a denser-grained Hypereutectic 290 alloy, you've got less thermal expansion to deal with and can set piston clearances tighter. Considering a piston tries to do a reasonable imitation of a salmon swimming for spawning grounds as it flies up and down, this

97

The extra beef of the linerless barrels doesn't cost much in terms of weight - the linerless barrel weights in at 5-1/2 pounds, roughly 8 ounces less than the factory unit.

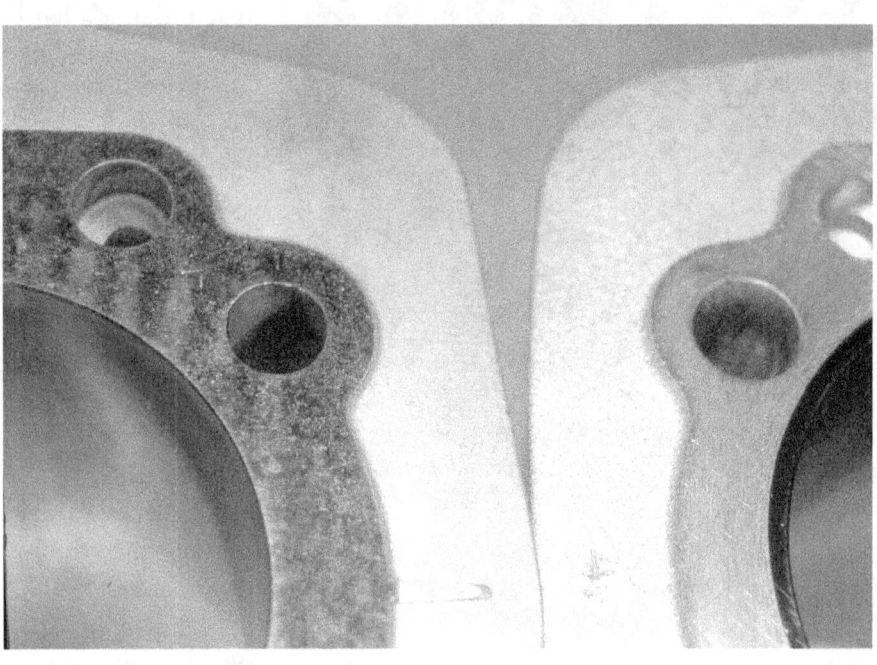

This close up shows the stock cylinder and its liner, and the linerless design from AAC (the cylinders from Millennium Technologies are very similar).

is an important resource for yet more power. If you eliminate the flopping and the popping goes smoother you just bought free improvement.

You can get away with a 0.0035-inch clearance with a linerless barrel, which at best would partly stick a stocker. Because, among other things, the 0.006-inch nickel-silicon-carbide coating is naturally olephyllic (that's oil retentive, for you anal-retentives) and so damn hard it takes diamond bit tooling to cut it. Wear it out? Probably not in your lifetime. But in a way that's the bad part of the deal. Should you knock a wound into one of these linerless cylinders, you can't bore it out. The only other negative is financial. A pair of these slick cylinders will set you back $990, with pistons. If you want barrels alone it's still a matter of $395 each. You wanna play, you get to pay.

Note: As we go to press, AAC was difficult to contact.

CONVERSION THERAPY 883 to 1200
Method one

Bore original cylinders, install factory 'flat-top' 1200 pistons, machine 883 heads to suit.

Method one (and a half)

Swap to ("black wrinkle" with "high-lighted" fins) stock 1200 cylinder assemblies, complete with pistons (#16447-88A), machine 883 heads to suit.

NOTES: Now, if you don't/can't buy heads don't panic, just be aware that the necessary 883 head machining for a 1200 conversion using factory flat-top pistons can cost close to half the price of a set of 1200 heads, and if you also need a valve job while the heads are off? Well, like I said, just be aware.

Method Two:

Replace cylinders with "conversion" barrels only (#16554-92A silver, #16871-99Y all black), use aftermarket or Sceamin' Eagle dished pistons, use stock 883 heads.

Piston Design

ANATOMY LESSON

There are several critical design elements of pistons that you'd be well advised to study before you make random swaps. Two of the most important would be weight and ring design. There are also cast and forged versions of most popular pistons for H-D performance applications. Two decidedly different animals How close the rings live to the crown is an issue, as well as the crown itself. Here are some basics.

Main Piston Dimensions
F - Top land width
S - Crown thickness
RL - Ring land width
CH - Compression
DL - Elongation length
TL - Total length
NH - Ring groove Axial height
BO - Pin Bore Diameter
   (piston pin diameter)
SL - Skirt length
UL - Lower skirt length
BD - Pin boss spacing
D - Piston Diameter
DH - Dome height
   (see illustration)

TYPE – CASTING ABOUT OR FORGING AHEAD?

Die Cast

Die cast means a high silicon alloy is melted in an electric furnace with extremely closely controlled temperature. The molten alloy is then poured into a multi-piece die producing a very accurately shaped piston casting. The casting die is manufactured so that when the metal has solidified the various pieces of the die can be extracted one by one. This means that undercuts and reliefs can be produced in the casting to reduce the piston weight. The cost of a die-cast piston is considerably less than that of a forged piston but their use is typically limited to street application, running pump gasoline. These pistons grow notably at operating temperature, so typical clearances are relatively large compared to forged pistons.

Forged

Quality piston forging is a more complex process than casting, and one of the more popular materials used is RR58 (2618A). Two other alloys are often used, one is a high silicon alloy and the other is a Metal Matrix Composite. The precise mix and spec of each brand remains proprietary and metallurgical details are generally top secret stuff. Raw material in closely controlled diameters is cut to billet size and all cut faces machined to a smooth finish. The billet is pre heated in an air circulating furnace to a temperature quite close to the operating temperature of the piston crown when the

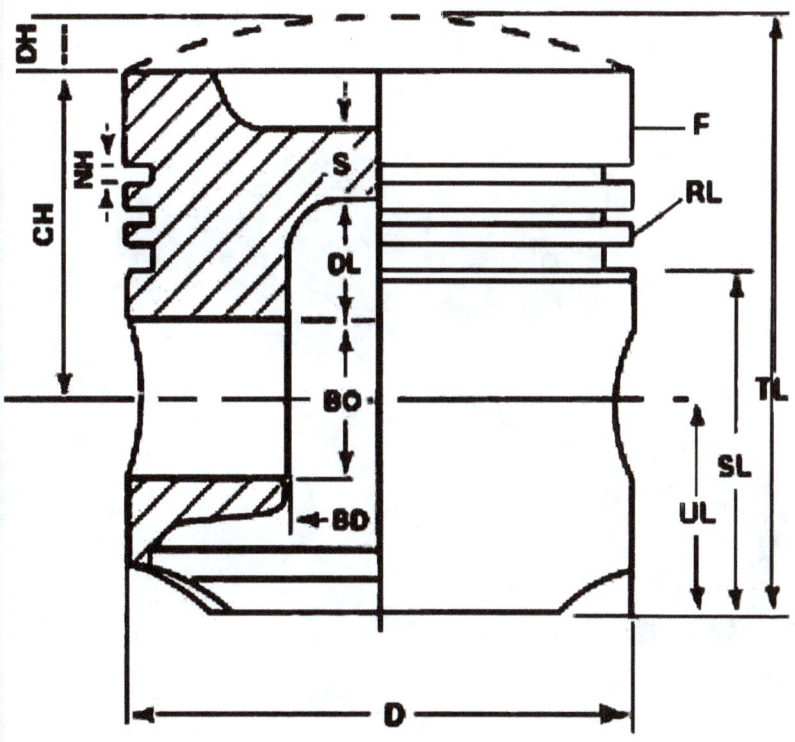

As you can see, the piston designer's job is never an easy one - a piston is much more than just a slug moving up and down in a matching cylinder.

Piston Design

engine is operating at full power. Again somewhat secret stuff, but generally over 1300-1400 degrees. This combined with speed in the forging process gives a dense and very fine grain structure. This fine grain gives forgings higher strength and fatigue life. After forging, excess material is removed and the forgings are then heat-treated and wet-blast cleaned. Forged pistons are shape and size stable, so clearances in the bore can be held more closely. This, along with the strength advantages they hold, makes them the common choice for serious performance.

Having determined what sort of material best suits your needs/application you want a piston that's as stable as possible to maintain effective and consistent ring-seal. Poor ring sealing equals poor performance. And none of this is helped by the relatively enormous distance from the wrist pin center to crown height on most H-D pistons.

Modern piston rings are generally of high quality materials and production tolerances. Standard ring widths are distilled down into certain operating envelopes. Extremely thin rings are used pretty much only for racing, as a way of reducing the 70-75% of the total internal friction rings are responsible for in an engine. They last about that much less time too. Most modern pistons have the ring packs and their position on the piston pretty much figured out too. It's worth knowing that the zone for distance from the top ring to the piston crown on an X-series engine is around 7mm. Higher than this and damage from combustion is likely, lower and detonation can be caused by excessive amounts of un-burnt fuel collecting here, then ignited by incorrect ignition timing or plain old heat retention in the crown.

Oil drainage from the oil ring land area should preferably be by drilled holes as these can be angled and strategically positioned to best use and minimize weakening of the piston. This form of superior oil drainage is one of the must-have features for a high performance piston. Unfortunately, this isn't usually practical on mass-produced standard pistons. Production pistons tend to have slots machined along the back of the ring groove at 90 degrees to the wrist pin axis, which also tends to make the piston run quieter by damping out resonance. Dandy for production motors, but not the hot tip for performance.

The vast majority of standard production piston pins are very thick walled with a parallel-bored center hole. Grossly over-engineered to easily cover 100,000 miles without failure, simple and cheap to manufacture. But very heavy. A better performance solution is a much thinner

Many 883 - 1200 conversion pistons (like this example from Wiseco) are dished so you can use stock heads without an excessive gain in compression.

Piston Design

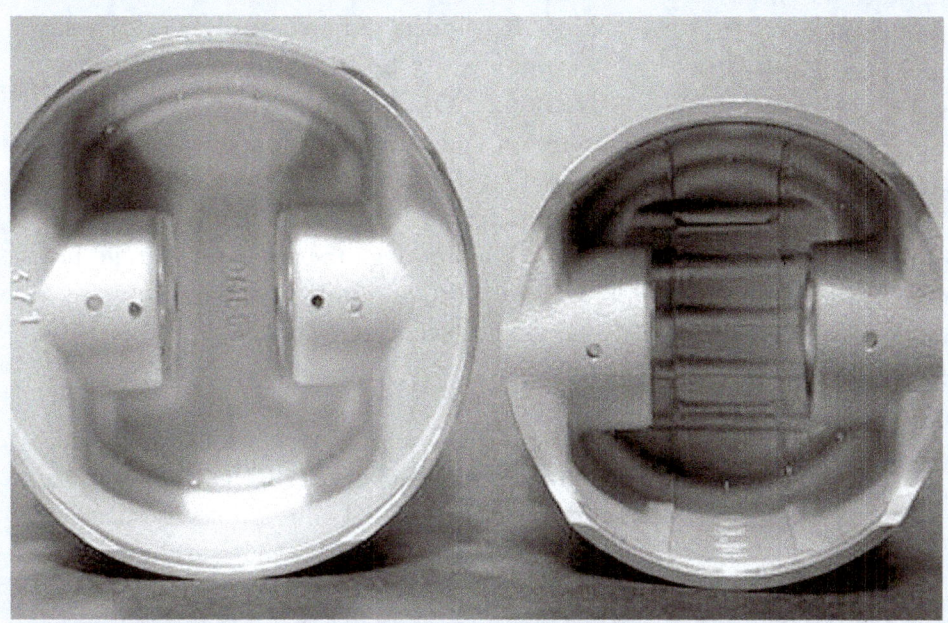

Sometimes you can tell more from the bottom of the piston than the top: The forged piston is on the left, note the eggshell finish and smooth underside of the crown. Cast piston on the right has ribs across the bottom of the crown. Though stronger, forged pistons are also heavier than cast designs.

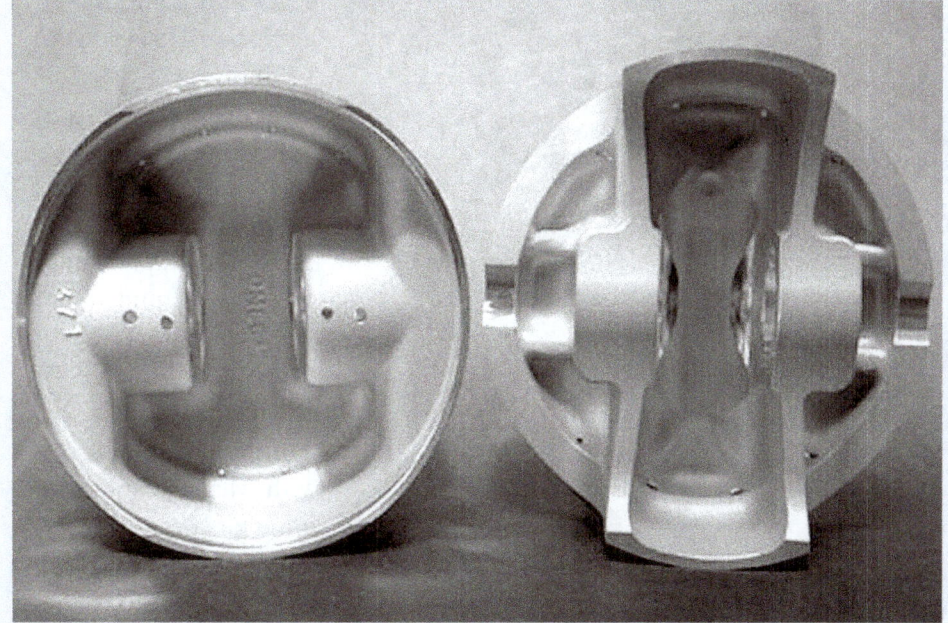

Real racers tend to trade in some excess weight (and often, durability) for reduced friction, as in this slipper piston on the right. There's quite a trend toward mini skirts in modern engines. The firebolt, with it's short stroke and higher speed design, takes advantage of this thinking.

walled, parallel-bored pin in superior material - light but expensive to build. The best compromise is a pin with tapered-bore ends.

Just for the record, pistons are rarely either straight (parallel) sided, nor round. They are machined like this to compensate for the massive running temperature differences between the crown and skirt, and pin axis to open skirt area - the piston crown being the smaller end of a tapered shape, mainly because this was the simplest shape that would get the job done. The idea was to fill the bore to greatest effect for minimum outlay. Technology came into play with the Evo and continues today, finding gains in hot/cold and in between performance, reliability and other areas, by making the piston barrel shaped - at least when cold. At temperature the shape grows to conform to the cylinder better than any design that came before. This design saved weight and expanded both the safe upper and safe engine speed ranges. And with it came more power.

NOTES: The other way to go is with dished top pistons and stock 883 heads. These conversion pistons with machined depressions in the crowns, eliminate the need for reworking stock 883 heads. They cost $200-$300 a pair, give or take ten bucks, whether aftermarket, like Wiseco, or the factory Screamin' Eagle pistons. The S.E. pistons are available in standard bore for a true drop-on installation, but Wiseco has traditionally had a cagey way of making you set clearance the way they want it, by making their pistons 0.005" oversized, so you must hone the cylinders to proper clearance. Thus, there's additional work/expense, and it's not quite the bolt-on proposition the stock parts are. Lastly, Wiseco offers two different ring groove widths. Unless you are fan of crowding the redline and frequent top end jobs, you want the thicker ones that will take stock H-D (Hastings) replacement rings. Even if you opt for the thin rings, you will need to set the end gap at about double the factory spec of standard thickness rings.

Method Three:
Use Lightning (Buell SI) or Screamin' Eagle cylinder heads (#16457-96B silver, #16458-96B all black), and flat-top pistons with any of the available 1200 cylinders or bored out 883 cylinders.

Note: Factory 1200 pistons are heavier than 883 pistons. Wiseco pistons are nearly as light as 883 pistons, and there are other aftermarket piston choices that run the gamut. If you don't go nuts with compression, and ensure that whichever pistons you choose weigh the same, you should not have to worry about excessive vibration. Crankshaft rebalancing is, or should be, a non-issue.

Method Four
Use Buell Thunderstorm pistons (or aftermarket pop-up equivalents with 10 to 10.5:1 mechanical compression), and Thunderstorm heads with any of the available 1200 cylinders or bored out 883 cylinders.

Method Five
Some combination of the above, but don't mismatch pistons to heads. Dished pistons only work with stock 883 heads. Standard 1200 heads and Lightning heads use flat-top factory 1200 pistons. Thunderstorm heads need pop-up pistons with 10:1 compression.

Method Six
S&S, Zipper's and probably a couple more aftermarket sources I haven't mentioned have complete 1200 kits. No figuring which heads go with what pistons, or in some kits even matching up a cam set and carb to go with it. Just buy the "program" from the source of your choice and install as per their instructions.

The Millennium Technologies 1250cc drop-on kit uses their own pistons and a linerless barrel. Barrel is coated with Nickel Silicon Carbide for reduced friction.

883/1200 TO 1250

Yes, there is as of this writing, one outfit who can supply you with the goods to do a drop on conversion to 1250cc. Millennium Technologies has a tiered approach to this unique conversion. You can buy dish-top 10:1 piston/cylinder set-ups, 10.3:1 flat top piston/cylinder set-ups, or 10.5:1 pop-up piston/cylinder set-ups, and add (or not) stage 2 or 3 ported Thunderstorm heads to the package. Ditto the SE536 cams.

XB9 TO XB1050

Millennium Technologies also has something to offer in a drop-on kit for the Firebolt, namely an 1050 conversion kit in three flavors. The first is a basic piston/cylinder arrangement weighing in at 10.5:1 compression. The second adds Stage 2 head prep and a new re-configured EFI controller. The third is the same thing, only the heads are Stage 3.

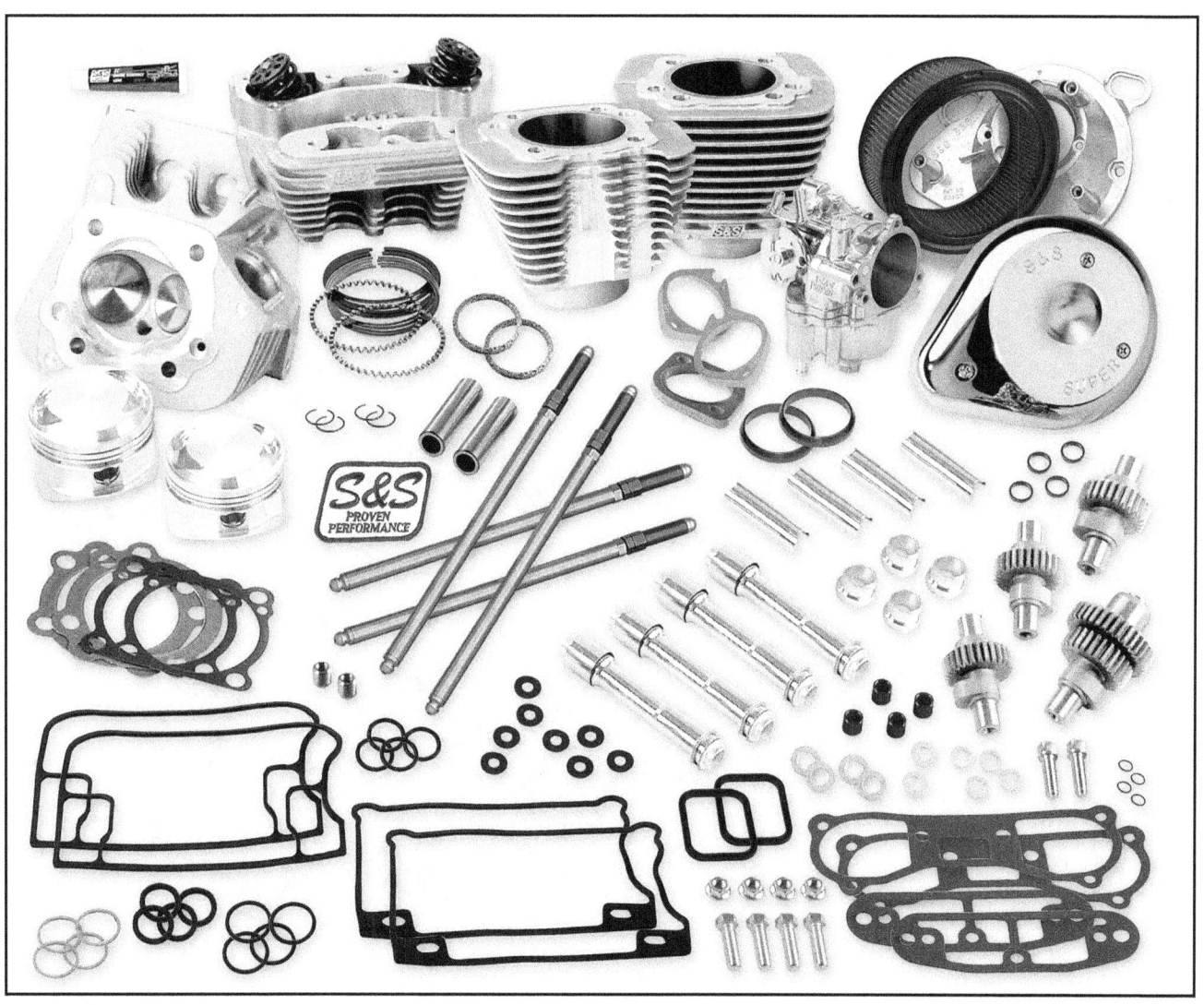

In light of the way each part interacts with all the others, it makes sense to consider a complete kit when increasing displacement. This assembly from S&S includes pistons mated to the heads, and cams designed to fill those bigger cylinders. With 3-1/2 inch pistons (1200cc) 883 flywheels do not need rebalancing. S&S

Chapter Twelve

Flywheels

Stored Energy

Once upon a time, H-Ds employed a built up assembly of separate, individual parts to create what, in lesser machines, would be called a crankshaft. These pieces consisted of connecting rods, big end bearings and cages, left and right flywheels, sprocket shaft, pinion shaft, and various washers and fasteners. This time honored arrangement lasted from, oh, about 1909, until 1986, where X engines are concerned. Then things changed. Mostly, the change involved integrating

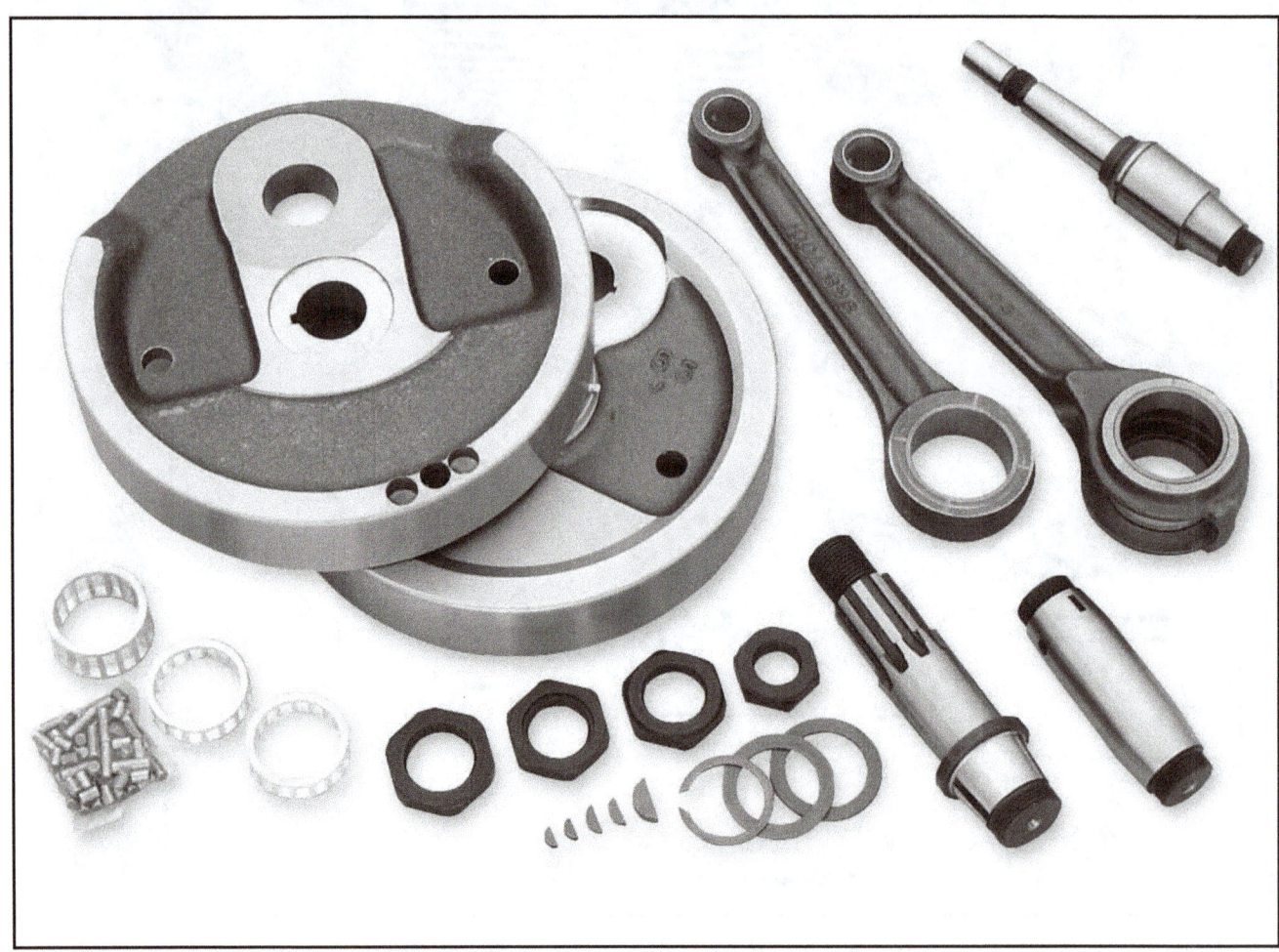

Though the new factory lower end assemblies use flywheels that are one piece with the pinion and drive shaft, assemblies like that shown here with separate flywheel and shaft, are available from the aftermarket. Biker's Choice

104

the two shafts (sprocket and pinion) with their respective flywheels. In short, each half is now one piece. This is a good thing insofar as it makes for a tougher, less flexible flywheel assembly, or crankshaft to anyone non-Harley speaking. Anyway, the real fly in this wheel ointment, is that should you be unfortunate enough to "damage" this assembly - you get to replace the whole thing.

If you look in the parts book you will notice that not only is the pinion shaft, or the sprocket shaft not available, the respective flywheel its mated to isn't either. You can buy a new set of connecting rods, but if the wheels are torched that isn't much help. A whole *Flywheel assembly*, on the other hand, will set you back several hundred dollars.

Most folks, when faced with this situation, resort to the aftermarket. There are a number of companies out there that will be glad to help with any specific component you need to get back on the road. The only thing is all they supply separate pieces. Even then, it can get expensive to replace a pinion shaft *and* a flywheel, with aftermarket parts, when the only thing you really need is the shaft. And suppose for rigid reasons, known only to you and The Motor Company, you want to *retain* the services of the factory-style integrated flywheel? It is a better design for strength and stiffness at

Here you can see the more modern one-piece flywheel and shaft assemblies. CCI

Build a stroker, with a flywheel assembly from S&S. Available with 7-1/4 or 7-1/2 inch wheels and strokes all the way to 5 inches.

105

high rpm. Well, call this another episode in the fine art of compromise in engine building. You can certainly stick with the factory arrangement, even if you crave extra displacement. Big bores are still open to you with the stock stroke and crankshaft.

Matter of fact there are two choices here, since the Sportster and the Buell 1200 cranks are interchangeable. The beauty of the Buell set-up is the lighter, more mass-centered flywheel design. This is the ticket for quicker revs and sharper throttle response. Look at Buell dyno charts alongside those of Sportsters, invariably the time taken to hit maximum engine speed is cut by a second or better. Meaning in two otherwise identical 85hp motors, with two otherwise identical chassis and drive train set-ups, its four bike lengths or better just to the top of fourth gear in a roll-on. A great performance option using factory one-piece stuff. There is also a benefit or two in terms of oil control, increased case volume (better pumping and less sensitivity to pressure fluctuations) and therefore less friction to compliment the reduced inertia.

Should you opt for the built-up multi-piece flywheel assembly there are at least two sources with a reputation for tough performance with this "obsolete" layout. Both Truett & Osborn and S&S are in the business of building crank components second to none. Either will supply the goods you need for anything from a stock stroke replacement, to a long-armed stroker. But, it requires more decision making. For example, S&S offers lighter Buell-style wheels, just like the factory. Actually, these are knife-edged, a notch better than the original equipment wheels for oil shedding, so maybe not just like the factory's. But, they offer them in stroker sizes only, unless special ordered otherwise. Now, one of the advantages is pretty well cancelled out by that very idea. Knowing that strokers can't rev as high, and that a built-up crank assembly will ultimately flex more – the only good news left is that an engine done with these wheels will take the wick well – will rev quicker than other strokers – but to a much lower upper limit. Still, it's a sensible alternative to standard Sporty wheels, in many senses. Less inertia is always a good thing and it's also the only way to fly if, in fact, your objective is a 79, 92 or 100 cubic inch Buell.

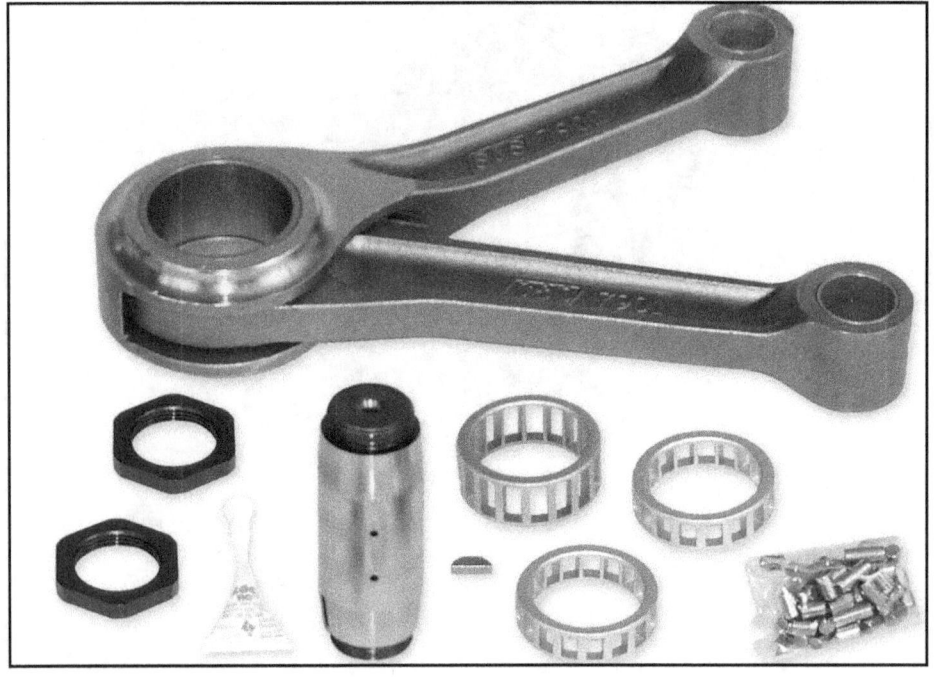

Connecting rods are available as shown with crank pin and bearings. All are forged from chrome moly or aircraft-grade chrome moly and then heat treated. S&S

This makes it sound like there's no real reason to opt for regular Sporty wheels, doesn't it? Well, admittedly it takes even more thought to make sense of the choice, but there are good reasons to go with heavier flywheels. Not least of which is that though slower to reach speed, once the mass of those wheels is spinning it creates a sort of damper for vibrations crated by the rest of the reciprocating mass flailing around in there. In short, less shock load to the engine, less rider fatigue, less abrupt throttle response and a smoother engine.

Plus, flywheels are where the torque is kept. Let me say this another way: I know of a dealer in the south that used to sell a lot of Harleys with one little trick. He had a standing offer every Saturday to play "Tug of War" with any of the latest greatest rice rockets that would care to try. He'd tie the Harley and the victim (er – "contender's") machine tail light to tail light and when the flag dropped, the mega-horse Superbike was seen smoking it's tires, bucking like a bronco and being dragged *backwards* by the poor ol' obsolete, mechanically inferior Hog. That's torque. And torque comes through flywheels. So, if you don't care to have an engine you throttle whip like a two-stroke, or you spend more time two-up pulling steep grades, in short, under load in the middle of the powerband all the time, flywheels can help. It all depends on what you want, need and can use.

BALL BEARING LOWER END

Pretty much since day one, Harley engines have featured ball and/or roller bearings in their built up crankshaft assemblies. This isn't unique, but it is fairly rare among modern four-stroke engines. Kawasaki's near bomb-proof, air cooled Z-series bikes, still popular among Drag racers, employ similar construction. However, *that* engine and virtually any other motorcycle power plant you'd care to name using ball/roller bearing construction, are wet-sump. The oil is contained within the engine and in most cases also lubricates the transmission gears. The upshot is Harley *is* virtually unique in it's use of a dry-sump system with a separate oil tank and high volume, low pressure, recalculating pump. Like many things about H-D motors, it wasn't necessarily planned that way, but how it turned out.

Way back in 1903, ball bearings not only made sense, they were the only game in town. Nobody had created an oiling system that was entirely reliable. *If* they had an oiling system we'd *recognize* as one, in the first place. This was the era of drip-feed and splash oiling. As primitive as it sounds (and was) it worked OK, primarily because ball bearings can live without a lot of lubricant. They also achieve their highest load ratings sitting still. Meaning that low speed engines weren't likely to overload them, no matter how spotty the oil supply. In short, ball bearings are tough.

This is in sharp contrast to plain bearings. Honda uses plain bearings to some advantage in most of their engines to make use of their hydrodynamic characteristics at five-figure engine speeds. The higher the better actually. As far back as the early '60's, Honda's GP *five cylinder* 125's were reliably spinning to 22,000 rpm, thanks to this characteristic. They're not the only ones. Practically every automobile or motorcycle motor out there these days uses plain bearings for both

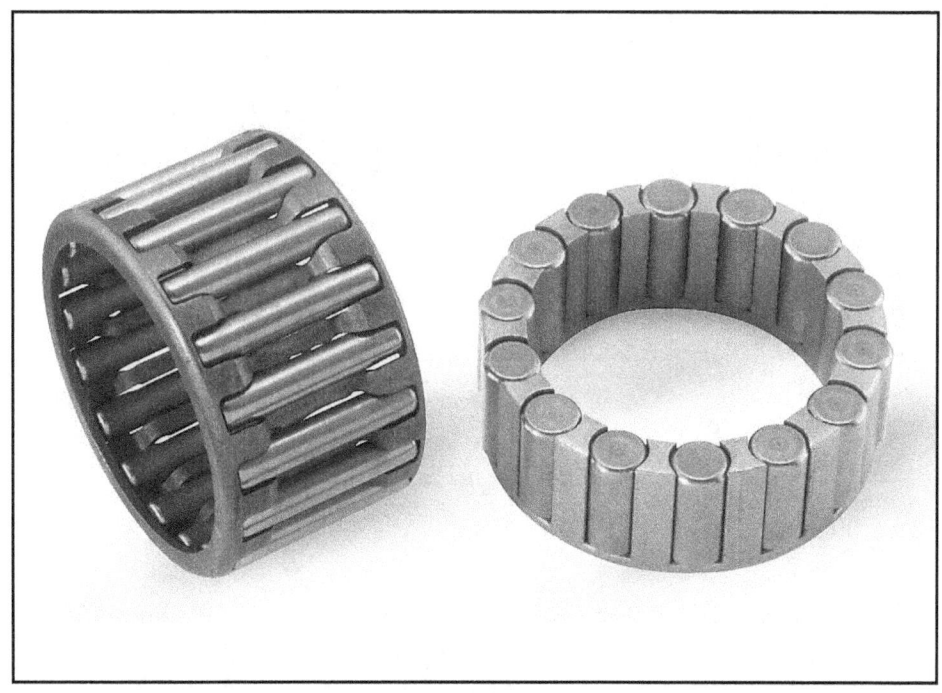

Though they might seem old fashioned, roller bearings are extremely durable and don't require the same type of high-pressure oil supply as plain bearings. Biker's Choice

rods and mains. The thing is, this requires a very sophisticated high pressure supply of clean oil.

Oil does two things for a ball/roller bearing. It keeps it cool under pressure and offers the balls something smoother than bare metal to roll on. Oil does *everything* for a plain bearing. At even nominal rotational speeds, oil throws itself down between the bearing surfaces, like Sir Walter Raleigh's cloak under Queen Elizabeth. No contact is the name of the game (not between royal shoes and mud, and certainly not between bearing shell and spinning crankshaft). This kind of behavior not only continues, but increases and improves, even at mega revs, because the oil film wedges itself 'twixt the parts down to the point of a molecule layer only microns thick. At that point, ironically, it's become a sheet of (literally) microscopic – ball bearings. God help you though, if the supply is impure or gets cut off. Dirty, contaminated oil, or an oiling failure, means almost instant destruction to the plain bearing engine. To top it off the loads on plain bearings work just the opposite of a ball/roller. Unless they're spinning pretty fast, plain bearings, basically, can't take any loads at all. Picture a Honda Four with the engine off, propped up on the center stand in gear. Bump the wheel around much and you've got metal to metal contact of the bearing and crank. Aren't you glad Harleys don't play these silly games?

SPEAKING OF SILLY GAMES

To picture the difference in the way these two bearings do their job, you'll need something that rolls and something that slides – or – let's keep it simple. Just take a penny out of your pocket. Use this as your surrogate for both style bearings. On edge it's a fair imitation of a ball bearing. Flat it will simulate a plain bearing, OK? Now, find a flat, smooth surface. The kitchen table will do. If you can balance the penny on edge, it will just take a slight nudge to get it to roll the length of the table. Lay it flat and give it that *same* little nudge. Didn't make it far, did it? Pour a little oil on the table. Do the edge roll once more. Notice any big difference? Once more with the lay it flat technique. The coin fairly flew across the table. Nudge it harder it goes faster, surfing on the oil film. Try thumping the penny harder while on edge. It probably made a fair little "rooster tail" while it plowed through the oil film, but still no

One of the problems with a 45 degree V-twin is the close proximity of the front and rear piston when both are at the bottom of their strokes. Kip Woodring collection

spectacular difference like there was on the oily flat nudge. If you tried a bottle as a roller or needle bearing, the oil might even slow things down. There is a lesson here.

Too much oil on a ball/roller can impede its ability to roll. The same wedge effect that lets a plain bearing surf *on* a thin oil film can, for a ball bearing, look much more like wading knee deep *in* strong surf. Therefore, a ball/roller will eventually hit a plateau wherein it's fighting so hard to turn through the oil that it simply cannot keep up with the very parts it's supposed to *assist* in motion. Don't misunderstand, ball bearing motors can succeed at high rpm. The fabulous and arcane straight eight in the Type 35 Bugatti race car, or nearly any high performance two stroke, comes to mind. But then so does the Black and Decker electric drill. It's just that most successful ball bearing engines like to barely keep their feet wet - not swim in the oil supply. It's more fun to slide gracefully on melting ice than to tap dance toward a fire hose, if you get my meaning. Friction is a funny thing. It's relationship to oil is even funnier. Ponder on this a bit before you automatically determine that you *need* more oil pressure in your Hog motor.

A HARD CASE

Suppose, just suppose, you wanted to build a monster X motor for use in your Buell. Or possibly you need new cases for your old 883 or 1200 Sportster because the last time you looked at the old ones they had a rod hanging out. Perhaps, you have a perfectly good motor that neither needs nor wants anything. Doesn't matter.

If you have the hots for a nasty noise maker and want to stick the stocker on the shelf for a spare. Or sell it to help pay for the "killer" engine you're just dying to build. Whatever you need/want, crankcases and though stock replacements are always an option, that option may be limited. Limited in that H-D/Buell won't sell you a set unless you turn in the originals, for instance. There's also the issue of strength.

For over forty years it was a rare thing to see a street four-speed X engine that made over 70 honest horsepower. Or if it did, that stayed together for long periods of abuse. All that has changed. 1200cc Evo X motors (four-speed or five) can and do make 90 horses on a fairly routine basis. More than likely they can make 100-110 reliably, stock cases included. That being the case why worry about better than factory alternatives? First, better can be a pretty subjective term and second, more to the point, you want more than the stock cases can offer.

The major limits to stock five-speed cases are more about displacement limits than anything else. Theoretically, one can build 96 inch engines with stock cases but the line gets pretty thin at that point, and beyond that it's invisible. Outfits

STD offers extremely strong, cast 4 speed cases with built in windage tray and flywheel scrapers. Available in two versions: for bores up to 3-13/16 inch or 4 inch. Either will accept a stroke of up to 5 inches. STD

like STD and S&S both build cases based on what they've learned by creating 120-160 horsepower X engines of enormous capacity.

STD has traditionally offered four speed cases, beefy stock spec style featuring 356 T6 A alloy construction and the highest tensile strength on the market. They also incorporate a flywheel scraper they refer to as a windage separator. The purpose of this little goodie is to keep power robbing oil drag on the crankshaft to a minimum. Another noteworthy feature is the sheer number of bolts holding the halves together. Those extra bolts make a difference.

S&S offers cases for both 1986-90 and 1991 and later XL and Buell applications – with a twist. All of them use five-speed transmissions and clutches. It can get a little confusing, since S&S offers several iterations of X engine crankcases.

The Super Stock crankcases *only* – in either 3 1/2" or 3 5/8" bore - are replacements for 1991 and later, 5-speed Sportster or Buell models in the first place. Meaning mostly that you can use stock crankshafts if you stick with stock stroke. Besides these are what S&S calls "Evolution Sportster and Buell Style Crankcases." Buell cases, whether 3 1/2 or 3 5/8inch bore, are only available with the five-speed cam set up. All the Sportster cases are also really five-speed-style cases with special reed valve breathers, which will not accept four-speed crankshafts, but some are machined to fit four-speed frames and/or use four-speed style cams.

For example, on the left side of all S&S cases behind the drive sprocket we have the five-speed type alternator set up, same as the Super Stock replacement cases. A very good thing, as anyone who's had to replace an over $400.00 clutch hub/cum rotor on a four-speed will attest. Then on the right, there is removable/replaceable tappet guides. (Another good idea as any stock five-speed owner who's torched a tappet bad enough to ruin stock cases will gladly announce.) Generally, S&S recommends switching to four-speed style cams, complete with 1986-90 cam cover and oil filter mounting. However, they can also be had, machined for the 5-speed cams, using 1991-97 cam covers. Still featuring special removable tappet guides and collapsible pushrod tubes.

And, there's yet another version. S&S' "Special Application" These, 356 T6 cases, in addition to all the other S&S elements, attempt to cover all the desired bases in giant X motor construction. (Right off the bat, you *know* they are not going to accept stock cranks, since these cases

Offered by S&S, these Buell flywheels are knife-edged to shed oil more readily, and lightened to rev faster. Available in strokes up to 4 inches, or more with a special order.

take a +.500" pinion shaft, standard.) These cases practically *require* little added attractions to complete an assembly. For five-speed owners we're often talking the four-speed cam set and cam cover, adjustable pushrods, pushrod covers, oil filter mount, tappets and tappet blocks, to name the biggies. You may also encounter the need for S&S's version of the tappet blocks, since stockers have different geometry that won't work on the 1/2" wider camside of S&S cases.

GOT HEADS?

Well, those who just popped for a set of Thunderstorm heads or are happily rockin' along with S1 heads or other choices, will need to machine the pushrod holes as well. S&S heads bolt right on. You can go as big as 4.635inches in cylinder spigot diameters on these so huge displacement is absolutely the name of the game. There's more. Since you must use a built-up crank (S&S by any chance?), you can choose to use either XL or Big Twin sprocket shafts, mostly depending on what transmission you run. Yup, the cases can even be had with no machining in the transmission cavity, or no cavity period. Of course, should you choose to keep a Sportster gearbox back there, you can order a trapdoor for the top that let's you inspect those brutalized gears after every run. It means giving up the electric starter though, so you might want to think about that one.

The message is clear. These cases are built to be "built." Come to think of it, S&S does practically anything you'd care to pay for, on special order. The wimps and the impecunious among us need not apply.

Which leads right back to the bad news. No stock four-speed crankcase was ever as strong as any of the new 5-speed cases are proving to be. That fact alone may be incentive for owners of these older models who are contemplating taking on the newer '91 and later stuff.

S&S reminds buyers that Buell and Sportster long blocks are not interchangeable, due to differences in mounting. You must order the right cases for the right bike. When installing a 100 inch engine in a Buell, S&S mounts must be used.

111

Pressing Matters

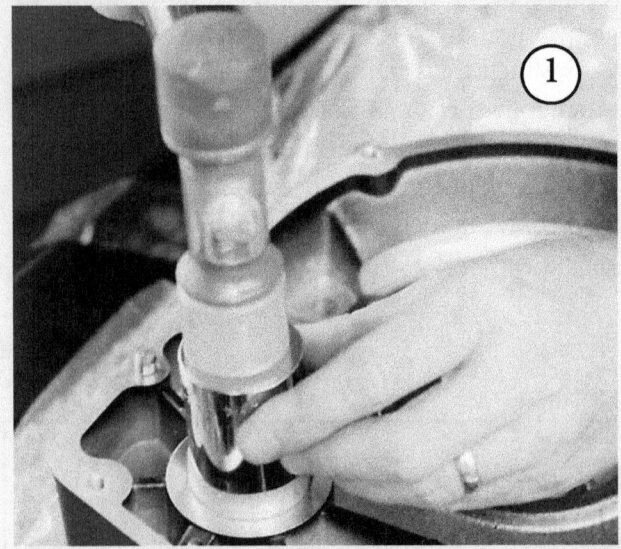

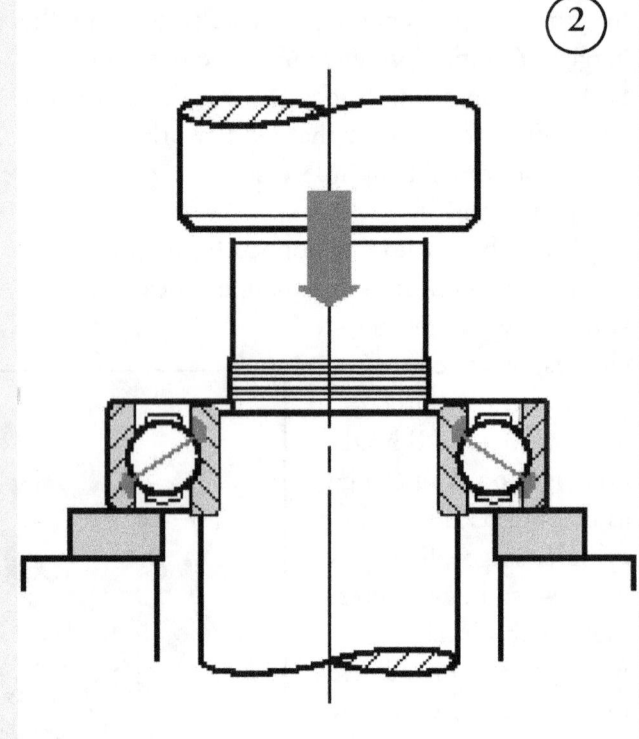

Incorrect Arbor Press Dismounting

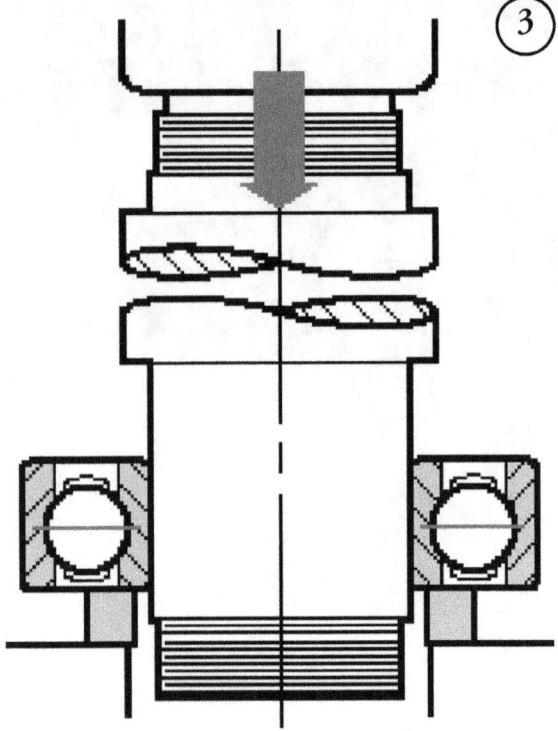

Proper Mounting Procedure

The support should be on the inner race as show to prevent damage to rollers and races.

Even when you do have a pressing engagement, there's a right way and a wrong way. This is not right.

The simple fact is, modern ball, roller and needle bearings, are tough and durable. Properly selected, installed, lubricated, and protected from abuse, they will likely last longer than the engine. The key word is – properly. There's a lot to learn about these seemingly simple, but truly sophisticated contraptions we take so much for granted. This little treatise is far from comprehensive and is intended only to make you aware of the more common issues, and get across the message that we can do ourselves more harm than good by improper handling of bearings we bet our lives on.

Pressing Matters

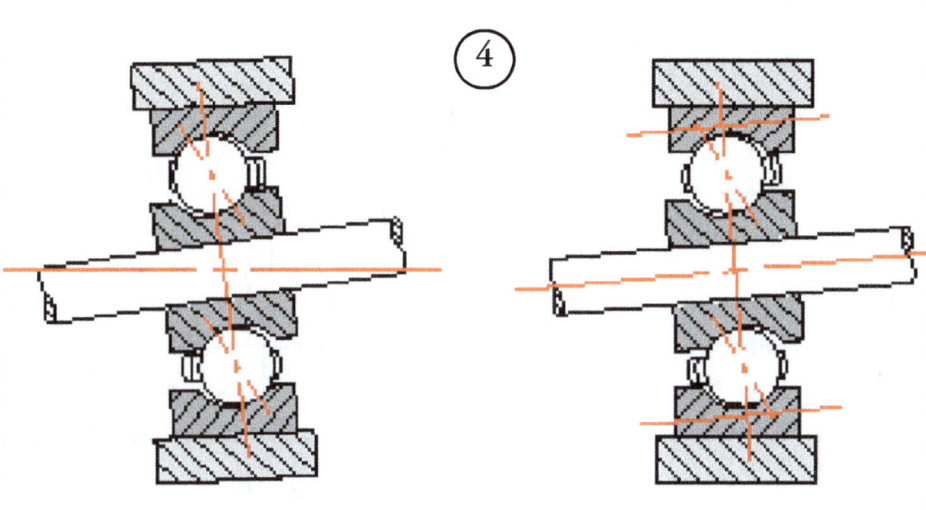

Shaft Misalignment **Housing Misalignment**

There's more than one way to mess up the installation of a bearing.

Example - of Ball Path Running from One Side of the Race to the Other Side

A bearing that's been in service often has a story to tell. When looking at used bearings, the race often tells a better story of neglect than the balls or rollers.

1) It's always better to press than pound. Not that folks don't get away with this behavior daily. It's just that it's a big risk, if you intend to have long lived bearings. Socked into a cavity like this, (or like a wheel bearing) is the more forgivable of evils when the tool matches the outer race diameter and there's no load on the inner race going in.

2) There's a right way and a wrong way. This is wrong. The loads imposed on the unsupported, inner race in this image amount to virtually guaranteed damage and/or short service life.

3) Here's the better way. The inner race, the one being severely loaded up by the pressure, is supported properly to prevent damage to the balls and the race.

4) There's more than one way to mess things up once the bearing is snug in it's new home too, as you can see from these exaggerated sketches. Don't take it for fact that new parts will align perfectly – check.

5) A bearing that's been in service under these conditions will tell you all about it, if you look. Here's an example of a race

113

Pressing Matters

with wear marks that indicate how crooked it has been for who knows how long.

6) Once installed, a new bearing should be squared away – literally. The shaft needs to be gauged to ensure that it's concentric, straight and have any shoulders squared at perfect 90 degree angles. The housing bores should be dimensionally accurate and true to the shaft.

7) Using a bearing with the right internal clearances is important enough, but lubrication is key. The quickest way to ruin a bearing is with the heat that accompanies a sky high thermal load.

8) There's plenty of heat involved in let-

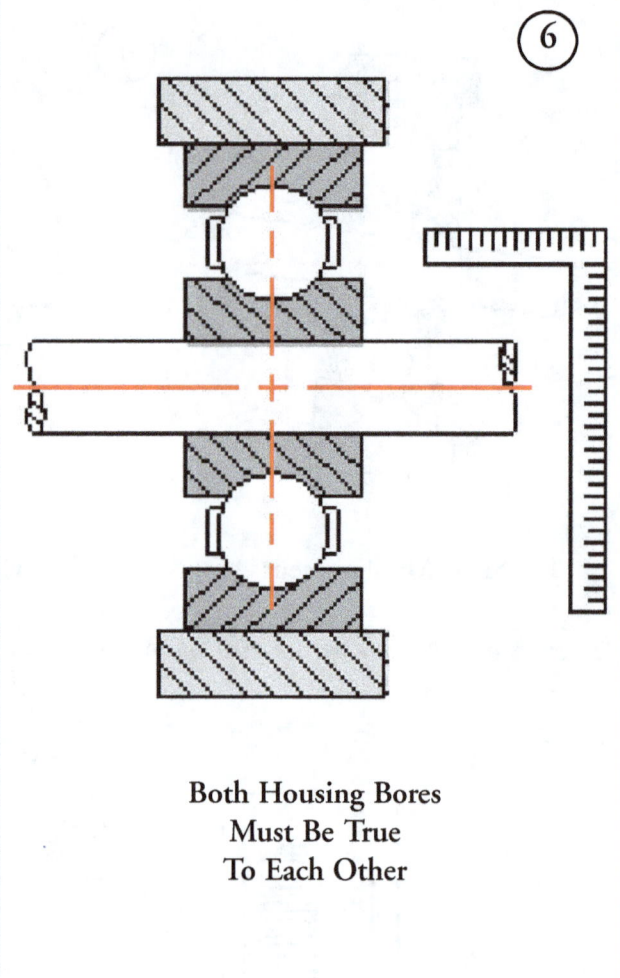

Both Housing Bores Must Be True To Each Other

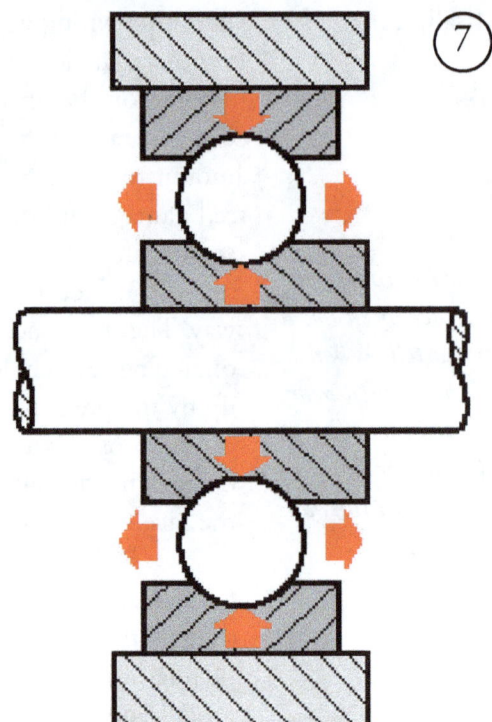

Lubrication Failures in Ball Bearings Are Usually Accompanied by a Thermal Expansion of the Components

Lubrication prevents metal to metal contact and ensures long bearing life.

A new bearing must be square in the bore.

ting a ball bearing do its job, when properly installed in the first place. But they are all built to handle their specific task, so it's not an issue with the right bearing in the right place.

9) Improper fit or insufficient internal clearance, especially in a thermally over heated, (thus distorted) aluminum housing can lead to flaking or sapling in a bearing prematurely. If a bearing of yours is similarly afflicted, it too will die young.

Any basic bearing failure amounts to the destruction of the hardened operating surfaces,

Pressing Matters

whether it's the races, the balls, or the cage retainer. There are several names for the various versions of this, usually coined to describe the speed or nature of the failure. Sapling, flaking, galling, pitting, fracturing, seizing and many more. Some are abrupt, some degenerative, all are pretty much unnecessary. There are plenty of expert resources available out there, on the internet, in shops, and at bearing supply houses. Should you suffer from a failure, be sure to take the time to have the carcass of the dead bearing autopsied by one of them, rather than risk a second failure.

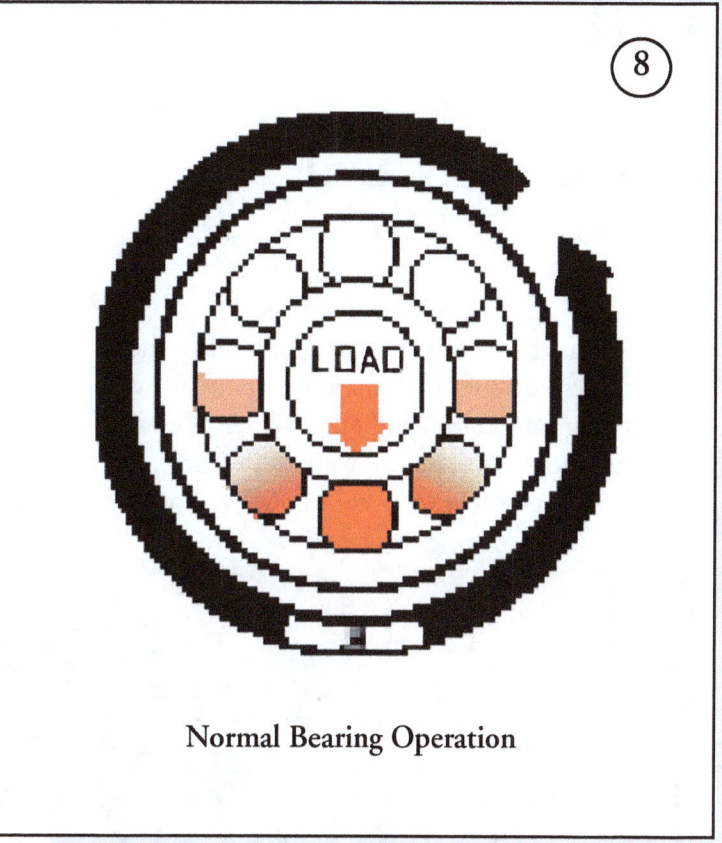

Normal Bearing Operation

Bearings are designed for a specific load and fit. Be careful with any bearing substitutions.

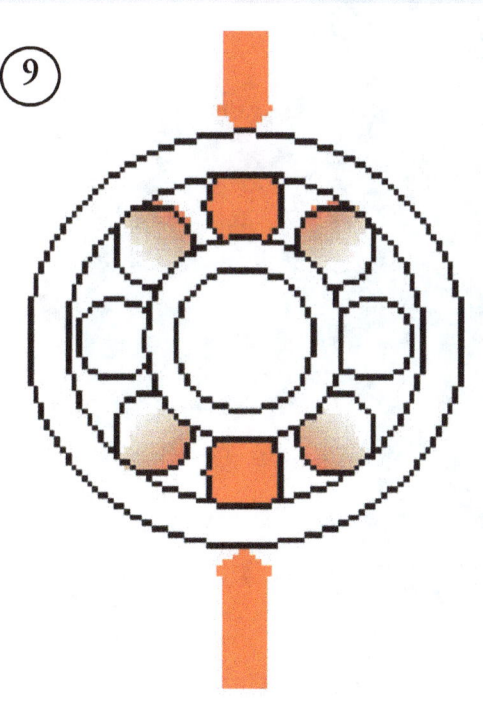

**Outer Ring
Squeezed by Housing**

A distorted housing will likewise distort the outer gearing race.

Chapter Thirteen

Oil

A Necessary Evil

It seems there's one more item to add to the list of topics you should never argue about. Now it's sex, religion, politics and oil. It's a never ending list of questions: Is there really any difference between motorcycle oil and car oil? Why should I pay extra for oil? What's the deal with synthetic oil, isn't it too slippery? The list goes on - complicated by changes in Society of Automotive Engineers (SAE) ratings, traditionally ignored by H-D, but recently addressed in a service bulletin.

It's hard to know which oil to buy for that V-twin, given the large number of possible brands and viscosities. There are two facts most "experts" agree on: use oil meant for air-cooled motorcycles, and buy multi-weight, not a straight weight.

Thing is, there's no real need to debate. All you need to know is a few basics, which are pretty much agreed to by all parties.

Oil analysis does not tell the whole story.

Okay, we can cut to the chase now. One burning issue for most of us Hog riders is, "exactly what's in Harley oil anyway?" It seems the compounding and chemical make up of the stuff is the most closely guarded secret since the formula for Coca-Cola. (See chart pg. 118)

H-D 20W50, the recommended engine lubricant for Buells and Harleys including the water-cooled V-Rod, is about 85-percent conventionally refined (by Sun Oil) petroleum oil base stocks, containing the additive elements seen in the page 118 chart (expressed in parts per million).

Told you that chemical analysis wouldn't give you the big picture. But, let's see if we can't make the picture we have somewhat clearer. First, if you want to know what all those elements with a ppm of less than 10 are, look them up. The rest of us are gonna concentrate on the concentrations. The amounts of these specific compounds are largely what makes Harley oil - Harley oil. The very first item on the list is the company's secret weapon in the oil wars - Calcium. The concentrations are literally about *twice* what other oils contain. This is a good thing, since Calcium fights acid. Acids are the bad boys that pop-up when you deal with "agreed upon" points 1,2,6,7,8, and 9. There's more to it than that, but we'll come back to it.

Next, we have Magnesium, which is another acid dispersant, and there's plenty of it, but not as much as some other motorcycles oils. That wad of Phosphorus you see listed has a much different

Thirteen Lube Laws

1) The worst thing you can do to an engine is start it. That 70-90 percent of all the wear and tear in an engine occurs on start up is a fact, so there's not much to argue with there.
2) Short hops, which don't warm oil to operating temperature, are as hard on engines as over-heating.
3) There are a few basic types of oil. For reciprocating engines they are castor, conventionally refined petroleum, hydro-cracked petroleum, and synthetic.
4) Additives are what make oil work. So called multi-viscosity oils are rated such because of them.
5) Additives are what wear out in oils. And they are what keep things from wearing out.
6) 212F degrees is considered the ideal temperature for oil, since it will boil off moisture.
7) At a constant 240F degrees you cut the oil's service life in half.
8) Every 12F degrees above 240F, cuts life in half again.
9) Air-cooled engines operate at temperatures as high as 350 degrees.
10) So- called straight-weight or single grade motor oils went out with high-button shoes and flat head engines. Use then at your own risk. (See- items 1-9)
11) Most modern multi-grade SAE-Rated oils have an EPA imposed cap on the added amounts of certain additives to prevent clogged catalytic converters. 20W50 isn't subject to these limitations.
12) Defining a given oil's performance by chemical analysis does not tell the whole story.
13) The frequent changing of both oil and filter are still the best insurance for engine longevity.

task to perform. It, along with its partner Zinc, function as sacrificial elements – AKA. anti-wear agents. It's their job to get in there and plate moving parts to prevent scuffs, galling, seizures, and other metal to metal accidents from happening when oil is literally squeezed out by extreme pressures. But even knowing all this, you still need to understand a few more things before you decide which oil is best for you and your engine.

H-D/Buell isn't and hasn't ever been, concerned with SAE/API ratings. They rightly conclude that's car stuff and of no relevance to air-cooled, ball-bearing equipped, V-twin engines. Especially with low-pressure, high volume oiling systems. Instead, they devised their own tests for motor oil. Ever wonder what the 360 on a bottle of Buell/H-D lube stands for? It's hours - as in hours on the dyno. It works like this: The company establishes their definition of worn out, essentially the point at which leak-down (compression sealing) gets below a certain reading. They strap the worn out bike to a dyno with the test oil in it, and run the thing at 4000rpm for 55 minutes with a fan simulating air flow. After which, the fan gets shut off and the motor idles for five minutes. Then its rev, idle, repeat, 24 hours a day until. Their own latest oil makes it *at least* 360 hours. Since some of the best car oils only lasted 80 hours, that's mighty good real world simulating. But, the fact remains, when they say change oil at 5000 miles max, they mean it, and smart folks will change it every 3000.

OPTIONS AND ALTERNATIVES.

We've basically determined that oil is made of three parts: First there's the raw oil or base stock. Secondly, and much more importantly, there's the additives package which includes more than just "elements." Things like co-polymers, which in the petroleum industry can be the chemical equivalent of anything from Styrofoam cups to nylon stockings in quality. These co-polymers and dozens of other chemicals and compounds even more exotic are there to help oil keep from shearing down it's viscosity (wearing out). They do other things too. Grouped into rough categories, we have.

Viscosity-Index Improvers: to keep oil from thinning too much under heat.

Dispersants: keeping contaminant's in suspension, to keep them off vital engine parts.

Detergents: soap, if you will, to prevent varnish build up and sludge, especially on the piston rings.

Antiwear agents: We've talked about those. Motorcycle oil should be full of them.

Antioxidants: to keep oil, which loves oxygen, from turning into tar. This becomes a big issue at high rpm, or pulling a heavy load in the heat.

Rust and corrosion Inhibitors: Again, something we've touched on. The worst under cold start, and ironically, hot shut off in moist cool climates.

Al = 2ppm	Na = 10ppm
Ba = 2ppm	Ni = 2ppm
Ca = 1410ppm	P = 1060ppm
Cr = 2ppm	Pb = 10ppm
Cu = 2ppm	Si = 2ppm
Fe = 2ppm	Sn = 2ppm
Mg = 751ppm	Zn = 1220ppm
Mo = 2ppm	

Get out your high school science book, here's the chemical analysis of the H-D oil.

Water actually likes the insides of an engine and a hot motor on a cold night makes coke-bottle sweat in reverse.

Friction modifiers: the new kid on the block, mostly an energy saving car thing. But remember those co-polymers.

Pour-point depressants: prevent wax crystals from forming in the base stocks in cold weather and, conveniently lowers the temperature at which oil remains a pourable fluid instead of a poor syrup.

Foam Inhibitors: similar to the stuff they put in fork oil to keep it from mixing with air. You wouldn't want your oil to suddenly become compressible, just when your motor needs a strong boundary layer of non-shear slipperiness.

Third is the actual process of refining oil base stocks. From the refining process to quality co-polymer additives, and in all the combinations available. Ultimately you still get what you pay for, but it doesn't have to be all that much. Take the new hydrocracking process for instance:

Invented primarily to allow petroleum oils to compete with synthetics at a much cheaper price. There are at present only three or so hydrocrack facilities in the U.S. The process amounts to pumping crude oil into a furnace heated to 600-700F degrees, then once up to temperature, pumping it into a still. The light gases and liquids rise to high "trays" in the still, while heavier oils settle on the lower trays. The heavy stuff is sent back to the cracker furnace and reheated to 800F degrees under nearly a ton of pressure. Add a few catalytic chemicals and bang. - the heavy oil molecules split into lighter molecules. The lighter molecules go back to the still. The net result is oil that resists oxidation as much as three times longer, generates 90% less acid, and because it's so pure, has 50% less sludge in it. That makes a better base stock. If the base oil does more of the work, the additives can be left to do their job, namely protect the engine.

SYNTHETIC OIL – NO SLIP UP?

People seem to have a natural aversion to things that seem too good to be true. Remember the 200 mile per gallon carburetor? How about the light bulb that never burns out? The trouble is that sometimes the story is absolutely true. You can't blame people for being slow to recognize technical advances either. Enzo Ferrari never did like disc brakes on his race cars, Soichiro Honda didn't want water-cooled engines in his cars or motorcycles, and Henry Ford never trusted electric starters. A lot of Harley riders could teach any of those three a lesson. It doesn't matter - because this particular "too good" is "too true."

The API ratings many of us have learned to look for on the back of an oil can are pretty much meaningless when considering oil for a V-twin. Some of the things that make an oil a good choice for a water-cooled V-eight, make it a less-than-ideal choice for an air-cooled V-twin.

Oil Pukin'

I don't mean to offend the three folks out there who *don't* have this problem, but it's not exactly a secret that five-speed Sportsters have a tendency to blow oil into the air cleaner. This is aggravated by prolonged high-speed excursions. Something like 75-100 miles at 75 mph usually does the trick. You get back from a run like that and your air cleaner is bleeding 20/50, right? Particularly noticeable, if it's a Screamin' Eagle/High-Flow set up. Well, I don't mean to imply that I've found a cure, but I do have a theory about the disease.

All V-twins have a positive pressure build up in the crankcase when the two pistons are on the down stroke. This pressure must be allowed to escape from the cases in a quick and timely fashion, or a real expensive aluminum balloon will burst, and the oiling system won't work properly. All this huffing and puffing is controlled by a timed rotating mechanism on Big Twins and early Sportsters. Somewhere along the way the Sportster engineers at the factory figured that it would be a better idea to design a breathing system that would let the pressure out whenever it wanted out, instead of trying to figure out when it *should* want out. So they did away with the rotating type of timed breather gear. The *non-timed*, asymmetrical breather design did work better. But, there's always room for improvement, right?

When H-D went to the five-speed transmission on XL's, they actually did a whole lot more than just stuff an extra gear in the box. It amounted to a complete redesign of the crankcases, *and the way they breathe.* The X engine family became what is known as "head breathers." Meaning that excess chuffing pressure in the crankcase was no longer vented from the crankcase. Instead, the pressure is piped up to the cylinder heads and vented into the airbox via two hollow bolts.

This was done with the EPA firmly in mind, since everybody knows that it's a heavy no-no to allow nasty, dirty, old oil to escape into the atmosphere. So, the breather bolts go straight from the cylinder heads into the air cleaner - for cleaner air.

So far, so good, engineering-wise. What nobody seems to have realized is that this arrangement effectively connects a high pressure zone to a low pressure zone - directly. Think about it, the oil/air mist that *should* simply escape from the cases is instead sucked into the air cleaner by the carburetor. At high rpm this can create quite a siphon effect. The faster you go, the worse it gets. Hey, if an open carb bell will suck your pant leg right in, it'll sure suck some oil in.

Here's what I suggest you do about it, and no it's not sanctioned by any factory engineer.

Late model Sportsters like this 2002, 883 are prone to "oil pukin'" when ridden long and hard on the highway.

Oil Pukin'

Remove the vacuum.

• First, you get a Screamin' Eagle air cleaner kit. You know, the one that leaks the worst. (No, I'm not nuts, just stay with me on this).

• Then purchase an Adapter kit H-D # 29281-91T, two exhaust studs # 16715-83, two 5/16" coarse Nyloc nuts, four 5/16" flat washers, two 5/16" X 1/4" spacers (chrome, if you like), two rubber washers # 5797, about three feet of 5/16" fuel hose, and maybe one of those little K&N crankcase filters.

• Drill and tap the head of the banjo bolts in the adapter kit to 5/16" fine threads. Use blue Loctite on the studs, and install the fine thread end of the two exhaust studs in the freshly tapped, and cleaned, holes in the banjo bolts. Run them in to the boss in the middle of the stud.

• Rip the air cleaner off the bike - whatever kind it is. Install the adapter kit *exactly* like the instructions tell you to, except for the hose. Next, put one of the 5/16" flat washers on the protruding end of the stud, followed by one of the 5/16" X 1/4" spacers. Take the backing plate from the air cleaner kit and install it as usual.

• This should leave you with a backing plate that sits flush and correct on the bell of the carb. If all is well at this point, you'll have the coarse end of two exhaust studs looking at you from the holes where the hollow stock bolts normally go. You will also undoubtedly notice that the studs are 5/16" diameter and the holes in the backing plate are bigger. No problem. Stick one of the rubber washers over each stud. Then the other flat washers, one on each stud.

• Run the Nyloc nuts onto the studs to about 7-10 foot-pounds of torque and hook up the rubber hose to the spigot on the adapter. Finish installing the air cleaner.

• Now, the tough decision. Where and how are you gonna route the rubber hose? You may elect to stuff it down behind the sprocket cover with the other hoses and wires that live there. Maybe you'll want to route it across the cases to the left side of the engine, and from there down between the back of the case and the swingarm pivot. Or, there's the notion of mounting that cute little K&N breather filter somewhere unobtrusive and connecting the hose to that.

Your carburetor will no longer suck oil out of the motor into the air cleaner. Whether it will still puke a little into the hose, I'm not prepared to say. However, if it does:

It just may be, especially if you have a '91-'93 model, that you'll need to install a "reversed" motor seal (#35151-74) and a tighter spacer (#40290-89), to help you nail down some more of your oil transfer gremlins.

The key part of any repair done to eliminate oil pukin' is to separate the head breathers from the air cleaner.

Though expensive, the new synthetic oil from Harley-Davidson is of very high quality and can be used in the engine, primary case or transmission. H-D

Synthetic oils (technically, Poly-Alpha-Olyphic or P.A.O. Synthetics) have been around since World War II. The Germans used it on the Russian front because conventional oil wouldn't even flow in those cold conditions. The stuff wasn't exactly perfected at that stage but obviously had at least one major advantage even then. In the last half of the last decade of this century, it has so many advantages it simply cannot be ignored. Synthetic oil molecules are superior to mineral-based molecules.

1) They resist heat better. It takes more than *600 degrees F* to vaporize the stuff. Regular motor oil begins to torch at more like 350 degrees F. Since air-cooled Harley engines run at 180-210 degrees F and have been known to get as hot as 240-260, that adds up to a *much* better thermal safety margin. That extra high temperature stability has lesser benefits, too. Your motor won't burn up as much oil and that also means less sludge and built up varnish in the engine.

2) They are slipperier. The molecules in synthetic oil are *far* more uniform in length, weight, size, and shape, than those found in nature, and that makes it much easier for them to slide over things, and one another. The resultant loss, of friction can actually be measured. It shows up as

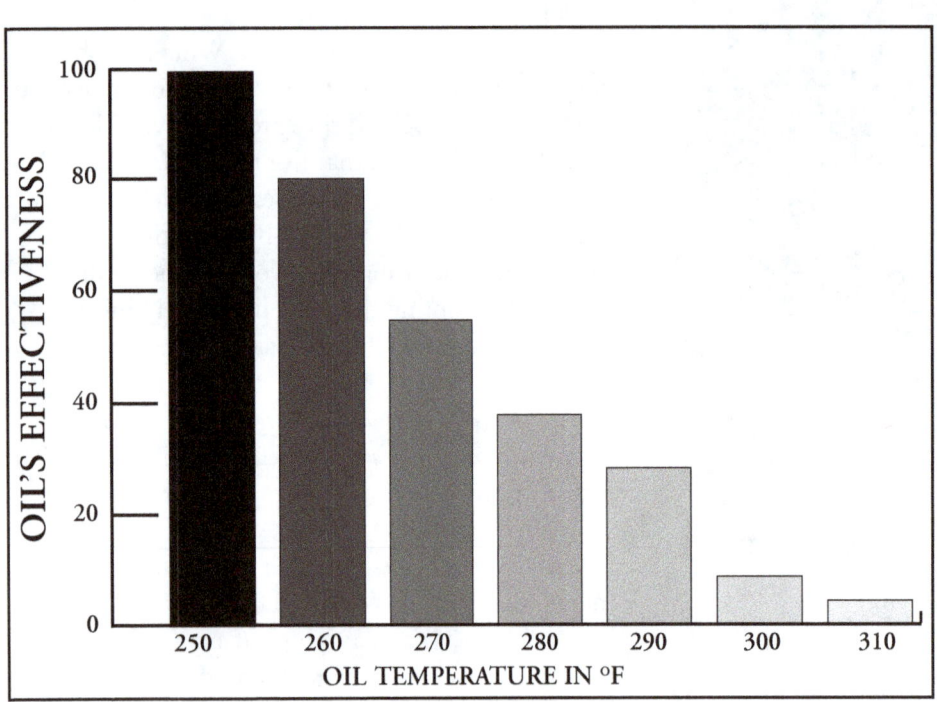

Here is what happens to your fossil oil's ability to lubricate above 250 degrees F.

more horsepower. What you do with this benefit is up to you: a tenth of a gallon at the gas pump, or a tenth off your ET.

3) They have film strength. This is the *real* payoff. Film strength is what keeps those little molecules from being pushed, or torn apart under extreme pressure. Regular oil is about done at 500 psi. Synthetics go about 3000 psi. In an area where two metals are trying their absolute best to destroy each other, where pressures and friction can go ballistic at almost any moment, Synthetics cover your bet six times over. There simply *is* no comparison! Film strength counts in another arena as well, and it's one of my favorite soapboxes. Cold starts.

Regular oil will *not* remain as a boundary layer on metal surfaces. When you shut the motor off the stuff heads for the bottom of the crankcase, leaving pistons and rings, valves and guides, cams and pushrods, in the lubrication lurch. I'd be willing to bet that a great many of the unexplainable tappet roller failures in Harley motors are a testament to this nasty little habit. Leave a bike parked long enough for the lubricant to drain off the rollers and the little needles in the tappet, and a little rust pit appears. Cold start the bike a month later and TAH-DAH. You've just knocked the rust off that dry roller *and* successfully jeopardized the surface hardening at the same time. You do that very often and oops, trashed engine.

For the disbelievers, those who are convinced that synthetics are "too slippery," it's worth noting here that GM and Ford have been using roller tappets in V-8s for years now, and failure is virtually unheard of. Besides, Motorheads with 5.0 Mustangs, Vettes, and Z-228's almost all run synthetics already. Vettes even come stock that way.

Bottom line is, wouldn't it be nice to have a strong and healthy powerplant at 100,000 plus miles instead of a used up chunk of scrap iron? Hold that thought whenever you light up your engine. Picture some mighty important metal surfaces crying out for lubrication in the time it takes for your oil pump to pressurize all of those bearings, lifters, passageways, and so on all the way to the rockers, nearly *eighteen inches* straight up hill. Then, count slowly to thirty. That's how long it can take for the whole motor to get lubricated, particularly on cold mornings. Now, picture that commercial where they run the engines without oil after they drain the synthetic. Lastly, envision the bonus benefit of extended change intervals. The expense of the stuff is offset by the need to change it about half as often. There's also an environmental dividend in that you don't generate as much toxic waste. If there's a down side I can't see it.

Multi-weight oil does a better job of lubricating under a wide range of temperatures. From that cool morning start up to idling through Sturgis traffic. And isn't that what you want for that new Sportster or Buell in the garage.

So, if this stuff is so great, why doesn't everybody use it? A few reasons come to mind. New engines actually *shouldn't* use it until they are broken in. The added friction and surface abrasion of mineral based oils help to seat the valves and rings and create even mating surfaces. The process generates lots of microscopic particulates (usually metallic) so frequent changes are necessary. Major manufacturers don't push the stuff, as a rule, because they'd like to sell you a new vehicle every few years, and wearing out the one you've got is a major motivator. Big oil companies (and Harley-Davidson) have been slow to come around to synthetics because building the stuff is a different technology and an expensive process. Now that they *are* into it, H-D will push it like mad.

But, the *biggest* reason by far, is that the would-be consumer is ignorant of the benefits and distrustful of the technology, even if they've known about it for years. They rationalize. "Yeah, my Grandaddy used 'ol Maximillion 105 weight Reclaim in his '26 JD, so I won't use nothin' he didn't. Family tradition, y'know. Besides, I can get the stuff right down the street, for 39 cents a quart." Or, my favorites, "The stuff is too slippery, it'll make my bike leak or my ball bearings fail." Usually coupled with, "I been usin' brand X for years. If I change now, or mix 'em, it'll blow my motor. Besides, oil's oil. I ain't payin' no five bucks a quart, no sirree, Bob, I ain't that stupid." Yeah well - there are times when wisdom *isn't* conventional, and what's conventional isn't wise.

P.S. - Harley-Davidson service bulletin #1065, states *flat out*, that car oil is no longer suitable for use in their motors. Basically, the newest API service rating for automotive oils is designed to protect catalytic converters - not engines. To comply with this rating, the major oil companies have removed most of the sacrificial elements (zinc, Potassium, Magnesium, etc,) in their additives packages that can save engines, but plug-up and burn out catalytic converters. Harley says that as a result of this, these oils will no longer work as a substitute for Harley (motorcycle) oil. The factory now recommends using either diesel oil or a good synthetic like Mobil One, or Castrol Syntec, or their own new synthetic.

Oil Filters

First, visualize what some of the better known bits in your engine do for a living. Gas and air are confined in the combustion chamber and lit. The explosion sends the piston down the cylinder wall in a Hell of a hurry. Said piston is "flexibly" attached by a connecting rod with an offset via a crankpin to your ever so essential flywheels, which fly around in a rotational fashion, giving up power at the end of the shaft in quantities directly determined by speed, size of piston, compression ratio, etc. All of this is taking place very quickly.

We've said it before, we'll say it again. Oil meant for automobiles is fine oil – for automobiles. Air-cooled engines have different needs and operate under a different set of criteria. Use automotive oil in your car and motorcycle oil in your motorcycle.

Oil is a Drag

First and foremost, understand that oil is a necessary *evil*. It would be flat terrific to abolish all need of it, and the first man to do so will either be the next Henry Ford, or whacked by some big Petroleum Conglomerate. Point is, though irreplaceable, the stuff is messy, behaves incoherently at different times and temperatures, and gets in the way as often as it helps out. Oh, and you *can't* compress the stuff. Physics says it doesn't succumb to pressure, so in tense situations it's the motor that suffers, not the oil. If something has to give, it'll be horsepower not fluids. Sort of the immovable object - irresistible force game. You figure out which is which, especially where V-Twin engine flywheels are concerned.

If oil cannot get out of the crankcase fast enough, those flywheels have a seriously severe battle on their hands. Dragging through that muck at 5-7 grand, is like you running hard through a swimming pool, the water could care less, while you wind up near dead from burning energy going nowhere. You want to boogie, drain the pool or buy a water slide. Same idea with crankcases. Get the oil down to skimming levels, instead of sloshing deep in it, and guess what, more speed and less energy used to get it. Easier said than done, precisely because oil is a *necessary* evil.

Oil *pumps*, on the other hand are so *unnecessary*, they had to be invented. That's right, early engines, lots of 'em, didn't have oil pumps, only gravity, and they ran okay, just splashing the lube around. Of course engine speeds in that era are this era's definition of a fast idle. To do better, to "be cool" with speedier reciprocating takes a pump.

The oil pump in a modern motorcycle engine works a little like a traffic cop at a busy intersection, telling circulating motor oil when to speed up, slow down, stop and start. The trouble is, there are other intersections throughout the engine where there's no cop on duty, and the bad guys will take a crack at "telling oil where to go" every chance they get. The biggest offender is the crankshaft assembly ("flywheels" to The Motor Company), but cam trains, and pistons flailing to and fro, are pretty offensive to oil control as well. Not unlike trying to fill a thimble with a squirt gun from 10 feet away, through the

It shouldn't be necessary to pull the exhaust, 5-speed Sportsters and Buells have good access to the oil pump.

It's a good idea to simply remove the screws and drop the pump, then worry about the hose clamps. Don't sweat draining the oil, you only lose a bit.

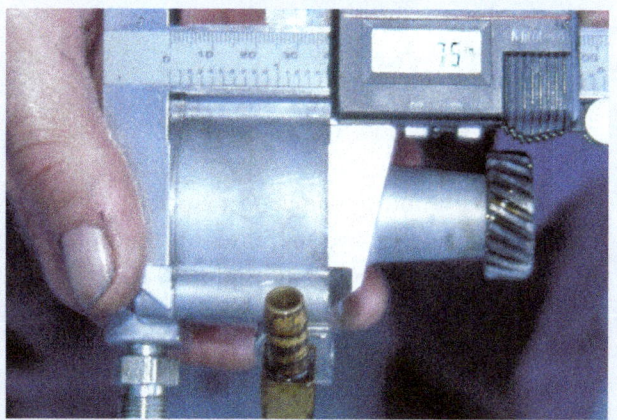

Your old (1991-1997) pump measures right at 1.4575" at the body. The new '98-style pump at 1.6400", is holding gears that are .200" taller.

125

Oil is a Drag

Notice the "trough" cut into the conical part of the new '98-style pump (left) from gear to body? That allows the oil to drop right, straight into the pump, instead of hanging around in the can cover. there's an additional cavity cut into the body, as well.

blades of a ceiling fan. All this apparatus moving about affects the ability of the oil to run its course.

Harley's proven high volume low pressure, oiling system compliments the rather unique ball bearing engine construction, so much so, that overly high pressure in the system can actually aggravate any short comings. (Think about that, before blindly bouncing your oil pressure readings as high as you can get them.) The arena for true improvement is in fine tuning the amounts of oil trapped in the bottom end or cam cover. Get the oil to the critical spot at the right time and then out of the way before it slows down, stops, or pools up and blows out. You don't need a cup full of the stuff lagging in the cases, dragging on flywheels. You don't need pools of the stuff backing up into the rocker boxes and puking into the air filter. You really don't need an extra few ounces backed up in the cam cover waiting its turn to drain back into the pump. You especially don't need widely varied powerful pulses of negative, then positive, pressure screwing around with the oil's direction of flow every nano second.

Since it obtained its fifth gear in 1991, the X engine, whether Sportster or Buell versions, has often as not, to one degree or another, had these oil control problems you don't need. All sorts of things have been tried, with various degrees of effectiveness. Drilling rocker box drain holes over-sized, flipping the motor seal 180 degrees, tightening up tolerance on the sprocket shaft spacer, all to minimum benefit. The problem persisted until 1998, and a clever redesign of the oil pump. And, guess what? It scavenges better, much better. It also bolts right up to older five-speed models. If you've got a Sportster or Buell built before 1997, this is an oil pump swap you *do* need. It is simply one of the best and most effective mods you can make for a couple hundred bucks and an hour or so of your time.

There was another minor update to the pump in 2000, and the new Buell Firebolt has yet another variant on board. This re-working of stock pumps should be plenty sufficient for most of us street riders. However, for road racers and/or drag racers that spend max time at max revs, it might be worth considering Zipper's aftermarket pump. This 3-stage racing pump is pretty much guaranteed to keep the bottom end of your engine as dry a bone. The other nice touch is that with the purchase of an adapter kit, you can use the Zipper's pump on 4-speed X-engines as well.

This Zipper's pump uses one geroter set for oil feed, another geroter for sucking oil from the cam cavity, and a set of spur gears for the main, "factory" scavenge area. It's also got a built-in filter.

Oil is a Drag

If you spend a lot of time at redline there are certain mechanical facts of life you should be aware of. First, the engine using up a lot of it's available power fighting off the drag of motor oil. It takes a lot of energy and time to move it out of the way. To your engine's crankshaft, it's like running hip deep in the ocean, trying to make any progress in the midst of both pounding surf and an undertow! Damn near impossible. Yet, you ask your Buell or Sporty to deal with a similar situation every time you visit the upper end of the rpm-band. Well, in sort of an "old trick for new dogs" twist" there has been a cure, the essentials of which date back - ah, at least to the early XR750, if not beyond. But hey - a fix is a fix.

You start by tearing the engine down to free the crank. Or, it can be performed as you build up a big-inch engine. Once done, it's necessary to scribe the case for proper clearance of the flywheel scraper. Notice the cut away case screw bosses at the bottom of the sump as well.

More work is required to evacuate oil from where it normally drops (and hangs) in the cam cover. The bottom of the cam case is tapped and plumbed with a new hose to let this oil fall straight to the basement The second hose below the sump is a short cut for the oil that's in there to get back to the pump quickly.

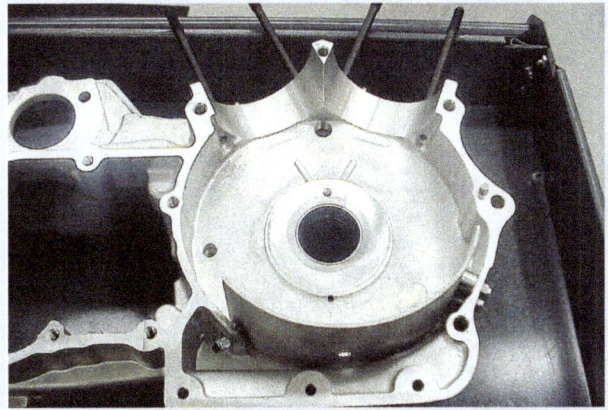

The scraper, once constructed, lives in the left case half. See the drain hole. The object of the game is to not only keep excess oil off the flywheels in the first place, but get rid of what remains, as soon as possible, after it's done it's work. At high rpm this means in fractions of a second.

A polished crank is a ton of work, and it borders on gilding the lily. But oil has a hard time clinging to that smooth surfaces. At least one aftermarket companies supplies flywheel assemblies already polished.

These oil filters combine a filter with drop in elements and a housing designed to double as an oil cooler. Biker's Choice

Much like the oil you use, pick an oil filter from a brand—name manufacturer. One that's meant for use on your motorcycle.

At 6,000rpm for instance, a four stroke engine is enduring 50 explosions every second in every cylinder. The crank turns 100 times a second and the piston and rod are screaming up and down slamming to a complete halt and reversing direction almost instantaneously at the same rate. Piston speed approaches 4600 feet per minute. Valves are opening and closing, springs are bouncing like mad and everything else in there is moving. Not that it isn't all terrifically well organized. The thing that makes it all possible let alone commonplace, the *real* magic in the motor, is oil. But, we *truly* take a lot for granted when we assume the oil doesn't need any help to do it's job. If we remain oblivious to all the hidden but frantic motion, and the heat, friction, and shock loads that go with it, the typical engine grinds itself to death. O.K., given that the oil is the magic, what's the trick? Oil filters.

In days gone by most motorcycle engines had at least three strikes against them in terms of longevity. They were air-cooled (wears out *three times* faster than water-cooled), filled with thick straight grade oil *and* had *no* oil filter worthy of the name. Considering all those bearings and shafts, rings and cylinders, valves and guides, and all that relative motion combined with close tolerances, you wonder how something as indispensable as a filter could be overlooked. Well, if you were to examine a sample of oil you wouldn't be very likely to notice the dirt because, hey, the stuff is too small to see most of the time. The few chunks you might see, ironically, are not usually the ones to worry about (as far as wear is concerned anyway) because they are too big to enter the tight clearance areas.

To see why this is so, consider a plain rod bearing with a typical diametrical clearance that averages .002 inches. The oil film layer, the separation between shaft and bearing, or thickness between perfect running and a blown motor, is slightly less than 10% of this, or about .00015 inches. A particle this size can and will scratch the bearing and shaft surface. Those particles suspended in the oil are in effect a lapping compound continuously wearing away engine surfaces while adding even more particles, thus compounding the problem. Some surfaces are soft enough that dirt will embed in the material creating a grinding wheel whenever it happens. It works the same everywhere else in the motor, the rings, ball bearings and so on. When you check oil levels, add or change oil, then airborne dirt or even the crud around the filler can fall in as well.

But cheer up, this has been going on since before any of us were born and in the good old days, our forefathers' motors needed overhauls more frequently than we *now* need to even bother changing oil. These dramatic increases in engine life are the result of the superior materials used in the construction of the newer motors, *vast* improvements in the additives packages in modern multigrade oils, and *the perfection and inclusion of good quality oil filters.* Dramatic improvements in engine life are *apparent* when full flow filters are used, with typical reductions in wear, relative to

Biker's Choice (and others as well) makes a line of oil filters that combine high quality internals with chrome-plated externals.

non-filter equipped engines, of as high as 90%.

No oil filter will remove *all* the particles in an engine, however. Filtration that fine would be extremely restrictive and cause high pressure drops across the element, not to mention excessively frequent filter changes. The happy medium, agreed to by most reciprocating engine manufacturers, seems to be filtration down to approximately 10 to 25 microns. Studies have shown this is an effective value for maximum filtration with minimum hassles. The details of filter ratings are pretty involved and include percentages of various sized particles that a given filter can stop. The interesting thing is that a 25 micron filter will take out many particles *much* smaller than 25 microns, so the ratings are pretty conservative. Then there is the issue of correct filters to use as replacements for O.E.M. specified so-called full flow filters. It's crucially important to realize that blow off pressure, volume of flow through the filter, and the actual cleansing capability that the engineers were after when they told you what filter to use, can be destroyed (literally and figuratively) if a different filter is substituted. Make no mistake, even if they look identical, two filters can function in a completely different fashion. The filter for a Buick V-6 turbo motor will screw right on, but there's no way it's worth taking a chance on a filter designed for a water-cooled, plain bearing, wet sump, auto engine with about 50-60 pounds of oil pressure, hot.

Factory filters are made by Purolator to H-D specs, and Phram #6022 is also for Harley motors. The latest (OEM #63798-99 or #63731-99), trap down to 10 microns and are a great retrofit idea.

Harley-Davidson also offers an inexpensive line of oil filters, called "Classic Motor Parts". These economy H-D/Buell filters are generically constructed with internal plates using six holes. The OEM filter has only four. There are likely to be other related design details that set this filter apart from the genuine article. We're not prepared to say whether the "Classic" filter is better, worse, or about the same in terms of function. We are saying the OEM/Genuine item is made in the U.S. of A., whereas the other filter is *not*. The two dollar difference in the retail price isn't the *only* difference. So be aware.

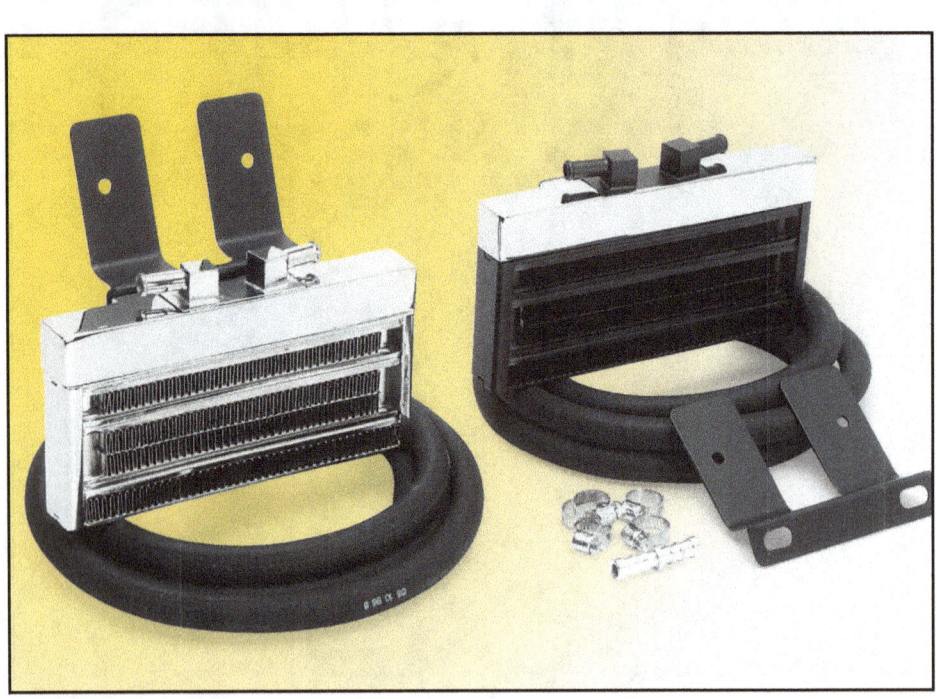

An oil cooler needs to be chosen not only for looks and how it fits but bike, but as to whether or not it contains a thermostat. Biker's Choice

Also, for those who persist in doing oil and filter changes 4 or 5 times as often as H-D recommends, "just to be on the safe side," it's worth noting that a filter is proven most efficient *after* it has operated a while and developed a so-called "cake," or coating on the element.

OIL COOLERS

Corporate Harley-Davidson will look you right in the collective consumer eye, and say flat out that Evo motors do not need oil coolers. Then they proceed to refer you to the shop manual, specifically the pages that discuss and describe what weight oil to use under given temperature conditions. You know, Summer, Winter and so on. Hmmm, where does that leave you?

It's fair to say that a stock under-stressed X engine, making all of 55-65 horses, probably doesn't need any help to stay in its prime operating heat range, somewhere between 180-220 degrees. It's also logical to believe that an oil cooler can do more harm than good, if the machine it's mounted on is used primarily for short hops - a situation that leads to the very real problem of not ever getting oil properly warmed up. Cold oil being as dangerous and deadly as hot oil ever thought of being.

You probably already know, thanks to TV commercials, that 90% of the wear and tear on engines is from cold starts, and you may have heard that too-cold oil can't "burn off" the acid by-products of internal combustion. Guess what? True. So, what do you do?

If you have an engine capable of generating, say 100% more power than a standard one and if you ride hard on long trips of 100 miles or more almost constantly, you should probably consider a cooler. If you really are aboard a stocker for no more than 20 minutes at a time you may still consider a cooler, at least in the hot months of the riding season.

If you're anywhere in between, as most of us are, consider this:

If you choose to install a cooler for any reason, you'd better have one with a thermostat. That way it won't bring the cooler on-line during short hops. This solves the too cool problem. And if you actually read the manual, and live in the initial decade of the 21st Century, you'll realize that a cooler, combined with a multi-viscosity 10-50 or 20-50 motor oil makes a hell of a lot more sense for the majority of riding environments than *any* heavy molasses-like 50-60w straight grade. In fact, the quickest way to wear out a top end is to use straight-weight oils in cool conditions, for short rides. It's that simple. The second best is to use a multi-grade on days when it's too hot, you have too far to go, and plenty of power to get you there, but you're stuck in traffic, smelling hot metal and cooked lubricant.

Nothing can cover you 100% for all riding conditions, but common sense tends to point out that using 10-micron oil filters, 20/50 Harley oil, or a good synthetic, and a quality oil cooler -*with a thermostat* - covers more of the bases than anything else.

These slim coolers from Lockhart are designed to be used with a separate thermostat (shown) so the oil bypasses the cooler until it reaches proper operating temperature. Biker's Choice

Chapter Fourteen

Transmission & Clutch

Get it in Gear

Sportsters kept their four-speed gearboxes for over 40 years, until "hell froze over" in 1991, and the new five-speed debuted. In terms of the basic design, and minor engineering updates aside, four-speed boxes are more hassle than their five-speed step children. The ratios are less than great in most XL four-speeds, (although you can help that), and the whole shee-bang had to survive the early years of busted trap doors and flattened main shaft rollers when you put them to abuse. Not sniping,

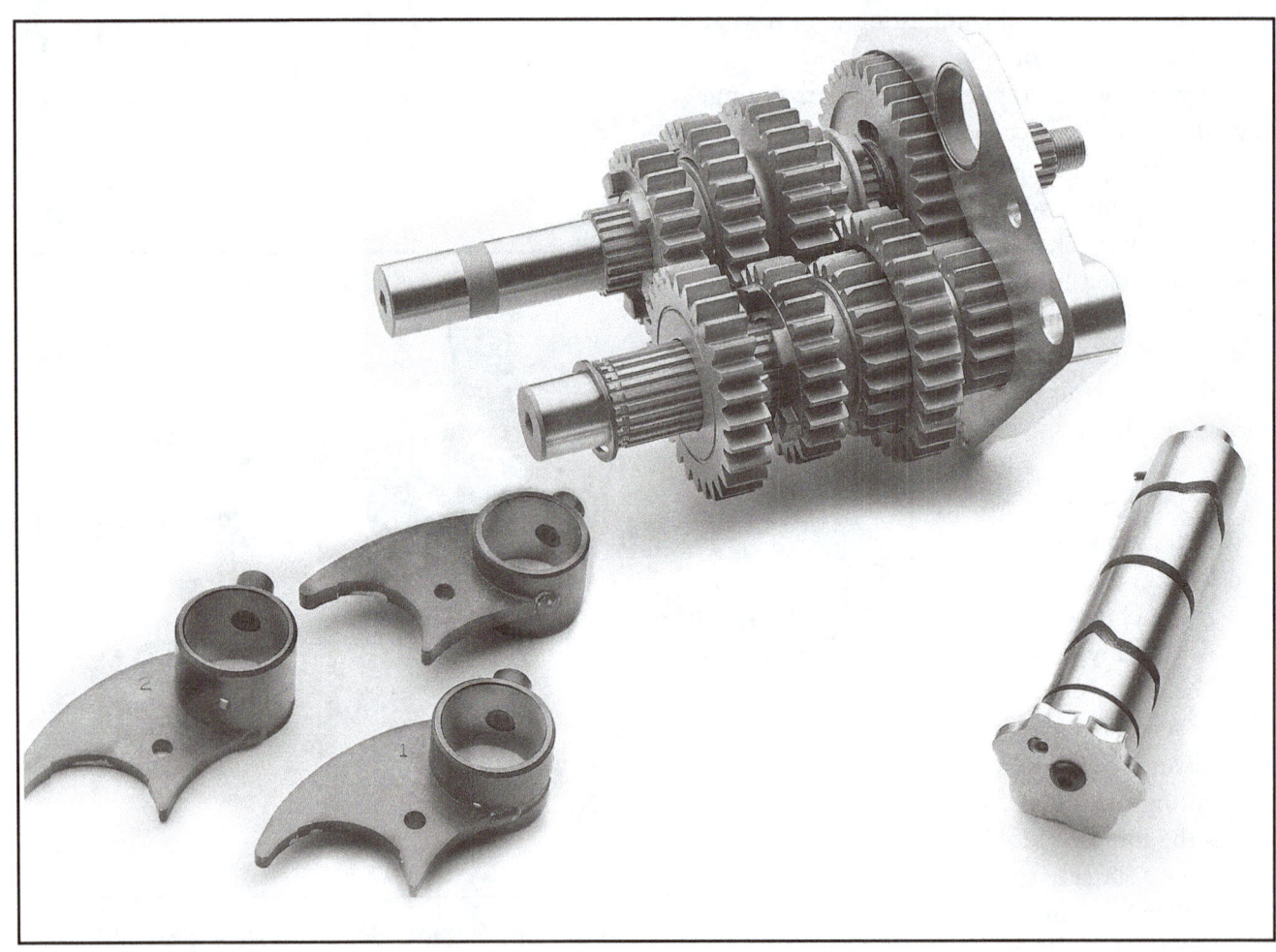

Yes, you can have a 6-speed Sportster or Buell with the addition of this 6-speed kit from Baker Drivetrain. 2nd through 5th gears are essentially the same as stock, but 6th is a .86-to-1 overdrive which knocks 500 rpm off at 75 mph. Fits '91 and up Sportys and Buells.

just letting you know what you might be in for. The four-speed is a labor-intensive unit to set up correctly, as well. All those shims, you see.

XL four-speed boxes, as fitted to Evolution Sportsters have damn little to apologize for. They were state of the art for decades, have a shift quality that shouts HARLEY, design upgrades over the years have all but eliminated the early problems, and properly set-up and cared for are virtually bullet proof.

The five-speed boxes are the result of late 20th century CAD/CAM manufacturing methods and of course marketing demands. Do you really think Harleys need five, or even six, gearbox ratios to choose from with that wide torquey powerband? The benefit of all this technology is one of the simplest, strongest designs you can imagine, superb durability, decent shifting, and the ability to be over-hauled by normal humans with almost no shimming. Still, top gear is top gear, and with straightforward 1-1 ratios for both, there's no real difference between four and five in that department. Six speed gearsets with an overdriven top gear are another story however, as you'll learn elsewhere in these pages.

Four-speed Transmission Chronology

Sportsters were blessed with four cogs to choose from since day one, 1957 to be exact. In the ensuing decades the ratios got messed with, the clutch went wet (and limp), the shifter swapped sides, the trapdoor got beefed up – I could go on.

But the big news happened in 1984 when H-D went to an alternator system on Sportys. The transmission access plate (trap door) changed (again), along with the clutch gear and the clutch design itself. (Much better!) The outboard bushing in the clutch gear was changed to a roller bearing. The cam follower was changed from a spring loaded pin to the rocker style. The shifter fork shaft, countershaft and thrust washers for the main and countershafts were also redesigned. First gear on the countershaft also got bearings instead of bushings. Last, but not least, the mainshaft case bearing went from loose rollers to a caged (torrington type) bearing. In 1985 the trap door was changed again, which in turn changed the way the clutch gear and bearing were mounted. The details can be found in factory service bulletin #894. Even though that was still the Iron Head era, this transmission was virtually identical in 1986 when the first Evo models were introduced.

1986 also brought a modification to 2nd and 3rd gears on both tranny shafts. The only way to spot the difference between these early and late gears is to measure them. The diameters are different, and the specifications for gear spacing are affected. Check out H-D service bulletin #906 if you need to.

Close ratio gears came along in 1987. The

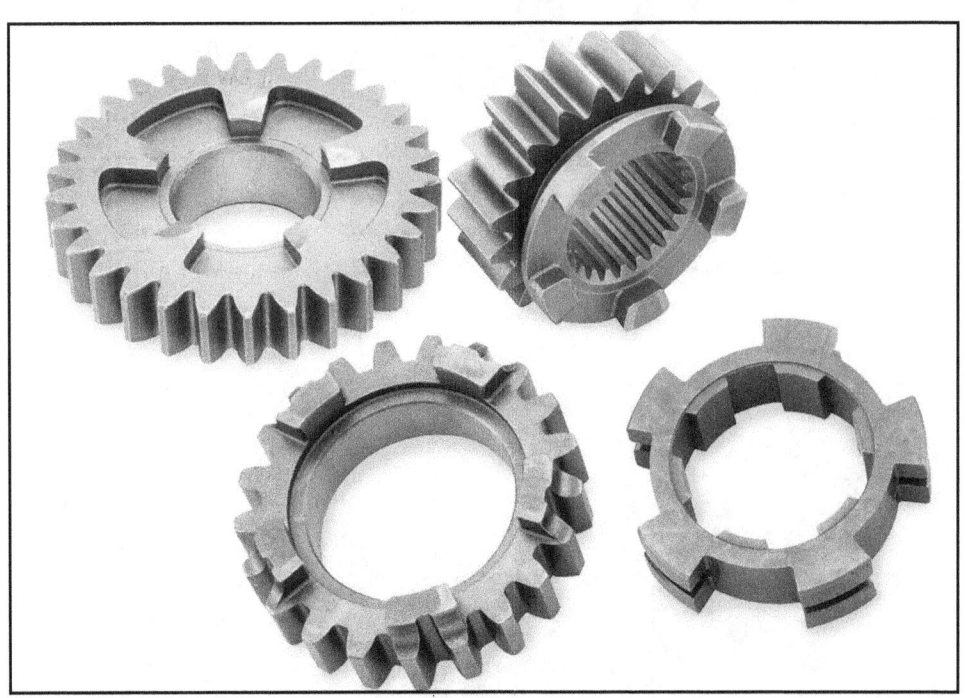

Replacement gears, shafts and shims are available for both 4 and 5 speed transmissions. Close-ratio gears are also available for both 4 and 5 speed transmissions. Biker's Choice

133

Before you get to this stage, you will have already checked the inside of the clutch basket for defects or damage to the alternator magnets.

Be cautious not to lose the gears off the shafts, slow and steady. Look for bits and pieces of metal in the gear teeth, particularly amongst the parts that stay inside the box when cartridge-style gearset is removed.

Look for signs of ordinary wear and tear. This shift cam for instance is looking pretty "buffed" along the slot but it's serviceable since the ramps aren't worn down. Get a second opinion of you're not sure.

clutch gear went from 17 to 18 teeth. Countershaft 4th from 27 to 26 teeth. These gears can be easily identified by a groove machined into the gear side face, and can be used to update older models. The close ratio kit consists of #37448-87 clutch gear and #35695-87 countershaft drive gear.

Second and third gears were changed again in 1990, along with the countershaft itself. The materials were improved and the shaft got a radiused shoulder. This meant that the washer had to have an increased (inner diameter) I.D. to accommodate the shaft change. You can update to these stronger parts with kit #35613-84B.

There's also the "bogie" of gear spacing, complete with rampant confusion resulting from the factory offering three sizes of shift forks. The differences in shift forks boil down to the dimension between the guide pin and the fork end that rides in the groove on the gear. So in neutral, the clearance between the sliding gears and the gear adjacent to it are measured. (Shift forks are available in Std., +.020 and -.020 sizes, and more from aftermarket sources, if/as needed.) A .020 fork on the mainshaft will move the slider gear closer to the clutch gear. On the countershaft, the same fork, will move the slider gear closer to 1st gear. This clearance must be at least .040inch, and not more than .080inch. Use the fork that gets the clearance within this range, it's that simple.

Last but not least: No version of the 40+ year old four-speed was ever designed to deal with anything like the horsepower and torque potential a strong 1200cc Evo motor is capable of, let alone some 100hp big bore with muscle enough to twist the box entrails up like a pretzel. Bear that in mind when you plan your build.

SOME ISSUES:

All-in-one clutch shell and alternator rotor. Clearly not The Motor Company's finest hour of design proficiency. The magnets can and often do come loose inside the assembly. Worse – it's an expensive piece to replace.

Camplate shifting mechanism. A flat piece of steel with slots and grooves cut into it is adequate but no more. It is a tad too notchy, balky and vague, as a rule. There are ways to improve the shift quality and the precision of this mechanism by modifying the slot contours and smoothing tricks here and there, but even then, not the best way to get from one cog to the next.

The shift pawl. Essentially a tin teeter-totter designed to transfer the movement of the shifter lever into movement in the shift mechanism. All but the last of these in 1990 (and the replacement part) were too soft a material, leading to premature wear and too often a broken part that made the box un-shiftable.

The trapdoor. Historically a weak link for high-powered applications, from 1957 to the end of it's days in 1990. The stock version wasn't bad towards the end, but still occasionally needs aftermarket upgrading in engines pushing the envelope.

Clutch Basics

We expect a lot from a clutch when you get right down to it. We want it to hook up, regardless of the power we transmit through it. Then we turn right around and want to be able to slip it mercilessly in slow traffic. We will not tolerate grabby, or abrupt engagement, yet want a two finger pull at the lever. We don't want the adjustment to change when we get the poor thing smoking hot. Nor, will we tolerate even the slightest creep or drag with the lever pulled. And, even under the terms of our abuse, if it won't last at least 60,000 to 100,000 miles we think it's junk. Truth is, most of the time it's us, not the clutch.

Take some responsibility. There are lot's of things you can do to extend the life of your clutch. First and foremost, use it properly: meaning at long traffic lights find neutral, don't sit there with the lever pulled and add unnecessary wear and tear to the throw out bearing. Obviously, excessive slipping is taking meat off the friction plates faster than you'll save the money for new ones. There are others like excessive heat, but mostly you need to maintain the thing - regularly. Simple stuff like this:

1. Make sure all components are properly adjusted.

2. Maintain proper lubrication of your wet clutch. Change its oil at regular intervals. Always use a good quality fluid, at the proper viscosity,

HERE…is the problem with this trans! It's one of the first things to check if you have shifting issues.

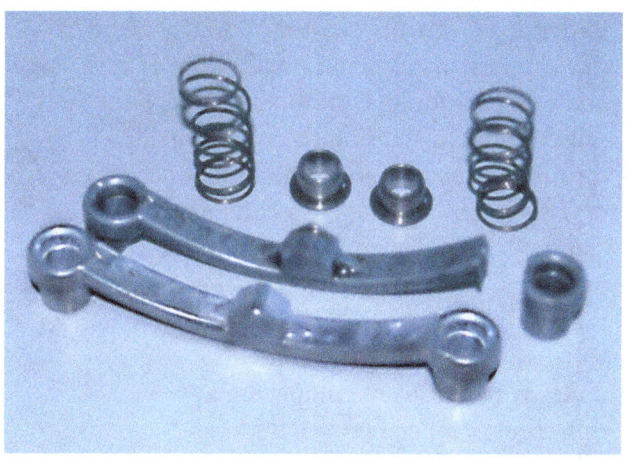

The new piece of a different alloy than the original design and much more durable for it! Replace the shift springs along with the cam follower.

As you check the wire leads for the stator to ensure there's good sound insulation, you might want to observe that your original part doesn't look like this.

135

Five-Speed Fix

The Sportster five-speed transmission was introduced in 1991 and designed to have its internal gear bits assembled without custom-fitting each gear to its shaft or stack of gears with assorted (and time-consuming) shimming, like the good old four-speed box of years gone by. When Harley eliminated the need to shim the new Sportster transmission, production went up, but shift quality could easily go down. It's better these days than it was the first couple of years of production, but still some will fail to nail a quick shift or feel sloppy between one gear and the next. This often indicates a loose clearance between the shifter dogs—usually between second and third on the countershaft. When the shift drum is in the second gear position, the measurement between the shifter dogs can be as much as 0.100 inch, whereas the distance between the other shifter dogs is closer to 0.050 inch. Moving the second gear on the counter-shaft closer to its third gear mate will usually improve things noticeably. Once the tranny is apart, just like the shop manual says, you'll see what you need to do to fix the problem. Simply use a thin thrust washer, between the left side snap-ring on the countershaft (the stock thrust washer is 0.070 inch) and second gear. Another needs to be put in on the gear's right side (of a thickness equal to the standard thrust washer minus the amount of the new thinner thrust washer that replaced it). There is no thrust washer at this position in the stock setup.

For example, you might need a spacer 0.030 inch thick where the stock 0.070-incher goes on the right side of countershaft second gear, and one about 0.040 inch thick where there isn't one at all on the left side of countershaft second gear.

But no spacer-washers of the right dimensions for this job exist in the parts book. You want 'em; you make 'em.

The easy way to make them, is to have the standard 0.070-inch Sportster five-speed thrust washers (#6003) ground to the thickness needed at a local machine shop that has a surface grinder with a magnetic table. Just tell them how thick you'd like the finished thrust washers to be.

Be aware that each measurement of each tranny may be slightly different, and plan to center the gear and tighten up clearances accordingly. In other words, what you take off one side, put on the opposite side. If you need a 0.030-inch thrust washer on the left side, you'll need a 0.040 inch on the right side between the second gear and the fifth gear on its right, and so on. Perhaps even vice-versa, so measure carefully.

It's not the easiest job, but if you want your Sportster to shift slicker than a hot knife through butter, and especially if the box has to come apart for some reason anyway it's worth it!

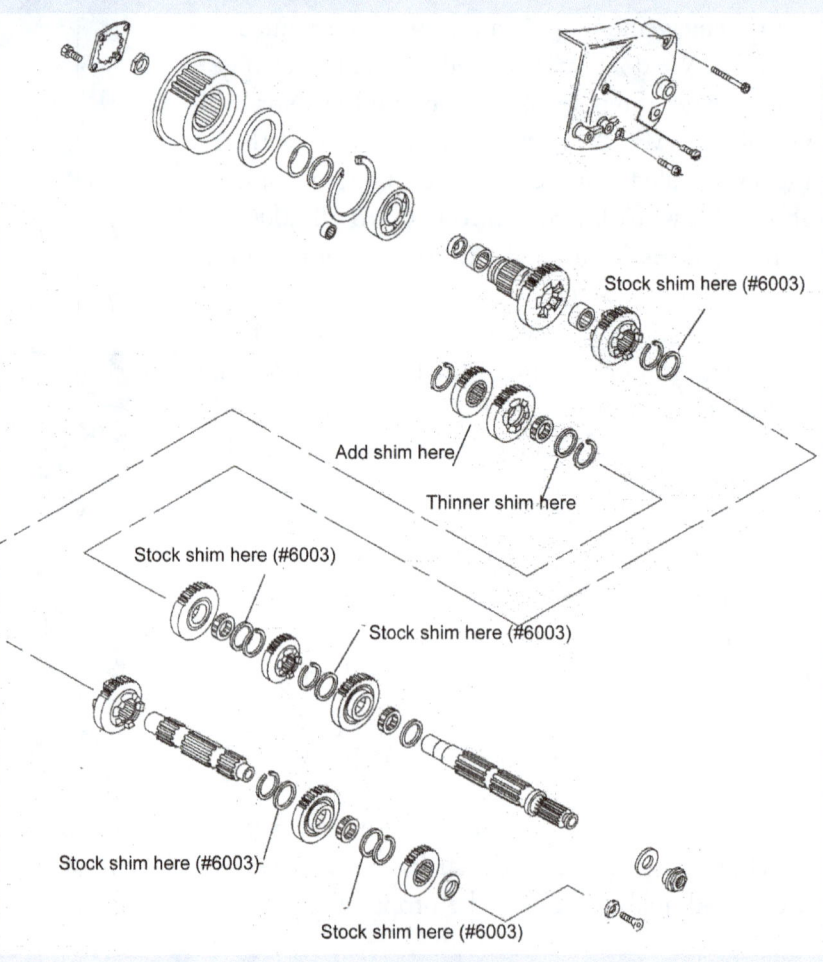

and do not be afraid of synthetics.

3. When clutch guts are replaced, always use the best parts available and replace all worn components. High quality clutch parts, whether stock or aftermarket, will save money in the long run.

CLUTCH "ADJUSTMENT" QUICKIE

Big mileage with little routine maintenance and adjustment can leave you feeling like your tranny doesn't seem to shift gears as easily as before. But don't panic, the problem is not likely be your gearbox. Look instead at your clutch, particularly the cable. More often than not a clutch that's out of adjustment, usually accompanied by a bone dry cable, can be the source of faulty or erratic shifts. It's sneaky, because it's a series of minor long term changes you don't notice until they catch up with you. By this time you've overlooked the basic simple stuff and start sweating major items. Don't. Just take a few minutes and deal with the most likely culprit.

Before you begin, support the bike in a level position to keep the transmission fluid in the primary case where it belongs.

The first step is to totally slacken the clutch cable by loosening the cable jam nut and threaded cable end adjuster until no threads are visible. After loosening the cable adjuster, check for free play by pulling the clutch lever. You should have tons.

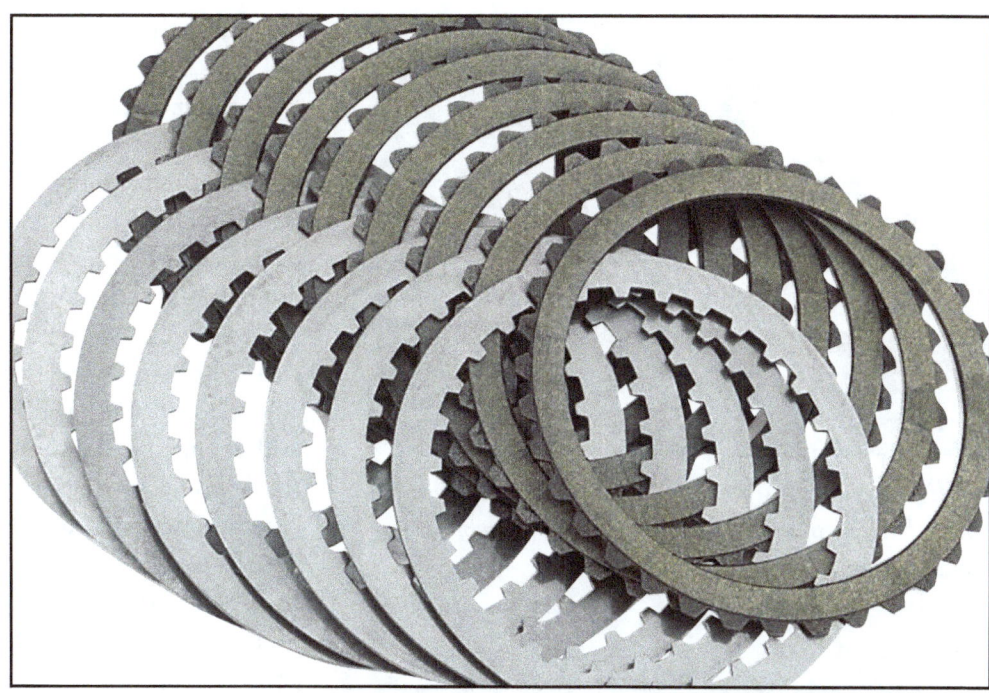

These "extra plate" kits from Barnett offer 20% more clutch surface area. The bar-flex friction material is designed to be run either wet or dry. Biker's Choice.

The one with the brass rivets, is the one you can do without in the stock clutch. It's there to keep noise down with the lever pulled.

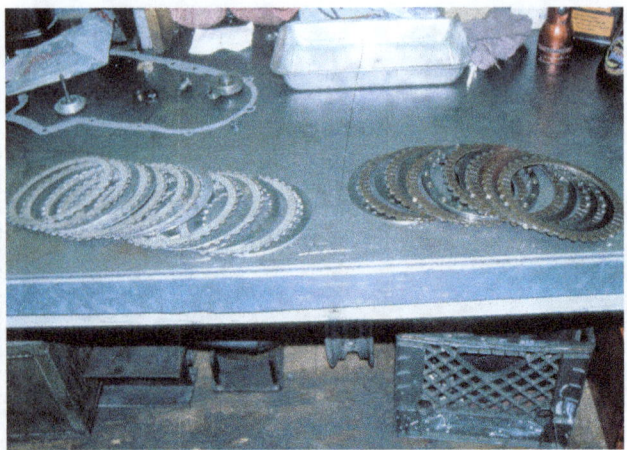

This collection of dry bits on the left contains one more friction plate than the soggy stock clutch, for a total of 9 sticky ones.

You need this gadget to compress the spring and continue disassembly. Keep the parts in order and clean for re-use during re-assembly.

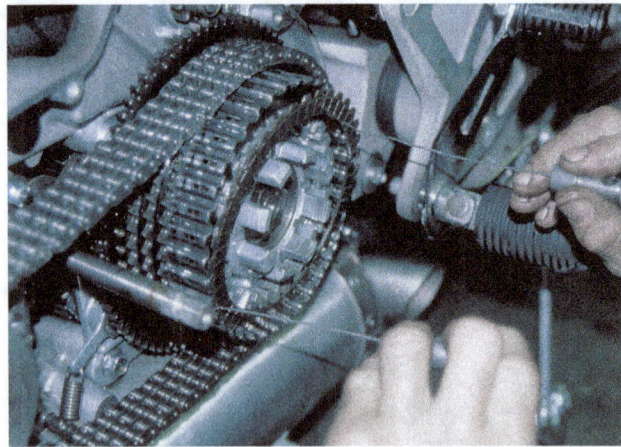

Sometimes it helps to have a tool like this to remove the plates. They can be bought or built…even though coat hanger wire is usually too coarse for the job.

Lube the cable. Dri-slide or chain lube or WD40 - take your pick, because it doesn't matter that much. What matters is to do it frequently with something that does the job for your particular cable. Repeat after me: Clean. Lube. Adjust. And don't buy into a certain hype about "linered" cables either! Linings, regardless of material used, are to reduce friction between wire and sheath for an easier pull – not eliminate the need to remain clean and slippery, via your periodic efforts.

Check fluid levels in the primary housing, and add/change fluid as needed. The upper level of fluid should just cover the bottom edge of the clutch plates and basket.

Re-adjust the clutch cable adjuster for 1/16-inch to 1/8-inch free-play at the clutch lever. Squeeze the clutch lever three or four times to re-seat the balls in the ramps. Tighten the cable jam nut at the adjuster. Oh, and by the way – if this slick trick doesn't make that old clutch work a lot more like new, you'll just have to do a real clutch adjustment.

FOUR-SPEED CLUTCH QUIRKS

All in all, the factory got it right. It's a very good clutch. Diaphragm spring, nice meaty friction plates, decent pull at the lever, good engage-disengage characteristics. Not great, but very good. There are plenty of upgrades available for "empowered" 4-speeds in need of stouter stuff in this department. Barnett even offers a double-extra clutch plate kit for severe duty.

But the biggest problem is that the factory moved the alternator rotor to an extremely hostile home in the back of the clutch basket. Over simplifying a touch, with magnetic waves and a "stack-up" issue when the various bearings in the assembly get a bit worn – it's a recipe for disaster. The whole program can get to wobbling like a hula-hoop headed uphill. When there's enough side to side going on the clutch basket encounters the stator windings. Make that a recipe for an expensive disaster if you don't stay on top of things. These clutches need routine maintenance and double checking like few before! Once every riding season is not too often to open and inspect, then R&R as required, while the fixes remain cheap. Other than this the only tip is to avoid extra strong clutch springs. The trick with this is to find the right plate set up, not put major pressure on the assembly. Most of what follows, in principle, holds true for 4-speeds as well.

FANCY FIVE-SPEED CLUTCHES

The stock clutch in the five-speed XL is a very sweet, sturdy unit, one of the best ever used on a Harley. Up to a point. That point is usually around 85-90 horsepower, or an equivalent 85-90 ft-lbs. of mid-range torque. In 100-plus-horsepower or big-inch torque monster X motors, the stock clutch can be pretty marginal.

Well, you can increase that safety margin by 12-13 percent simply by using an Extra-Plate high-performance clutch kit whether, Barnett's or the factory's own Screamin' Eagle. In fact, this is a good alternative to a stock clutch replacement when that time comes.

What you give up is a fairly useless oddball located right in the middle of the clutch pack. Called a "spring plate" by the factory, its main function in life is to prevent clutch rattle. Once you've installed this Extra-Plate kit, you will find it not only works superbly, but it's not noticeably noisier.

Here's a tip or two on how to put this kit in your Sportster:

1) The first thing is to soak the Barnett friction plates in a good quality primary fluid for about 1 hour before installation.

2) Next, open your shop manual to the clutch section and read the part about the spring compressor tool (JIMS #38515-90 and -91 or the equivalent).

3) Back all the adjustment out of your clutch cable.

4) Remove the clutch inspection cover (1994 and newer models) or remove the clutch inspection plug in the primary cover if you don't have the derby, being very careful not to loose the little coil spring that sits on the adjuster lock plate.

5) Turn the clutch adjusting screw clockwise to release the ramp and coupling mechanism, and then remove the primary drain plug and drain the fluid.

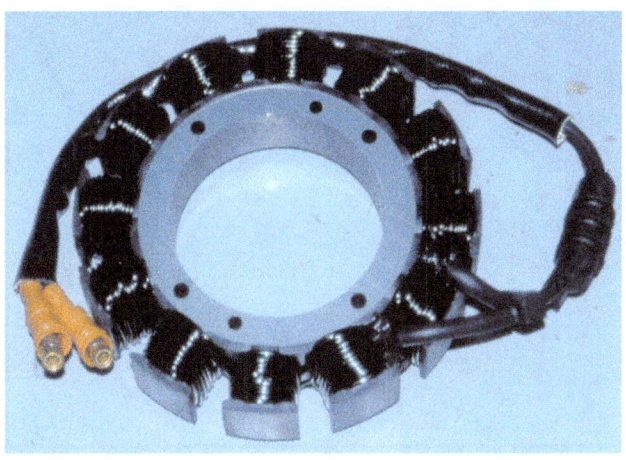

Take a hard look at the stator windings and leads. Any insulation that's cracked or rubbery will need to be replaced.

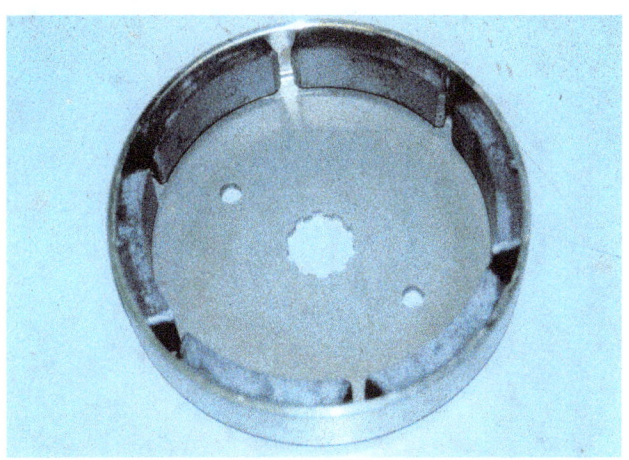

Check for sharp, solid edges on the rotor splines, magnets that aren't loose, damaged or holding lots of little metal shavings.

Last minute check for the threaded rod sticking out of the clutch pack. Take time to be observant, meticulous and thorough — before screwing the cover back on!

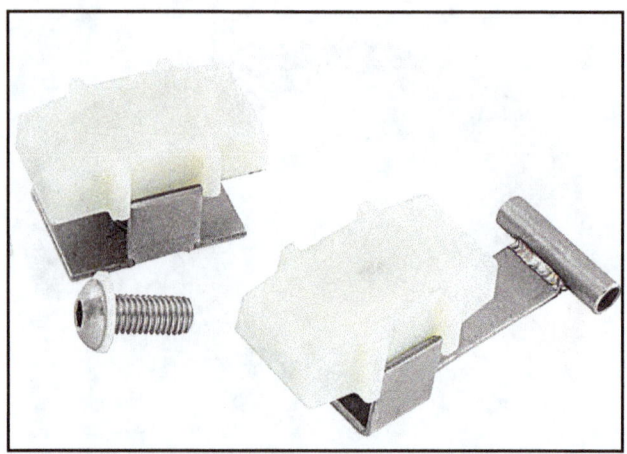

The Hayden M6 in two XLnt choices, four-speed on the left, five on the right is spring loaded, has a constant adjustment feature and is too logical to pass up.

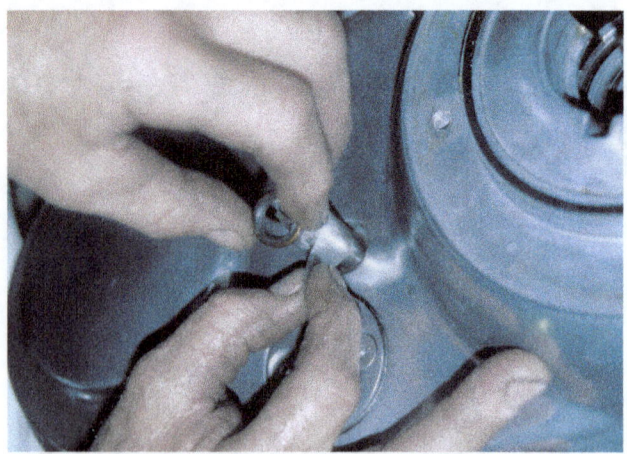

Cover the shaft splines with tape to keep from damaging the seal lip and "installing your next leak" by accident.

Keep things oily when replacing the seal. You can use a deep socket the same O.D. as the seal for an installer. Tap, don't pound, in a slow rotation until the seal bottoms.

6) Remove the shifter using a flat blade screwdriver and a rubber mallet to spread the arm, and then slide it off the shaft.

7) Finally... remove the primary.

Now you're back at the snap ring that holds the adjusting screw assembly in place. Compress the clutch pack with the tool, and remove the snap ring and spring seat from the groove in the clutch hub. Remove the clutch-plate stack. Keep track of the order—steel, fiber, steel, fiber—and which was first in line.

Once it's out, take the time to inspect your drive (steel) plates if you plan to reuse them. They need to be flat. Warped steels will thwart your best efforts at a good clutch. If they are blued or horrendously gouged or grooved, get new ones. If they are otherwise okay, glass bead blast them or rough 'em up with fine emery paper.

Reassembling your clutch pack is the reverse of disassembly. Start by installing a friction plate and then a drive plate and continue until you get to the spring plate (between the fourth and fifth friction plates). The spring plate is two steel plates riveted together with a wave washer between them. Lose it. You've just done your clutch a favor, especially if the rivets are loose. Add the extra Barnett friction plate, thus increasing your pleasure and peace of mind by over 10 percent. Finish installing plates, apply a new primary gasket, do a little wrenching, and first thing you know, it's time to adjust your new clutch.

First, adjust at the primary via the adjusting screw assembly, and then at the cable to set freeplay. Set primary chain tension to 3/8 inch to 1/2 inch, (unless you add or have an M6 tensioner) and check it in several different spots by rotating things a bit, even if you have to stick it in gear and bump the wheel a bit.

You're still wondering why there's no talk here about heavy-duty clutch springs? Actually, for drag racing there's probably some merit in boosting pressure by the seemingly requisite 20-30 percent. This is not the case for street clutches. Better to add friction material, as we've just demonstrated. That, or get ready for carpal tunnel and trashed clutch internals on a regular basis.

If you try the extra plate kit and still don't find that it's adequate and if you're talking major torque, like 100 ft-lbs. or more - then what? How about a Pro-Clutch? This high performance clutch from Rivera/Primo offers the features and benefits we need along with all the performance capabilities we want - abuse included.

Case in point: With no increase in spring pressure, pull at the lever, there's literally double the surface area. That 100% increase means slippage is a virtual non-issue. Put another way, 25% even 50% more spring doesn't do as much as this increase in friction surface will. At this stage in the proceedings your clutch can likely take more torque than your engine can produce (nitrous and blower bikes excepted). And for those who need more clutch than this, I submit you need a professional license to go with it.

Of course, professional drag racers already know about "lock-up" specialty clutches. They are certainly available, Rivera Engineering for instance has a good one. But that goes directly into an area that is so specialized you'd best consult the vendor, not this book.

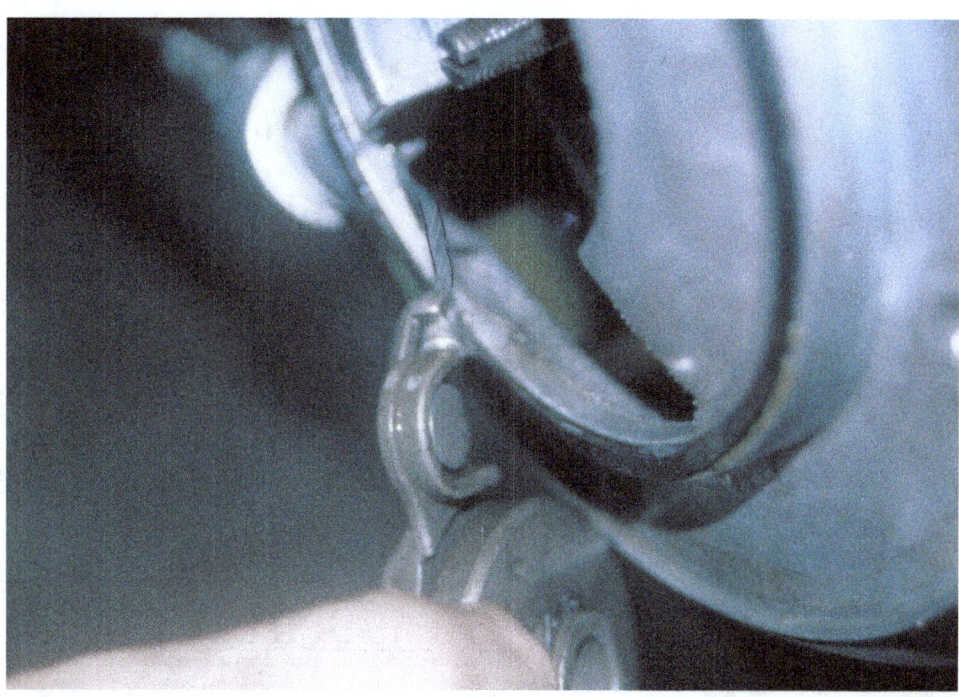

Hope you paid attention to the hook up here, when you took this apart, as it can become something of a chinese puzzle to put together again. H-D has changed the design, some link up in a sort of mirror image of others. This 1994 model does go like this however.

There is a certain amount of "touch" or finesse involved when interpreting the term bottom out lightly. A little time and tenderness spend on this adjustment will pay huge dividends in clutch feel and performance.

Wolfgang Books On The Web
http://www.wolfpub.com

HOW-TO BUILD THE ULTIMATE V-TWIN MOTORCYCLE

It's back. The book from Timothy Remus and Wolfgang Publications that helped to kick start the build-a bike-at-home phenomena, is in publication once again. Though the aftermarket offers new engines and frames not available when this book was written, the basics of building a bike remain the same. A quality frame remains a quality product. Safe rake and trail dimensions have not changed, and neither has the need for safe brakes that will stop you when that car runs a stop light or stops unexpectedly in the middle of the block. So for anyone who yearns to build a V-Twin at home, How-to Build The Ultimate V-Twin Motorcycle remains an essential tool. Build Your Own with this timeless how-to book from Wolfgang Publications.

Ten Chapters   144 Pages $24.95   Over 400 B&W images

HOW-TO BUILD A CHEAP CHOPPER

Choppers don't have to cost $30,000. In fact, a chopper built from the right parts can be assembled for as little as $5,000. How to Build a Cheap Chopper documents the construction of 4 inexpensive choppers with complete start-to-finish sequences photographed in the shops of Donnie Smith, Brian Klock and Dave Perewitz.

Least expensive is the metric chopper, based on a Japanese 4-cylinder engine and transmission installed in a hardtail frame. Next up, price wise, are 2 bikes built using Buell/Sportster drivetrains. The recipe here is simple; combine one used Buell or Sportster with a hardtail frame for an almost instant chopper. The big twin chopper is the least cheap of the 4, yet it's still far less expensive than most bikes built today.

Eleven Chapters   144 Pages $27.95   Over 400 photos, 100% color

HOW-TO BUILD AN OLD SKOOL BOBBER

Kevin Baas begins the second edition of his How to Build an Old Skool Bobber book with a little history, the history of bike building at home, as seen through the eyes of a young man watching his Vietnam-Vet father build a chopper at home in 1970. In his father's eyes, and Kevin's as well, the engine and frame should to be old skool - and genuine Harley-Davidson if possible - but the rest can and should come from swap meets, or the sweat of your own two hands. Kevin lays out the basics of bike building, starting first with the ideal components: which engine, which frame, and the differences in the various years. Next, things to watch out for when buying old parts, and how to fix the parts you do buy. Additional chapters describe brake systems, both early and late, tires and wheels, and frame geometry. Four complete start-to-finish bike assemblies round out this hands-on book.

Thirteen Chapters   144 Pages $27.95   Over 400 photos, 100% color

KOSMOSKI'S NEW KUSTOM PAINTING SECRETS

Jon Kosmoski - the King of Kustom Painters - puts over four decades of experience into Kosmoski's New Kustom Painting Secrets. The metal prep discussion includes the use of two-part fillers and how to get the panels really flat.

Jon explains the advantages and disadvantages of single and two-stage paints, and which is the best choice for a person working at home or in a small shop. The paint discussion moves on to cover candy and pearl paints, how best to utilize and spray these custom coatings, and how to mix up your own unique color.

How to pick, adjust and use spray guns makes up the next chapter in Jon's new book. As Jon explains, "you need to have the gun adjusted properly, and the way to do that is with test panels done before you start the paint job."

Eleven Chapters   144 Pages $27.95   Over 500 photos, 100% color

Wolfgang Publication Titles

For a current list visit our website at www.wolfpub.com

ILLUSTRATED HISTORY
Sturgis 70th Anniversary	$27.95

BIKER BASICS
Sheet Metal Fabrication	$27.95
How to FIX American V-Twin MC	$27.95
How to Build an Old Skool Bobber Second Edition	$27.95

COMPOSITE GARAGE
Composite Materials Handbook #1	$27.95
Composite Materials Handbook #2	$27.95

HOT ROD BASICS
How to Air Condition Your Hot Rod	$27.95
How to Chop Tops	$24.95

MOTORCYCLE RESTORATION SERIES
Triumph Resotoration - Unit 650cc	$29.95
Triumph MC Restoration Pre-Unit	$29.95
Harley-Davidson Panhead Restoration	$34.95

AIR SKOOL SKILLS
How Airbrushes Work	$27.95
How to Airbrush Pin-Ups	$27.95
Air Brushing 101	$27.95
Airbrush Bible	$29.95

PAINT EXPERT
Advanced Custom Motorcycle Painting	$27.95
Advanced Custom Painting Techniques	$27.95
Advanced Pinstripe Art	$27.95
Kustom Painting Secrets	$19.95
Custom Paint & Graphics	$27.95
Pro Airbrush Techniques	$27.95
Pro Pinstripe Techniques	$27.95

SHEET METAL
Advanced Sheet Metal Fabrication	$27.95
Ultimate Sheet Metal Fabrication	$24.95
Sheet Metal Bible	$29.95

CUSTOM BUILDER SERIES
How To Build The Ultimate V-Twin Motorcycle	$24.95
Advanced Custom Motorcycle Wiring	$27.95
Advanced Custom Motorcycle Assembly & Fabrication	$27.95
Advanced Custom Motorcycle Chassis	$27.95
How to Build a Cheap Chopper	$27.95
How to Build a Chopper	$27.95

TATTOO U Series
Tattoo Sketch Book	$32.95
American Tattoos	$27.95
Body Painting	$27.95
Tattoo - From Idea to Ink	$27.95
Tattoos Behind the Needle	$27.95
Advanced Tattoo Art	$27.95
Tattoo Bible Book One	$27.95
Tattoo Bible Book Two	$27.95

HOME SHOP
How to Paint Tractors & Trucks	$27.95

NOTEWORTHY
Guitar Building Basics Acoustic Assembly at Home	$27.95

Sources

Accel Performance Products
8700 Brookpark Road
Brooklyn, OH 44129
Phone (216) 398-8300
www.mrgasket.com

Andrews Products Inc.
431 Kingston Ct.
Mount Prospect, IL 60056
Phone (847) 759-0190
Fax (847) 759-0848
www.andrews-products.com

Axtell Sales Inc.
1424 S.E. Maury
Des Moines, IA 50317
Phone (515) 243-2518 or
1-800-704-3201
www.axtellsales.com

Baisley High Performance
5511 N. Interstate
Portland, OR 97217
Phone (503) 289-1251

Barnett Tool & Engineering
9920 Freeman Avenue
Santa Fe Springs, CA 90670
Phone (310) 941-1284
www.barnettclutches.com

Bartels' Performance Products
3237 Carter Avenue
Marina Del Ray, CA 90292
Phone (310) 578-9888 or
1-800-747-1151
www.bartellsperformance.com

Branch Flowmetrics
5556 Corporate Drive
Cypress, CA 90630
Phone (714) 827-5340
www.branchflowmetrics.com

Cometic Gasket Inc.
8767 East Avenue
Mentor, OH 44060
Phone (216) 974-1077 or
1-800-752-9850
www.cometic.com

Compu-Fire Ignition Systems
20290 Carrey Road
Walnut, CA 91789
Phone (909) 598-5485
www.compufire.com

Crane Cams Inc.
530 Fentress Boulevard
Daytona Beach, FL 32114
Phone (904) 252-1151
www.cranecams.com

Custom Chrome
16100 Jacqueline Court
Morgan Hill, CA 95037
Phone (408) 778-0500 or
1-800-359-5700
www.customchrome.com

Drag Specialties
9839 W 69th Street
Eden Prairie, MN 55344
Phone (952) 942-7890
www.dragspecialties.com

Dynatek
164 S. Valencia St.
Glendora, CA 91741
Phone (818) 963-1669
www.dynaonline.com

Dynojet Research
200 Arden Drive
Belgrade, MT 59714
Phone (406) 388-4993 or
1-800-992-4993
www.dynojet.com

Earl's Performance Products
189 W. Victoria
Long Beach, CA 90805
Phone (310) 609-1602 or
1-800-533-1320
www.earlsperformance.com

Edelbrock Corp.
2700 California St.
Torrance, CA 90503
Phone (310) 781-2222
www.edelbrock.com

Extrude Hone AFM
8800 Somerset Blvd.
Paramount, CA 90723
Phone (562) 531-2976
www.extrudehone.com

Fast Company
835 7th Avenue
Kirkland, WA 98033
Phone (206) 828-4130

Flo Dynamics
1150 Pike Lane #2
Oceana, CA 03445
Phone (805) 481-6300
www.flodynamics.com

Feuling R & D
2521 Palma Drive
Ventura, CA 93003
Phone (805) 650-2598
www.feuling.com

Gerolamy Company
3250 Monier Circle
Units G & H
Rancho Cordova, CA 95742
Phone (916) 638-9008
www.bcheads.com

Harley-Davidson Inc.
3700 W Juneau Avenue
Milwaukee, WI 53208
www.harley-davidson.com
Phone (414) 342-4680

Tom Hayden Enterprises
8439 White Oak Ave #109
Rancho Cucamonga, CA
Phone: (909) 944-3211

Head Quarters
3665 Dove Road
Port Huron, MI 48060
www.head-quarters.com
Phone Parts: 519-289-5990
Phone Service, Sales & Tech:
519-289-5229
Fax: 519-289-2046
e-mail: info@headquarters.com

Holeshot Performance
311 Chestnut Street
Santa Cruz, CA 95060
www.holeshot.com

House of Horsepower
1190 Griffith Street #2
Louisville, KY 80027
www.houseofhorsepower.com
Phone (541) 767-9089

Hyperformance
5152A N.E. 12th Avenue
Pleasant Hill, IA 50317
Phone (515) 266-6381
www.kingofcubes.com

James Gaskets Inc.
637 Bangs Avenue
Modesto, CA 95356-9517
Phone (209) 578-3599
www.jamesgaskets.com

JE Pistons
15312 Connector Lane
Huntington Beach, CA 92649
Phone (714) 898-9763
www.jepistons.com

JIMS
555 Dawson Drive
Camarillo, CA 93012
Phone (805) 482-6913
www.jimsusa.com

Kent-Moore
28635 Mound Road
Warren, MI 48092-3499
Phone 1-800-345-2233
www.spxkentmoore.com

Kosman Racing
55 Oak Street
San Francisco, CA 94102
Phone (415) 861-4262
www.kosmanracing.com

KuryAkyn USA
P.O. Box 37
Stillwater, MN 55082
Phone (715) 247-5008
www.kuryakyn.com

Mackie Engineering
2065-H Sperry Ave.
Ventura, CA 93003
www.davemackie.com

Manley Performance Products
1960 Swarthmore Ave.
Lakewood, NJ 08701
www.manleyperformance.com

Mikuni American Corporation
8910 Mikuni Avenue
Northridge, CA 91342
Phone (818) 885-1242
www.mikuni.com

Millennium Technologies
1404 Pilgrim Rd.
Plymouth, WI 53073
920-893-5595
Fax 920-893-4830
www.mt-llc.com

Motion Software, Inc.
535 West Lambert, Bldg. E
Brea, CA 92821
www.motionsoftware.com
Phone (714) 255-2931

Mr. Gasket Inc.
8700 Brookpark Road
Brooklyn, OH 44129
Phone (216) 398-8300
www.mrgasket.com

MSD Ignition
1490 Henry Brennan Drive
El Paso, TX 79936
Phone (915) 857-5200
www.msdignition.com

Nallin Racing Head Service
3770 Puritan Way, unit E
Frederick, CO 80516
Phone (303) 833-4500
Fax (303) 833-4450
www.nallinracing.com

Performance Plus
11901 E. Old Highway 66
Evansville, IN 47712
Phone (812) 985-7892

Performance Trends, Inc.
P. O. Box 530164
Livonia, MI 48153
www.performancetrends.com
Phone (248) 473-9230

Polymer Dynamics, Inc.
4116 Siegel
Houston, TX 77009
Phone (713) 694-3296
www.polydyn.com

Red Line Synthetic Oil Corp.
6100 Egret Court
Benecia, CA 94510
www.redlineoil.com

Rowe U.S.A.
P. O. Box 7409
Santa Maria, CA 93456
Phone (805) 349-1932 or
1-800-531-9901
www.roweusa.com

S&S Cycle Inc.
Route 2, Box 215
Viola, WI 54664
Phone (608) 627-1497
www.sscycle.com

S.T.D. Development Inc.
9601 Cozycroft Ave., Unit 10
Chatsworth, CA 91311
Phone (818) 998-8226
www.stddevelopment.com

Sputhe Engineering Inc.
11185 Lime Kiln Road
Grass Valley, CA 95949-9715
Phone (916) 268-0887
www.sputhe.com

Storz Performance Inc.
239 S. Olive Street
Ventura, CA 93001
Phone (805) 641-9540
www.storzperf.com

Sudco International Corporation
3014 Tanager Avenue
Commerce, CA 90040
Phone (213) 728-5407
www.sudco.com

Thunder Products
P.O. Box 61
Patascala, OH 43062

Trock Cycle Specialties
13 N 417 French Road
Hampshire, IL 60140
Phone (847) 683-4010

Truett & Osborn
3345 E. 31st South
Witchita, KS 67216
Phone (316) 682-4781
www.truettosborn.com
www.50megs.com

Wiseco Piston Inc.
7201 Industrial Park Blvd.
Mentor, OH 44060
Phone (216) 951-6600
www.wiseco.com

XRV Performance Products
10428 Burbank Blvd.
N. Hollywood, CA 91601
Phone (818) 762-5407

Yost Performance Products
P. O. Box 33408
Minneapolis, MN 55433
Phone (612) 755-0398
www.yostperformance.com

Zipper's Performance
    Products/Red Shift Cams
6655-A Amberton
Elkridge, MD 21075
Phone (410) 579-2100
www.zippersperformance.com

www.ingramcontent.com/pod-product-compliance
Lightning Source LLC
Chambersburg PA
CBHW082125230426
43671CB00015B/2810